« EVERYDAY ECOFASCISM »

Everyday Ecofascism

*Crisis and Consumption in
American Literature*

ALEXANDER MENRISKY

University of Minnesota Press
Minneapolis
London

The University of Minnesota Press gratefully acknowledges the generous assistance provided for the publication of this book by the University of Connecticut Humanities Institute.

Portions of chapter 3 and the second Interlude were previously published in a different form in "Hicks, Homos, and Home Cooking: Literary Recipes in Queer Appalachia," in *GLQ: A Journal of Lesbian and Gay Studies* 28, no. 3 (June 2022): 413–37, copyright 2022, Duke University Press. All rights reserved. Republished by permission of the publisher, www.dukeupress.edu. Portions of chapter 4 were previously published in a different form in "Hallucinogenic Ecology and Psychoanalytic Prehistory in Margaret Atwood," in *Mosaic: An Interdisciplinary Critical Journal* 52, no. 3 (September 2019): 19–36.

Published by the University of Minnesota Press
111 Third Avenue South, Suite 290
Minneapolis, MN 55401–2520
http://www.upress.umn.edu

ISBN 978-1-5179-1867-5 (hc)
ISBN 978-1-5179-1868-2 (pb)

A Cataloging-in-Publication record for this book is available from the Library of Congress.

Printed in the United States of America on acid-free paper

The University of Minnesota is an equal-opportunity educator and employer.

UMP BmB 2025

Contents

Everyday Ecofascism

Environmentalist Storytelling and Its Threshold Objects

> [F]ascism is an analytic category—not a fixed,
> objective thing. Definitions of fascism help us clarify
> what we mean, but they aren't objectively true—just
> more or less useful in helping us understand the
> differences and relationships between various political
> movements.
>
> —Matthew Lyons, *Insurgent Supremacists*

> Liberating the "nature" within or without us has been
> a constant theme of emancipatory discourse. . . .
> But we should not forget the irrationalities and
> repressions to which this "nature libertarianism" can
> also lend itself. . . . [A]n aesthetic of "nature" as source
> of purity and authentic self-identification has been a
> component of all forms of racism . . . and nationalism.
>
> —Kate Soper, *What Is Nature?*

In August 2019, a young man (self-identified as a white U.S. citizen) murdered twenty-three people and injured twenty-three more, most of Mexican nationality or descent, in El Paso, Texas. "Whites needed to be protected with their own border, like an endangered species," he wrote in a manifesto just before the attack. "My whole life I have been preparing for a future that currently doesn't exist." That future, he explained, has crumbled in the wake of unsustainable resource exploitation, the related disaster of global climate changes, and an ecological outlook he believes so dismal he can't imagine living through it. These phenomena are, for the shooter, hurried less by corporate accumulation and the consumption patterns of the Global North than by immigrant-driven overpopulation—what he referred to as an "Hispanic invasion." Three years later, in Buffalo, New York, another gunman slaughtered ten grocery shoppers, all of them Black. His motivation bore more than proximate resemblance to the first shooter's. In a manifesto of his own, the man plagiarized both the El Paso murderer and, to a greater extent, yet another who massacred fifty-one people at a mosque in Christchurch, New Zealand, also in 2019.

Writing and narrative played a subtle yet outsize role in these mobilizations. Each man cut and pasted a familiar set of protagonists and antagonists, settings and conflicts, from declarations made before his own. Each one not only understood the world through the lens of this story, but also, in repeating it, contributed to its writing himself. All three men subscribed to white-nationalist "replacement theory," the notion that nonwhite immigrants and citizens actively conspire to displace white Europeans from Europe itself, as well as its settler colonies in North America and Oceania. In his own act of plagiarism, the Christchurch shooter adopted the title of his screed, "The Great Replacement," from a 2011 book by French white nationalist Renaud Camus, but also added a caveat: "[T]here is no nationalism without environmentalism." For him, as for others on the far right, alien others represent a threat not only to an idealized, naturalized, and racialized national identity but also to that identity's environmental dimensions. Self-styled fascists, especially, have historically attributed nation and race to a uniform, autochthonous nature—a matter, the political philosopher Daniel Woodley writes, of "unquestionable essence."[1] Two of these three murderers indeed declared themselves fascists—*eco*fascists—illustrating how matters of environment and identity can converge to genocidal effect in the wake of particular cultural narratives about nature.

As the local and regional challenges posed by global climate change have intensified in the twenty-first century in the form of unprecedented heat waves, fires, weather anomalies, sea-level rise, and other phenomena, far-right figures in the United States and elsewhere have begun to more frequently frame anti-immigrant, anti-Indigenous, or otherwise white-supremacist sentiment in terms of environmental as well as national survival. Popular and academic media increasingly use the term *ecofascism* to describe this orientation. The word itself is not particularly new. It emerged in critical retrospectives on the close relationship between conservation and German National Socialism in the 1920s and 1930s. But recently, it has experienced a swift resurrection among twenty-first-century commentators searching for a vocabulary to account for the seemingly baffling adoption of ecological themes by political actors otherwise steeped in a rhetoric more often associated with climate change denial and antienvironmentalist conservatism. And though it began as a derogatory reference, it has also acquired cachet among self-proclaimed ecofascists themselves. As such figures attract media attention, their rhetoric has revivified blood-and-soil nationalism across a variety of environmentalist conversations in the United States.

Still, the scope of the term *ecofascism*, like *fascism* itself, remains fraught and contested. In news and magazine writing across North America and Europe, as well as online conversation, detractors often wield the word like a cudgel rather than treat it as a subject of analysis itself. Some dismiss the concept outright as a fearmongering tactic, a sensationalist vision of an unlikely world in which ecofascism comprises state ideology, a form or arm of fascist governance that scapegoats racialized others for environmental harm and ethnonational decline, framing their persecution and elimination as the means to the cultural and ecological rebirth of a privileged national identity (a situation typified by the *blut und boden* of the Third Reich). But current usage often casts a wider net, labeling a range of hypernationalist and/or white-supremacist activity rather than a regime. Such patterns indeed merit attention, but the sheer diversity of their origin, intent, and effect seems to mystify rather than clarify what ecofascism is. At the same time, scholarship in American studies and the environmental humanities has begun to follow the lead of scholars of race and Indigeneity, attending more closely to the white-supremacist dimensions of U.S. environmental history, policy, and representation and their relationship to the nation's settler-colonial foundations. Such work is indispensable as the far right steadily mobilizes environmentalist messages, but what little of it directly engages the concept of ecofascism tends to focus on the Nazi example at the expense of present phenomena—an oversight that demands attention, given the term's growing popularity, vexed definition, and adoption by some white nationalists themselves.

In short, recent commentary on ecofascism applies the label to a nebulous range of activity. It also overwhelmingly focuses on overt expressions of hypernationalist environmental sensibility by baldly racist actors on the radical right. But permutations of their perspectives in fact resonate across the political spectrum (and have historically animated U.S. environmentalism across partisan lines), perpetuating white supremacy in numerous contexts and effacing the asymmetrical impacts ecological disruption continues to have on marginalized peoples. Calls for border closure or deportation as means to reducing strain on national resources increasingly circulate on message boards hosted by democratic socialists as well as neo-Nazis, even in contexts in which race appears to be a blatant factor. And the critic Sarah Jaquette Ray reports that, following a lecture on climate anxiety, a student emailed her "to say she was so distressed that she'd be willing to submit to a green dictator if they would address climate change," teasing a future in which increasing numbers are "willing to sacrifice democracy and human rights."[2] Likewise, when the social scientist Joseph Henderson prompts students to imagine a solution to climate disruption, "overwhelmingly they say it's population control. . . . [W]e need to thin the herd." They are almost never, he adds, "talking about themselves, even though when you look at who impacts ecosystems the most, it tends to be white Westerners with high incomes."[3] For this sample of students, at least, decisions about who can stay and who must go play out implicitly along lines of nationality, ethnicity, race, and class. Such examples illustrate nothing if not the difficulty of detecting any "precise threshold one crosses at which the designation of 'fascism'" (eco- or otherwise) "becomes meaningful," as the antifascist Out of the Woods Collective puts it.[4] These students' perspectives emerge not from a central ideological or institutional source, but at intersections among racial, territorial, economic, environmental, and other sociocultural discourses that circulate in quotidian ways.

Everyday Ecofascism accordingly makes a case that we should approach the evasive notion of ecofascism not as a uniquely right-wing political program, but instead as a network of discursive and nondiscursive expressions of power, including subtle, everyday speech acts as well as overtly, physically violent actions. In other words, I'm proposing that we understand the concept much as we have come to conceive of race-supremacist ideology and other forms of social injustice, which, as structural, systemic phenomena, implicate even the most well-meaning people, reproducing in commonplace assumptions and utterances, including in environmental art, writing, and politics.

Approaching the concept in this manner might seem to further muddy its definition. Some critics indeed advocate for a far narrower interpretation. Peter Staudenmaier, for example, argues that the term best refers to a particular subset of far-right environmentalism: groups and individuals with explicit, active connections to fascist thought—what Bernhard Forchtner and Balša Lubarda refer to as "eco-fascism 'proper.'" At the same time, however, Staudenmaier acknowledges not only that fascism, as a self-conscious movement, has become more diffuse since 1945 but also that "less virulent forms of the same ideology" espoused by proud ecofascists "can be found in mainstream circles" as well. "Naïve beliefs about nature . . . take on a harder edge at the right end of the spectrum," but are "just as common among Greens, progressives, New Agers, and the like."[5]

As I explain later in this Introduction, such "naïve" beliefs among ordinary folks in fact played a crucial role in the formation of fascist regimes of the early twentieth century. Fascism is, historically speaking, not so much a centralized program but rather, as Glen Sean Coulthard (Yellowknives Dene) writes of settler colonialism, "the sum effect of the diversity of interlocking oppressive social relations that constitute it."[6] It is for this reason that the late comparative historian Walter Laqueur noted in 1996 that fascism, classic or contemporary, "is not primarily an ideology or a political party." It is more of "an alternative way of life," articulated in part through consistent patterns of storytelling about who and what different people are, are not, and/or should be—which can reasonably be said of any politics.[7] What distinguishes fascism is not necessarily (or not only) top-down imposition of authoritarian power, but its particular grassroots synthesis of existing, nonpartisan ways of representing the world. This process of accretion, involving otherwise well-intentioned people as well as far-right agitators, historically constituted what we call fascism, not merely the explicit violence (or regime) that was its endgame or result.

For these reasons, we might likewise productively conceive of ecofascism not as a stable ideology or program, but (much as scholars have come to understand fascism more broadly) as a phenomenon or process, or even an outcome—a pattern not just of material violence but also of cultural narrative. In part, then, ecofascism is a matter of political genre, or of the representational frameworks through which "social subjects come to understand their everyday lives, their political landscapes, and the broader spaces that they—and others—inhabit."[8] Genres are identifiable by their consistency: they are "repeated, detailed, and stretched while retaining [their] intelligibility," Lauren Berlant writes. For this reason, a genre "promis[es] that the persons transacting with it will experience the pleasure of what they expected"—including, for example, a sense of secure attachment to place.[9] For the geographer Kai Bosworth, it is because of this affective dimension that genre also "condition[s] political struggles"—and therefore has material effects.[10] All forms of discourse are political. Language, genre, and narrative have concrete impacts on the world and the people and nonhuman others who live with it. By the same token, all politics involve discursive as well as nondiscursive elements. Rhetorical and physical acts of political violence committed in the name of environmental, national, and racialized purity, undertaken by the state or movements and individuals operating independently of it, do not occur in a vacuum. These scenarios—what we might indeed call "ecofascism proper," or even *ecofascist effects*—proceed from certain ways of representing the world that encode existing assumptions about race, nation, and environment that transcend conventional ideological distinctions in contexts both fanatical and banal.

It is precisely these less zealous circumstances that interest me in this book, chiefly because the "drama of the everyday," the critic Min Hyoung Song writes, "doesn't just remain at the level of the everyday." It provides both backdrop and buttress to conditions of oppression and overt acts of violence. As recent scholarship such as Eduardo Bonilla-Silva's *Racism without Racists* (2003), Christina Sharpe's *In the Wake* (2016), and Dylan Rodríguez's *White Reconstruction* (2020) demonstrates, casual, even unintentional iterations of supremacy provide infrastructure on which acts of overt violence take place. Take, for example, the sheer number of social media users who proclaimed in spring 2020 that the death tolls of Covid-19 augured nature's recovery from a pernicious *human* virus—a stance the journalist Ketan Joshi refers to as "lazy ecofascism." This "sentiment that the world would be better without humans in it," Song writes, "might seem like a typical misanthropic statement." But to suggest that "the world would be better without humans," he adds, "leaves open the possibility that it would be ethically permissible to allow many humans to die, as their absence would enable greater human flourishing—a suggestion that . . . allows eugenic thinking to come into play, as some groups of humans might be seen as more disposable than others."[11] Covid-19 deaths indeed surged most catastrophically among poor, marginalized communities, raising important questions about seemingly impartial misanthropy. What groups of people must die so that "nature" might live? What social forms live within that charmed circle of "nature," and which are inimical to it? Who, in any given context, decides the answers? What stories do they tell to justify them? This book asks these questions of such diverse cultural precincts as back-to-the-land communalism, regional food movements, New-Age psychedelia, and others.

Everyday Ecofascism, then, is not a book about state ideology or even the far right. It is, rather, about the political genre or narrative pattern that "conditions" (to borrow Bosworth's word) "ecofascism proper." Throughout the rest of this Introduction—and indeed the book as a whole—I identify and explore that pattern as a series of nonpartisan cultural narratives (a) in an apparently antimodernist or antiestablishment mode that (b) link certain environments with certain people through appeals to nature and rebirth in ways that (c) actually reinforce existing patterns of power and inequality and, traced to their logical conclusion, (d) entertain or actually culminate in political violence. After a period of ecological decline, a chosen population positions itself for rebirth at the expense of others who don't qualify. Ecofascism, then, centrally concerns what Nira Yuval-Davis calls the "politics of belonging," or the ongoing and variable "maintenance and reproduction" of "the boundaries that separate the world population into 'us' and 'them.'" As a facet of identity, belonging is a matter of constant social construction and negotiation—one that is particularly prone to rhetorical naturalization, especially when the group in question believes its integrity to be under threat. But despite their perceived immutability, such identities are still in large part "stories people tell themselves and others about who they are," where they come from, and where they are going.[12] As a political genre, ecofascism might delimit belonging at the level of the nation, as in classical fascism, or at other units of scale, small or large, from a bioregion to the planet itself. Regardless, it invokes several consistent, core themes: an entitlement to land, a fetish for "purity and natural order," and a willingness to at least entertain mass death (if not perpetrate it).[13]

These themes do not proceed from a central ideological source. They are, again, products of nonpartisan narrative elements that, when combined in certain ways, synthesize broader racial, national, environmental, and/or economic discourses. That said, "the effects of genres of politics," Bosworth notes, are, like their origins and development, "nondeterministic."[14] Genre structures movements, communities, and societies, but remains historically contingent in terms of evolution and consequence, due not only to world-historical events but also to variations in the context, attitudes, intentions, and decisions of those who engage it, as well as the fact that the identities it articulates "shift and change," are "contested and multiple."[15] It is true that all politics involve discursive elements, just as all forms of discourse are political. But patterns of storytelling are not reducible to material acts of violence any more than those acts are reducible to narrative. It is for these reasons that I favor the word *prefigure* to express the relationship between genre and "ecofascism proper." To prefigure is not necessarily to predetermine, anticipate, or orchestrate—although it certainly can mean these things. It is, more broadly, to articulate an idea or relationship in a form that is nondeterministic yet consistent across contexts, some of which might indeed sponsor acts of or movements organized around political violence but others of which, depending on intention and other factors, do not.

The figures I study throughout this book chiefly (but not exclusively) fall into the latter category. Many of them do indeed feel menaced by numerous crises, not least ecological collapse. Throughout, I examine how, in response, they construct themselves and others as what Benedict Anderson describes as an "imagined political community"—one with an essentially privileged relationship with the earth.[16] But for the most part, they neither explicitly nor intentionally promote political violence, and often understand themselves to be actively fighting against social inequity. Nonetheless, many of them participate in—while others slyly lampoon—forms of storytelling that reify assumptions about social and ecological (im)purity, delineate territorial boundaries according to them, and shift blame for ecological disruption from political and economic systems onto those most likely to suffer their effects. Faced with a slew of ecological anxieties, these writers channel received patterns of politics and identity in new ways that can unintentionally telegraph white supremacy and other forms of domination. But ecofascism is a muddy field of insinuation, action, and neglect, difficult not only to define but also, as is the case for many if not all facets of human–environment relations, to discuss in terms of responsibility.[17] Who is at fault when a self-identified fascist appropriates (or might appropriate) ideas by writers or speakers who explicitly identify as *anti*fascist? It would be unreasonable to blame the originator wholesale or to dismiss their work as merely inadequate. Rather, the point of cultural critique is to consider "from what conditions such shortcomings emerge rather than . . . hastily dismiss them."[18] My intention, then, is not to cast a broad ecofascist net over diverse cultural phenomena. It is to trace those received narrative patterns I mentioned before—deeply rooted in U.S. politics of environment and national identity—and their contemporary manifestations, transformations, and implications. In some cases—such as the wellness industry's imperative toward self-optimization, which I address in chapters 4 and 5—these patterns straddle standard political boundaries in ways that clearly flirt with overt calls for ecofascist violence. But in others—such as the cooperative living and food arrangements featured in chapters 2 and 3—similar storytelling patterns proceed in numerous directions, some more oppressive and others more liberatory.

Those patterns derive from diverse historical sources (which chapter 1 explores in earnest), but it is my contention in this book that, in the context of the late twentieth- and twenty-first-century United States, it is a specific trope of *consumption* that arranges existing discourses on race, nation, environment, and other matters into a narrative form that prefigures ecofascist effects. Throughout, I consider representations that feature the consumption of what I call *threshold objects*: tokens a speaker consumes to attain or to prove—or to cross a threshold into—privileged access to an ecologically "pure" community. Each of the following chapters accordingly focuses on a single object—land, tools, foods, drugs, and contagion—and certain stories told about it.[19] That said, not all of these objects can be straightforwardly described *as* objects, let alone consumed in any conventional—that is, economic or bodily—sense of the word. For example, land, despite its commodification, resists objectification across U.S., environmental, and literary history. For this reason, it is worth noting that I use the word *consumption* somewhat loosely. In some cases, consumption proceeds literally in economic or bodily terms. In others, the action in question might resemble consumption or approach it but remain to some extent distinct from the activities we typically associate with the word (we do not, for example, typically think of humans as consuming bacteria or a virus). But in all of the examples I study, the assimilation of certain ideas about these objects, if not the objects themselves, plays a crucial role in articulating certain attachments to place. To be clear, my point is not that such objects are themselves "ecofascist." It is that certain ways of *talking about them* condense existing discourses on environment, nation, race, gender, and other social forms toward ends that we can, in some cases, meaningfully label *ecofascistic,* even when such expressions do not self-evidently announce an ethnonationalist stance. As I argue in chapter 1, these patterns emerge from the United States' settler-colonial history. The United States has indeed never adopted ecofascism as an ideological platform, but its extirpation of Native inhabitants furnishes a prototypical example of what I mean by the phrase *ecofascist effects.* Consumption of land occasioned not only settler-colonial genocides to begin with, but also an enduring perspective that Euro-Americans were (and are) better stewards of that land. Contemporary narratives that invoke similar acts and attitudes displace that consumption onto other, seemingly innocuous objects. I do not mean to suggest that this trope alone prefigures ecofascist violence, but I've chosen to focus on it due to the sheer consistency with which it arranges identitarian narratives that do.

It is precisely because identities, belonging, and relations with environment largely take shape through storytelling that I approach the concept of ecofascism through the lens of literature (though other scholars might do and have done differently). Creative works trace not only the rhetorical consolidation of identities but also the process of their creation, as well as contradictions and counternarratives. To study patterns of storytelling is not the same as seeking to explain, fully and finally, the origins or effects of a phenomenon like ecofascism. It is, in this instance, the study of just one aspect of its (potential, nondeterministic) promulgation. There are many others (as this Introduction goes on to explain) and therefore many other avenues of study I do not take up.

But as I contend in the following pages, for the term *ecofascism* to offer any precise critical value, we must understand its referent as a series of processes and effects rather than as a stable ideology, made possible by broad sociocultural conditions and irreducible to those who blatantly champion it. In this respect, ecofascism is a thing that can (and does) happen in various national contexts in similar ways. But because such milieus are socially and historically specific, the material and narrative conditions that prefigure ecofascist effects will differ depending on the circumstances. As such, any study of ecofascism must be situated or comparative. This is not to say that cross-cultural influences do not inform distinct narratives of national identity, let alone explicit ecofascist violence. As the case of the El Paso and Christchurch killers illustrates, transits across borders indeed (perhaps ironically) disseminate ecofascist ideas worldwide. What I mean to suggest is that such influences are largely a matter of structure rather than substance—that is, of genre rather than story. The narrative template—detailing an invading horde of foreign agents—remains the same, but the cast of characters changes depending on national preoccupations. The same is true within national boundaries as well. Some chapters of this book are regionally nuanced. Others are not. But in all cases, I examine how different writers and speakers work with the genre across contexts and scales—and often to radically different ends.

My most ambitious goal for this book, then, is to advance a new argument about the term *ecofascism*'s value—not as an ideological label but as a heuristic. I intend to be provocative: to invite response, debate, and (better yet) deliberation rather than to settle the matter, not only so I might better understand the phenomenon myself, through future conversation, but also so that all of us together might more effectively counter it. The left "often unwittingly cedes the space for fascism to creep into the mainstream," writes Alexander Reid Ross.[20] But the question this book investigates is not how figures on the right seduce those on the left and at the center. It is, instead, how everyday acts of consumption and the stories told about them *already* reproduce logics of entitlement, purity, and belonging that erupt in rhetorics and acts we refer to as ecofascist.

The remainder of this Introduction begins that project by elaborating on ecofascism's contentious discursive history, situating it within the study of fascism more broadly, and outlining its utility as a heuristic, as well as pinpointing consumption as a connective trope among acts of or appeals to political violence in the name of environment. Throughout, I seek to define ecofascism in a mostly searching and open-ended manner, admittedly offering more questions than I do answers. In chapter 1, which extends the Introduction, I pivot to concrete examples—answers rather than questions—that trace the social conditions and narrative patterns that underwrite overt acts of ecofascist violence today. I then turn in later chapters to contemporary, "nondeterministic" iterations of the same genre, some of which risk endorsing ecofascist violence themselves, some of which splinter into surprisingly liberatory alternatives, and some of which engage the genre in order to critique it altogether. I aim, in other words, to illuminate how writing functions as a site of contest over ecofascist effects and the cultural narratives that ground them, not just their consolidation. Seeds for more equitable environmentalist visions lie in the soil of U.S. ecofascism's own narrative conventions—and have indeed sprouted time and again.

Ecofascism as Ideology, Movement, and Debate

What *is* ecofascism? I ask this question plainly because the term's crispness belies the incredible diversity of writing, speech, and physical violence to which observers have affixed the label, discrepancies in its use as either an epithet or badge of pride, and ongoing disagreement regarding its scope (not to mention the scope of fascism more broadly). Popular commentary often frames it as *New Statesman* writer Sarah Manavis does: as a hypernationalist and "Malthusian take on the impact of population growth" that advocates "a culling of the population, and specific races within that population"—through deportation, sterilization, or even genocide—as "the only way to ensure the planet survives."[21] The term has become something of a catch-all descriptor, referring broadly to an ad-hoc ideology identifying ecological health with a specific racial, ethnic, national, or other privileged body, premised on the enforced exclusion of others perceived to threaten both that body and its presumptive environment.

It is unclear, however, how the concept fits into conventional models of political affiliation. The Swedish activist-intellectual Andreas Malm and the Zetkin Collective favor the term "green nationalism" to describe the perspective I just summarized as it manifests across far-right movements in Europe.[22] Others have preferred alternatives. The political historian Jonathan Olsen, for example, has proposed "right-wing ecology" as an umbrella term that synthesizes distinct yet often allied positions such as "eco-organicism" (the identification of an elect group with a certain locale), "eco-naturalism" (an application of cherry-picked evolutionary theory "as a blueprint for the social order"), and "eco-authoritarianism" (the perspective that a charismatic leader and/or a totalitarian state is necessary to address ecological problems).[23] More broadly still, Sam Moore and Alex Roberts refer to "far-right ecologism" to name "all manner of highly variegated attempts to produce . . . and enforce racial hierarchies *in and through* natural systems"—a big tent that encompasses activity among bygone eugenicists, existing (even mainstream) far-right parties, fringe movements whose organization takes place chiefly online, and active terrorists.[24]

Looking to such figures does not necessarily offer insight into a unified ideology. To begin with, the designation "far-right" comprises both "differences and similarities between the anti-liberal right and the anti-democratic extreme right," Forchtner notes.[25] Environmental proposals along this axis have ranged wildly in tone and intent from the casually racist to the nakedly genocidal. On the one hand, during his presidency, Donald Trump framed plastic pollution as a distinctively immigrant threat, casting desperate asylum seekers as a greater risk to ecosystem stability than the construction and presence of a militarized border wall in the U.S. Southwest (his signature policy priority).[26] On the other hand, U.S. neo-Nazi and early Trump cheerleader Richard Spencer wrote in a manifesto that the radical right has "the potential to become nature's steward," disseminating the argument across web platforms such as Twitter, 4chan, and Stormfront (a candidly fascist forum). It is principally within such decentralized spaces that one can find avowed ecofascists (including the El Paso and Buffalo shooters) trading memes, hyping conspiracy theories, and prognosticating impending social collapse. "Such memetic chaos defies easy summarization," Moore and Roberts write, "but it consistently combines refusal of a world . . . beset by degeneracy, race mixing and consumerism with exhortations to brutally enforce traditional gender roles and strive for racial honor, purity and purpose."[27] It also illustrates that the continuum between partisan bluster and genocidal manifesto is more condensed than it might at first seem. One end informs and reinforces the other. For scholars such as Moore, Roberts, and Staudenmaier, the term *ecofascism* designates a specific ideological point along this spectrum: one that identifies self-described fascist insurgents whose aim is institutional ethnic cleansing.

But the stances of self-identified ecofascists vary widely, inconsistently evoking eco-organicism, eco-naturalism, and eco-authoritarianism. Some yearn for a strong state while others promote decentralization. Some embrace capitalism, others socialism. Simply locating common ground in Malthusianism also seems to insufficiently define ecofascist ideology, given that, though some far-right environmentalists decry population growth wholesale, many maintain the necessity of selective reproduction to bolster white numbers (as the Buffalo shooter wrote in his manifesto, "If there's one thing I want you to get from these writings, it's that White birth rates must change"). To further complicate matters, participants in such conversations often disagree vehemently not only on programmatic questions but also on the usefulness of the term *ecofascism* to describe their stance.[28] Commentary has compensated by focusing less on ideology than on common themes, including veganism, anti-multiculturalism, nationalism, and Nordic mythology, all as expressions of a bodily purity synonymous with racial identity rooted in place.[29] Mainstream coverage, in other words, has come to apply the label to people, expressions, and other activities that proceed from markedly different political contexts, some of them ideologically rigorous, but most only loosely related according to shared rhetorical features. The best answer such an understanding offers my question above—*What is ecofascism?*—might simply be a bathetic *I know it when I see it*. The phenomenon itself—its origins and implications—remains vexingly unclear.

And yet the term nonetheless persists, doubtless due to what Staudenmaier calls the "close proximity" between "Nazi programs for ecological renewal and . . . racial extermination" prior to World War II.[30] At the very least, this continuity attests to the identity politics at the heart of ecofascist rhetoric and, more specifically,

the extent to which the articulation of that identity and its ostensibly privileged, exclusionary relationship to a particular place
takes shape in response to perceived threats. Identity "with nature
itself," one Nazi wrote, is "the true essence of National Socialist
Thought"—a sentiment that inspires numerous right-wing environmentalists in the twenty-first-century United States. For example, the Pagan Liberation League bluntly argued in 2000 that
"the true Green movement had its most . . . holistic germination
during the Third Reich," declaring itself "to be in a Spiritual War
with what we call the Judeo-Capitalist Status Quo." The statement
draws explicitly from the Nazi example, in which conservation
proceeded as part of a seemingly "undifferentiated condemnation
of modernity," a condition personified by the Jewish population.[31]
Nazi leadership contended "that the change from an agrarian to an
industrial society had hastened the decline of the race. In contrast
to nature, which engendered the harmonic forms of Germanism,
there were . . . cities, diabolical and inorganic."[32] In this crucible,
Germany's Jewish population exemplified a figure that Ray calls
the "ecological other"—one that takes shape in narratives that describe "which kinds of bodies and . . . relations to the environment
are" and are not "ecologically 'good'" along lines of "purity and pollution."[33] In the Nazi rendering, Jews comprised "a rootless, wan-
dering people, incapable of any true relationship with the land."[34]
The ethnic German *Volk,* by contrast, romantically aligned itself
with authentic (yet threatened) nature. Against the backdrop of
Aryan supremacy, a Nazi "politics of nature" organized around the
figure of an ecological other, becoming, as Olsen puts it, "a politics
of identity."[35]

What is also worth emphasizing, however, is that populist Nazism responded to what Janet Biehl refers to as "a very real sense
of alienation" that proceeded from the massive economic and geographic dislocations occasioned by rapid industrialization. Even as
the party itself shepherded the nation through its transformation,
it advanced "a mythology of racial salvation through a return to
the land" governed by an "unmediated application of biological
categories to the social realm." This Social-Darwinist "fetishization
of natural 'purity'" supplied "not merely a rationale but an incen-
tive for the Third Reich's most heinous crimes."[36] Nazis committed genocide in the name of preservation—of both nature and the
race. A "conflation of capitalism with Jews," Staudenmaier writes,

"personaliz[ed] capitalism, making an opaque and abstract system seem more concrete" by reducing it to "a straightforward story of good guys and bad guys. . . . cast in terms of an idyllic vision of restored nature," all while leaving actual, material hierarchies more or less intact.[37]

In recent years, similar configurations have become more prominent in the United States—and for analogous (though historically distinct) reasons. As the next chapter illustrates, ecofascist violence in the contemporary United States rests upon existing cultural narratives about race, nation, and environment, but largely takes shape in response to dislocations occasioned by interlinked crises of neoliberal globalization and rapid ecological change, just as Germans reacted to disturbances prompted by abrupt industrialization and the ecological costs it incurred. As Ruth Wodak notes, perhaps the most consistent rhetorical convention of right-wing populism in general, despite its ideological diversity, is a recurring trope of "*looming crises* . . . threatening 'the people.'"[38] It is when perceptions of those crises intersect with existing, reductive assumptions about race and nation, Blair Taylor suggests, that movements "resurrect" old, marginal, yet still consequential "traditions of the antimodernist, revolutionary, and fascist right . . . that attack liberal democracy, the state, and the 'mongrelizing' . . . forces of global capitalism."[39] Self-styled ecofascists overwhelmingly observe this pattern, mapping their environmental commitments over antiestablishment, anti-multicultural, and anti-industrial attitudes, including a rejection of mainstream conservatism.

Many of the sociocultural anxieties powering this response, however, cut across standard political divisions. Figures across the ideological spectrum have criticized what Anthony Giddens describes as neoliberal globalization's "disembedding" effects on local communities, as well as its concentration of neocolonial power in the hands of elite capitalist interests.[40] They have also done so in highly uneven ways, regardless of political affiliation, with respect to attention to complex material and discursive histories of settler colonialism, racial formation, land ownership, and local or national sovereignty. Staudenmaier clarifies, however, that where *radical* critiques "embody an emancipatory outlook that strives to create new social forms," right-wing *reactionary* critiques "reflect a nostalgic vision of returning to a simpler . . . communal life" marked by racial purity and heteropatriarchal hierarchy as well as ecological integrity.[41] To be clear, my goal in this book is not to vindicate the socioeconomic status quo myself (quite the opposite), but to scrutinize one particular critique of it: a form that racializes certain interactions with environment, naturalizing specific features and behaviors while "unnaturalizing" others in ways that justify political violence.

But what I want to emphasize is that, far from clarifying the lines of a right/left binary, this tendency in fact troubles them, and has done so for well over a century. Positions, ideas, and appeals often identified or claimed as ecofascist not only circulate increasingly in media at the left and center but also historically transcended ideological bounds. For starters, U.S. preservationism has roots in blatantly crypto-fascist intellectual traditions. As chapter 1 will explore in more detail, one of the greatest influences on Theodore Roosevelt's Progressive-era environmentalism was the eugenicist Madison Grant, author of the virulently white-supremacist *The Passing of the Great Race* (1916), whose other pupils include not only self-described ecofascists in the twenty-first century but also Adolf Hitler himself. In the late nineteenth and early twentieth centuries, preservation and immigration policy proceeded together under the assumption that pristine natural spaces reflected not just the integrity of the nation but also the racial superiority of white Anglo-Saxon Protestants.

A number of critics have also pointed out that, despite the blatant racial chauvinism of such figures, right-wing actors have increasingly—and successfully—"tr[ied] to seduce progressives by channeling environmental concern into support for anti-immigration policies," for example.[42] But such stances have permeated the politics of nominally progressive environmentalists for decades, including the population scientist and geneticist Garrett Hardin, cofounder of Earth First! Dave Foreman, and ecophilosophers Bill Devall and George Sessions, who elaborated a biocentric "deep ecology" to oppose "shallow" green consumerism in the 1970s and 1980s. The most militant acolytes of deep ecology even developed a reputation for advocating nonconsensual population control to facilitate nonhuman survival, attracting the ecofascist label from the social ecologist Murray Bookchin as a result. Bookchin, however, was not the only critic to submit that charge. Others have balked at the "implicitly fascist strain" in biocentrism's philosophical antecedents, especially the work of

Martin Heidegger.[43] Conservative pundits lobbed the same epithet in the 1990s, railing against environmentalism's supposed "valuation of ecosystemic concerns relative to human rights." The critic Lawrence Buell rightly notes that such claims "oversimplify the diversity of actual ecocentric positions, exaggerate their authoritarianism, and proffer a cartoon version of Nazis as Greens."[44] But they nonetheless help to demonstrate the fact that ecofascism is a term troubled by its ubiquity, to the point that the sheer number of examples said to illustrate it appears to obscure any precise understanding of its meaning or scope.

Given ecofascism's flourishing prominence as political shorthand, these variations suggest that a better question than *What is ecofascism?* might instead ask what benefit the term can offer the study of contemporary environmental politics and rhetoric (if it can offer any at all). "Do we need the term 'fascism' for any of this?" Moore and Roberts ask, pointing out that the word "was not required for a host of oppressive, authoritarian actions carried out . . . over the course of the twentieth and twenty-first centuries."[45] To what extent can an idea like ecofascism refer to such a diverse collection of activity? Why not eco*nationalism,* eco*racism,* or eco*xenophobia?* Why not a whole cornucopia of designations for a variety of phenomena? What does the term eco*fascism* specifically offer? How does it differ from "right-wing ecology" or "green nationalism"? These questions resonate with Matthew Lyons's epigraph above: we must approach ecofascism, like any "ism," not as a "fixed, objective thing" but as "an analytic category."[46] What makes ecofascism a useful heuristic for describing, analyzing, and connecting acts of or appeals to environmentally motivated political violence? In short, what does or should the *fascism* in *ecofascism* mean?

Fascism as Heuristic

As its own "analytic category," fascism writ large has remained hotly debated since its coinage. Lyons himself defines it as a "revolutionary form of right-wing populism, inspired by a totalitarian vision of collective rebirth, that challenges capitalist and cultural power while promoting economic and social hierarchy."[47] But as the concept's history attests, the real-world phenomena to which such definitions apply—including not only the full-fledged regimes of interwar Europe but also a series of related yet atomized movements that both anticipated and have since succeeded them—defy straightforward categorization. Some scholars, like the sociologist Michael Mann, contend that fascism "was essentially a product of post–World War I conditions in Europe and is unlikely to reappear in its classic garb."[48] The word emerged to refer specifically to Benito Mussolini's regime in Italy, but as its prompt migration to German National Socialism attests, observers immediately found broader descriptive value in the idea, establishing a long conversation over what, precisely, fascism is if not just Italy's Fascio d'Azione Rivoluzionaria—one that deliberates over how to understand historically and geographically distinct movements, regimes, and rhetorics in terms of common ideology, features, and/or conditions of emergence.

The precise form, content, and scope of that phenomenon—and utility of its definition—have been subject to debate ever since. Can we, for instance, reasonably refer to France's Nouvelle Droite or the New European Right more broadly as *fascist,* as many do? By what criteria? To begin with, Walter Laqueur suggests, one must acknowledge that during the interwar period neither "everyone who oppose[d] further immigration" nor "every anti-Semite" or "every ultranationalist" identified with local fascist movements, though their priorities might have intersected.[49] One must also recognize that fascist party members "originated from the political right, center, and left alike." In light of this diversity, scholars such as Mann and Laqueur have attempted to pinpoint the idea by turning to the conditions of classical fascist movements. Several transnational crises precipitated the rise of the Italian and German regimes, including the social and economic consequences of World War I, rapid industrialization, class conflict enflamed by a global Great Depression, and, as Mann puts it, "a cultural sense of civilizational contradiction and decay" that emerged in reaction to these factors. In distinct yet homologous ways, the regimes proposed a "Third Way" distinct from liberal democracy and radical socialism: one in which "[n]ations, not classes, were the true masses."[50]

But despite these similarities, both classical Italian and German fascisms lacked an orderly political philosophy. This is not to say that avowed fascists do not gesture to specific intellectuals. They do.[51] Such sources, however, are more opportunistic than systematic. Despite relatively consistent elements—a "mix of nationalism, militarism and regenerationist myth"—fascist movements, Daniel Woodley writes, have marched without "a coherent theoretical core," a definitional challenge compounded by tensions between "anti-capitalist and anti-socialist themes" and strong-state and decentralist emphases.[52] One cannot limit fascism to extreme conservatism (which *can* be read in terms of an intelligible philosophical tradition), despite a shared commitment to social hierarchy. That fascist leaders achieved social transformation through grassroots upheaval set them against conventional conservatives invested in family, church, rank, and property. As such, one can hardly boil fascism down to traditional authoritarianism, either, given that fascist leaders generally lack any established, inherited, or otherwise assumed claim to rule. But nor does it seem sufficient to privilege fascism's populist elements. Populism, Kai Bosworth points out, might itself be better conceived as political genre than as ideology: one that "stages a fundamental difference between the people and the elites"—a performance the left as well as the right enacts.[53] Populism is, in this regard, akin to nationalism, which has also historically manifested in conservative, liberal, and leftist (as well as imperial and decolonial) forms, and as such also seems an incomplete candidate for fascism's definition. Despite their commitment to conservation and preservation, the Nazis were hardly Luddites, either. For all its appeals to the soil, the party was more "reactionary modernist" than it was primitivist, welding essentialist visions of land and people to profoundly technocratic regimes of social and ecological management.[54]

In other words, it is difficult to argue for fascism as a stable ideology. Any attempt to identify, define, and distinguish *eco*fascism from right-wing environmentalism writ large requires recognition of this point. Fascism's classical forms did not rest upon any established theoretical foundation, but rather functioned like "scavenger[s] which attempted to co-opt all that had appealed to people in the . . . past," George Mosse writes: "romanticism, liberalism, and socialism, as well as Darwinism . . . were integrated into a coherent attitude" nonetheless marked by apparent inconsistencies that disrupt comprehensive definitions of what fascism *is*.[55]

Broadly speaking, comparativist scholars of fascism have navigated this challenge through two alternative approaches to definition. The first is to establish what the historian and political theorist Roger Griffin calls an "ideal type" or "common core of fascist phenomena which can be treated as its definitional minimum."[56] This route seeks to consolidate the features most commonly associated with fascist movements: their tendency to divide a population into an *us* and a *them* through appeals to racial and/or cultural distinctions, to naturalize hierarchies based on these differences, to fabricate what Jason Stanley calls a "mythic past to support their vision," to incite and foment grievance and victimhood among privileged in-groups, and to promote law-and-order rule.[57] Griffin thus defines fascism as "a genus of political ideology whose mythic core . . . is a palingenetic form of populist ultranationalism"—a typology whose key qualifier ("palingenetic") refers to "regeneration after a phase of crisis or decline." The nation appears, in this telling, "as a 'higher' racial, historical, spiritual or organic reality" that has been "contaminated" by immigration, miscegenation, and other "'alien' forces . . . unleashed by 'modern' society," including consumerism, feminism, and LGBTQIA+ advancement. The combination of these elements, Griffin argues, is what makes fascism unique.[58]

Others, however, have accused this approach of ignoring the concrete social, political, and cultural conditions that shape fascist movements and regimes. Fascism, "far from static," Robert O. Paxton writes, "was a succession of processes and choices."[59] One of its earliest interpretations advanced this perspective. For interwar and immediate postwar Marxists, fascism represented the culmination of the capitalist system in crisis, boiling over the heat of its inequities yet ultimately consolidating class rule. But important gaps riddle the teleological Marxist narrative, which largely ignores fascist movements' cross-class support and hostility to the cosmopolitan bourgeoisie, which, for fascists, "neglected the interests . . . of 'the nation as an organic whole.'"[60] Later critics like Paxton and Mann emphasize the rhetorical and physical tactics by which fascist movements have acquired influence, highlighting especially the roles played by propaganda and "cleansing" paramilitary violence.

Two key themes emerge across comparative fascist studies as a field, despite its internecine disagreements. The first is the fact that it actually concentrates on two distinct yet related objects of inquiry: what fascism ultimately "looks like" and how it comes about. Both elements, however, are arguably indispensable to a useful definition of a phenomenon whose complexity cannot be

reduced to a stable ideology. One can hardly "take into account social and institutional factors" without first normatively clarifying
what fascism "looks like."[61] Doing so crafts a frame without which
the study of how fascism comes about would be impossible. A definition such as Griffin's might function as a "point of departure
rather than the end result" of an inquiry into fascist forms—not
just of movements or regimes, but also of the material conditions
that shape them and rhetorical processes that inform them.[62] It is
insufficient, in other words, to define fascism as *just* an ideal or *just*
a process. It is an unfolding series of events that potentially (but
not inevitably) gathers momentum because of the second of the
two themes I mentioned: the fact that its historical success derived
from mass appeal. "Fascist movements could never grow without
the help of ordinary . . . even conventionally good people," Paxton
notes. They installed the few regimes they did because "great numbers of ordinary people accommodated to them in the ordinary
business of daily life."[63]

Fascist violence proliferates, that is, in part because enough
"ordinary" people support or at least stomach it—enough that
classical fascist regimes succeeded primarily through established
political channels. It is no coincidence that fascist movements
arise in conditions of rapid class stratification and attendant social
crises. Fascism might just be the word for one (ostensible) solution
to such plights: the promotion of an essential national identity to
paper over them, deflect attention from their material origins,
and forcefully eliminate anything that interrupts the illusion—
including any people who are, for any reason, incapable of satisfying the requirements of national belonging. This combination of
crisis and identity narrative helps to account for classical fascism's
mass allure: "cultural expressions of the true community," Mosse
writes, "moved to the forefront," promising a privileged group not
oppression but safety, security, and prosperity—and doing so by
"annex[ing] and bend[ing] to its purpose, rather than chang[ing]
concepts deeply rooted in the national consensus."[64] Fascism is indeed a process, one crucial part of which is the mobilization yet
reconfiguration of existing cultural narratives to "appeal to subjects not as individuals or class actors, but as 'the people.'"[65] That
identity requires constant maintenance (sometimes orchestrated,
as in the case of Nazi Germany, but sometimes accumulative, as
among the U.S. "alt-right") in the form of cultural products whose

transmission reinforces its value. Fascism shares this feature with nationalism writ large but is specific in that it cuts across partisan lines yet manifests in what appears to be doctrinal right-wing extremism, culminating in an incitement to identitarian violence.

It is in this respect that fascism is more of a political genre than a partisan ideology. The features most often associated with it—antiestablishment, hypernationalist, and race-supremacist violence—do not comprise a coherent right-wing platform, but a constellation of consequences that stem not just from the rise to power of impassioned movements but also from quotidian representations that reinforce the notion that only "certain similarities should count as *the* definition of political community," to the extent that exclusion and other forms of political violence come to appear attractive or necessary.[66] Populist identities, Bosworth notes, are always "actively constructed: 'the people' as an identity did not preexist its assembly." But in "composing a normative subject," *any* populism, on the left or right, is "liable to reproduce generic conventions" of race and nation (and elide class politics, too).[67] Even when "ties to ancient ethnicities can be traced," as in the German example, "such identities are *effects* to be explained rather than assumed," Woodley writes.[68] For this reason, comprehending fascism is in large part a matter of understanding how and why these identities might coalesce in a given context. Approaching these questions through the lens of literary analysis enables us to discern that phenomenon's narrative and other representational tributaries.

What makes fascism unique is that it emerges from certain social conditions and the stories told in reaction to them, not from a central theoretical source that mobilizes only true believers. In other words, not all far-right politics are fascism—but nor is fascism reducible to the far right. Any definition that omits this characteristic is incomplete. One might describe fascism as an emergent quality of political life—one that has historically organized in conjunction with the nation form but, given its definitional malleability, can develop across scales of political community whenever an already empowered group of people, under perceived threat, culturally reinforces an exclusive, naturalized sense of identity in ways that at least implicitly promote rebirth through violence against already disenfranchised populations. Properly understood, the concept is inclusive of both these effects and the representational as well as political processes that prime them yet also mostly remain obscure—not because they take place conspiratorially, among earnest agitators alone, but because their mechanisms turn subtly, in everyday contexts. This quotidian dimension comprises just one among many elements of fascism as a process, but one that still contributes to its material effects. It is on this facet, in contexts of ecological disruption, that I focus in this book: a logic of belonging, conflict, and rebirth that suffuses environmentalist storytelling in the United States, across the extreme right but also beyond it.

Ecofascism as Process, Genre, and Frame

The *fascism* in *ecofascism* requires that we likewise understand the concept in part in terms of its nonpartisan genre, which I defined previously as one that links certain environments with certain people in ways that reinforce existing patterns of inequity and entertain, if not outwardly advocate, political violence in doing so. After a period of ecological decline, a chosen population positions itself for rebirth at the expense of those who don't qualify. I am largely approaching ecofascism, then, as a blend of ecologism with classical fascist narrative elements.[69] It is distinct from various other forms of identification with or expressions of attachment to place in its emphasis on essential, even biological purity, its almost technocratic (if sometimes antitechnology) account of how one achieves or proves their belonging, its circular reading of existing social hierarchies into ecological phenomena and back again into social forms, and its intimation (if not plainspoken, final solution) of cleansing violence. This book, in other words, does treat ecofascism in somewhat normative terms. But it also testifies to the fact that to meaningfully name, analyze, and trace its emergence requires a dependable conception of its form. Ecofascism consists in acts of or appeals to political violence stemming in part from the narrative reinforcement of the notion that certain qualities constitute *the* definition of ecological belonging, mapped over existing discourses of territory and/or race. Again, these effects do not proceed from a central ideological source, but from existing narrative elements within a given culture that, when combined in certain ways, synthesize broader discourses on people and place into a distinctive form. As for fascism in general, not all far-right environmentalism is ecofascism—but nor is ecofascism reducible to the far right.

Any study of ecofascism must therefore acknowledge that an actor need not be avowedly fascist—in the sense of actively subscribing to fascism as a stable ideology—to work within this genre and potentially, if unwittingly, contribute to ecofascist effects. The example of deep ecology is again instructive. The steadfastly anti-Nazi Norwegian philosopher Arne Næss originated the "ecosophy" as a radically egalitarian perspective that all organisms possess inherent self-worth—a position that might seem at odds with the priorities of classical fascism. And yet deep ecology's emphasis on the "self-realization" of one's "ecological consciousness"—extended by thinkers like Bill Devall—has often been read, both approvingly and critically, as a potential reinforcement of human hierarchy, an argument that some people are consubstantial with their environments to a degree superior to others. At least one self-proclaimed ecofascist has expressed outrage that "everyone associates deep ecology with . . . far left ideologies deeply rooted in industrialization."[70] Like other far-right environmentalists, the speaker "translat[es] deep ecology's concern for habitat loss and species extinction into fears about 'white genocide' and the displacement of 'indigenous' white people by 'invasive species.'"[71] Counter-Currents Publishing, the predominant white-nationalist house in the United States, has sought to institutionalize this reading, revitalizing Næss's work for a far-right audience, shelving him beside fascist luminaries like Savitri Devi and Jorian Jenks. The left, and its broad attention to social inequities, appears, for such figures, synonymous with a blanket modernity that threatens a nature in which far-right environmentalists ground themselves.

Despite its partisan distinction, this statement illustrates nothing if not the extent to which present-day far-right environmentalists in fact share something in common with the left-identified radical environmentalism of the late twentieth century that Næss helped to stimulate, whose "great shortcoming," Keith Makoto Woodhouse writes, was a persistent (though by no means ubiquitous) "neglect of social issues," even a tendency to blame the social writ large for ecological disruption.[72] Perhaps no figure better captures such narrow misanthropy than the Unabomber Ted Kaczynski, whose political malleability has made him a nearly universal point of identification for sworn ecofascists. But it also, in the 1990s, resonated with the activity of many left-leaning groups, such as Earth First! Kaczynski's actions fall squarely within the legal category of "ecoterrorism," which the U.S. Federal Bureau of Investigation defines as "use or threatened use of violence of a criminal nature against innocent victims or their property . . . for environmental-political reasons."[73] So do the El Paso shooter's. That man's fixation on race arguably illustrates the line between ecofascism and ecoterrorism more broadly, committed most often in the late twentieth century by left-leaning environmentalists. But members of organizations like Earth First! were not immune to racialized distinctions, to the point that schisms over such matters dominated their politics in the late 1980s and 1990s. Despite his affiliation with the left, Devall argued something similar to the white nationalist quoted above, portraying immigration (specifically from the Global South) as a symptom of "misplaced humanism." Janet Biehl contends that, regardless, the man was "certainly not a fascist." Peter Staudenmaier likewise writes that attitudes like Devall's "do not take an openly fascist form but bring together reactionary ecological themes with anti-immigrant sentiment, eugenic policies, and a nationally or racially tinged defense of the land."[74] It would be unfair to call Devall an ecofascist—a label Sam Moore and Alex Roberts rightly find inapplicable to "any present political actor, except a few on the margins."[75] But we still might meaningfully consider the degree to which figures like him engage the same narrative forms taken as justification by those ecofascists proper, as well as what cultural traditions inform their logic.

Popular and academic commentary alike often typifies ecofascism as a heterogeneous yet indisputably right-wing program for which "proximity between the discourse about the nation and the discourse about the environment . . . leads to a rejection of so-called 'invasive species,'" including certain types of people as well as animals and plants.[76] I don't necessarily disagree with this description. However, I do think the concept is improperly applied. Many observers identify any coexistence of environmentalist and racist sentiment on the right as ecofascist while ignoring other speakers entirely, limiting analysis to overtly white-supremacist activities alone. Ecofascism is not reducible to Jonathan Olsen's right-wing ecology, Andreas Malm's green nationalism, or Moore and Roberts's far-right ecologism. But neither is it merely a specific instance of any of them. It is broader than the right, even if, in form and function, it resembles it—and that fact is precisely what renders the concept distinct and useful.

I am not suggesting that we condemn place-based narratives or politics tout court. There exists a range of vibrant forms of attachment to and identification with place—even myths of origin and rebirth. Many of them self-consciously prioritize emancipation, egalitarianism, and critical self-definition rather than recapitulate or escalate enduring forms of domination. Consider, for example, Indigenous politics of "resurgence," which, for Glen Coulthard, involve "reconnect[ing] with the landscapes and places that give [Native peoples'] histories, languages, and cultures shape and content," "revitalizing land-based . . . practices like hunting, fishing, and gathering," and "assert[ing] our sovereign presence" according not to hierarchy but to *a system of reciprocal relations and obligations.*"[77] Such approaches acknowledge the deep complexity of environments and seek to work with it, rather than to flatten it according to standards of "purity." Even in more ambiguous settler accounts, such as that offered by Ernest Callenbach's 1975 novel *Ecotopia* (the centerpiece of chapter 2), flexibility and entanglement appear as alternative values to purity and exclusivity. There are countless ways to celebrate place, and the designation *ecofascism* involves both *eco* and *fascist* elements—facets that, in examples such as *Ecotopia*'s, must be disentangled rather than thrown out altogether. Historically, it would be just as inaccurate to reduce the *fascist* to the *eco* as it would be to conflate *eco* with *fascist*. Nazi exhortations to "return to the soil" expressed not so much a flat critique of industry, capital, or "progress" writ large as they did an ambivalence toward it. In the interwar period, "the leading elites of the right rallied generally to technology" in "a posture of domination of nature," Christophe Bonneuil and Jean-Baptiste Fressoz point out, "whereas the critique of technology was more associated with an egalitarian and emancipatory thought" articulated by intellectuals such as Lewis Mumford and members of the Frankfurt school.[78] Nazis' seeming care for environment was bound up with efforts to manage, order, and control it, as well as its human inhabitants—a project geared more toward creating purity than protecting it. The precise tenor of a given perspective on place (and a people's relationship with it) depends on other political priorities and narrative influences. Emancipatory politics will tend to formulate place in emancipatory ways. Fascist influences frame it in terms of purity, technocracy, hierarchy, and violence.

As a political genre, ecofascism also intensifies what Rob Nixon calls the "slow violence" of everyday environmental injustice as a prelude to the spectacular violence of overt ecofascists.[79] Its narrative logic not only reproduces patterns of heteropatriarchy and ableism as well as racism and nationalism, but also places blame for ecological disruption on marginalized populations who least contribute to it. Bosworth and others suggest that, much like "green capitalism," ecofascism will always fail to substantively address ecological challenges "because it will forever be unable to understand that the crisis stems . . . from racial and national systems it takes to be 'natural'"—namely, entitlements derived from the institutions of settler colonialism and what Cedric Robinson calls "racial capitalism," which have not only generated wealth for the United States at the expense of nonwhite populations but also spurred vast ecological turmoil in the process.[80] This point clarifies classical fascism's ambivalent relationship with capitalism, too. Despite being "the source of much that fascism finds appalling," Moore and Roberts write, capitalism is also "the real motor of the domination that fascism affirms."[81] Put differently, despite fascism's pretension to buck the economic status quo, it ultimately reinforces it. The same is true for its green resonances. The difference "between saying 'climate change does not exist' and 'climate change is caused by poor people living in the south and coming towards the north,'" Malm and the Zetkin Collective write, "is rather like that between saying 'the earth is flat' and 'the earth is a golf ball.'" We might view the argument, that is, as yet another "shade of denialism."[82]

It is for these reasons that we can distinguish ecofascist articulations of people and place from others that might also appear exclusionary—namely, Indigenous anticolonial struggles of the sort I mentioned before. For Indigenous groups worldwide, a measure of exclusion can become not merely sensible but also necessary to resist the dramatic enactments of asymmetrical power inherent in imperialism, colonialism, settler colonialism, and genocide. Such arguments mobilize identity and place to protect ways of life threatened by such systems, including iterations of pluralism that nonetheless disempower or eradicate (such as global capitalism). Candid ecofascists parrot this line of reasoning, but in doing so paper over the lopsided power relations detailed above, which not only disenfranchise Indigenous peoples but also marginalize alternative, nonexploitative ways of living with the earth. Appeals to "blood" and "land" are indeed among what Chadwick Allen refers to as "the complicated, multiperspectivist, and sometimes controversial maneuvers . . . employed by indigenous minority writers and activists" to assert claims to place and resources, as well as to "maintain some level of cultural and political distinctiveness."[83] For Coulthard, such tactics challenge both universalist narratives of global liberation (often couched in a Marxist idiom that presents capitalism, and therefore settler colonialism, as a necessary step on the way to revolution) and glib antiessentialist critique. Place-based identities aren't merely figurative. They have real, material grounding in historical relations with specific environments and the nonhuman organisms that share them. This is not to justify forms of inequity "in the name of community self-determination," as some have attempted to do in past decades in terms of gender, especially.[84] Coulthard points to other Indigenous writers and activists, such as Taiaiake Alfred (Mohawk) and Leanne Betasamosake Simpson (Anishinaabe), who insist "that we remain cognizant of the pitfalls associated with retreating into an uncritical essentialism in our practices of cultural revitalization" even as they stress what Alfred refers to as the "values and principles that form the persistent core of a community's culture."[85] Such an attitude toward place, identity, and belonging is critical and self-reflective rather than static, recognizing the fact that traditions are concretely rooted in material conditions and histories but can, do, and indeed often should change in light of "the larger contemporary political and economic reality."[86] It also informs various movements that seek to abolish state-sanctioned racial capitalism and settler colonialism, reestablish political and cultural autonomy, and reject the nihilism and disaster fetishism that (as chapters 4 and 5 will explain) so often pervade right-wing and mainstream environmentalisms. Every community observes norms that regulate inclusion and exclusion. Not all are fascist. Those that are emphasize not just rebirth but rebirth through (implied) violence—directed, in the context of the United States, specifically against the populations most negatively affected by racial capitalism and settler colonialism to begin with.

Everyday Ecofascism seeks to expand critique to quotidian contributions because such contributions have profound, if profoundly unassumed, consequences. Just as "mapping out the trajectory between . . . micro and macro forms of racism" can demonstrate how "the path from merely 'innocuous' words to violence is swift," as Raquel Kennon puts it, charting similar relationships in environmental rhetoric can help us to understand how, for example, the El Paso shooter exemplifies a thoroughgoing rather than superficial phenomenon, embedded in tenacious cultural narratives about national identity in the United States.[87] It is in this sense that I use the word *everyday* in the title of this book. I do not quite mean it to evoke the methodology of everyday life studies (although I do engage work of this sort from time to time, particularly in chapter 3). I use it more capaciously, to refer to how racial inequity, for instance, "is reproduced through . . . practices that are subtle, institutional, and apparently nonracial," as Eduardo Bonilla-Silva writes.[88] As the work of the environmental justice movement amply demonstrates, this atmosphere has always involved matters of environment.

But as the history of fascist politics illustrates, not just inequity but also political identities themselves are everyday matters of social production and reproduction. Processes of what Michael Omi and Howard Winant call "racialization"—the "extension of racial meaning to a previously racially unclassified relationship, social practice or group," or the ongoing rearticulation of an existing one—structurally negotiate the boundaries of racial identities and, when territorialized, national ones.[89] Throughout this book, I consider how a variety of identity formations take shape along lines of *us* and *them,* in terms not just of existing racial politics but also other, seemingly minor distinctions between who is sufficiently "natural" and who is not. Storytelling plays an important role in this process. Narratives are "important occasions and repositories for the values, political and ethical ideas, and sets of behaviors that determine how we perceive and interact" not just with ideas about race, nation, or other social forms, but also, Erin James and Eric Morel write, "with ecological homes."[90]

Writers and speakers will, as a result, come to the same political genre for different reasons and, depending on context, tell markedly different stories within it. Contemporary German and Scandinavian ecofascisms, for instance, revolve around myth-images of a more-or-less ethnically specific people bound to the landscape. Similar expressions in the United States might stem in part from kindred circumstances (such as economic globalization and its repercussions) but also distinct historical conditions and narratives told in relation to them—specifically the nation's settler-colonial history, which has involved not merely an identification with land but also an active, violent appropriation of it. The word I favor is *consumption* of land, given that the term broadly connotes not only acts of possession but also incorporation or assimilation—that is, interaction with and/or representation of an object in such a way that rhetorically establishes or enhances a form of identification with or through it. One might almost (loosely yet suggestively) describe that identification as technocratic: it is managed or effected by some special knowledge or effort that, from the subject's perspective, others do not possess or have the ability or wherewithal to pursue.

Consumption might otherwise seem a surprising trope in the context of contemporary ecofascism. Much of modern environmentalist activism seems preoccupied with the problem of *too much* consumption by an unsustainably large population, as both a symptom and driver of resource extraction and related emissions, as well as a condition for nonrecyclable or degradable waste. But as John Levi Barnard points out, even though environmentalism constitutes a diverse field of thought, activism, and policy in the United States, the turn-of-the-twentieth-century conservation movement from which its mainstream iterations proceed "has never been at odds with consumption per se"—that is, consumption-as-commodification, the conversion of what Kyle Powys Whyte (Potawatomi) calls "reciprocal obligations" into patterns of purchase, ownership, and sale.[91] The next chapter will explore in more detail how conservation and preservation efforts in the late nineteenth and early twentieth centuries organized around consumption of the frontier landscape, the seizure and reconstitution of Native lands as private and public assets and sites of national and environmental mythmaking. On game preservations, wealthy recreationalists feasted on bison, further staking their claim by ingesting food that was "*authentic* in its indigeneity and the manner of its preparation," even as federal forces drove buffalo to functional extinction in overtly genocidal campaigns against Native peoples.[92] Ingestion, too, came to function as a mode of consumption yoking environment to identity, especially in national, regional, and racial registers. By *consumption*, then, I don't just mean the trade in or theft of commodities in economic and imperial terms alone. I use the word in a dual sense to refer to both the circulation of objects and their incorporation into the self, by a variety of means, as a matter of identity. To the extent that U.S. narratives of consumption, broadly conceived, proceed as acts of self-indigenization that announce one's authentic belonging at the expense of others', they also articulate (even as they obscure) a racialized entitlement to land.

Sites at which environmentalists perform such acts in less overtly imperial contexts are the focus of the following chapters, which survey how this narrative gets displaced for contextually specific reasons onto a variety of seemingly innocuous objects other than land itself. In narratives of environmental crisis, engagement with these threshold objects—including certain commodities (chapter 2), foodstuffs (chapter 3), organic drugs (chapter 4), and even microbes (chapter 5)—functions to rhetorically "return" the subject to a state of ecological innocence and absolve one of complicity in that crisis. The subject, that is, "palingenetically" crosses an avowed threshold from a state of modernity to a state of nature (think the antediluvian apple in reverse). The consumption of these objects prefigures ecofascist effects specifically when its representation articulates a sense of place-based identity; asserts the consumer's innocence of complicity in ecological crisis (including climate change); effaces, excludes, condemns, or ultimately calls for violence upon others who do not or cannot conform to the narrative, for whatever reason, as a matter of ecological necessity; and fortifies existing power imbalances in terms of nation, race, gender, sexuality, and other social forms in doing so. To reiterate, these narratives are not deterministic. They do not "produce" real-world ecofascist violence. But they are consistent with its logic, even when a given writer or speaker has different intentions. In all cases they at least imply that whatever happens to a given environment, or even the earth writ large, certain of its inhabitants, sanctified by suitable consumption, can and will survive even as others die—even, perhaps, *because* they do.

Crisis, Consumption, and Narrative in the United States

As an unfolding and historically contingent phenomenon, ecofascism's progression is uneven from context to context. But framing it in terms of genre enables us to identify ecofascistic storytelling in incipient forms and trace its sociocultural influences, if not deterministically link those examples to possible outcomes. *Everyday Ecofascism* traces such instances in the form of threshold object narratives from the rise of the modern environmental movement in the 1960s to the present. As I mentioned before, each of the coming chapters focuses on a single object—land, tools, foods, drugs, and contagion—and certain stories told about it. I have chosen these sites in part for their effective ambiguity. In many cases they help to organize politics oriented toward laudable, equitable ends, as in the case of food justice coalitions and psychedelics' encouraging applications for public health crises such as addiction and depression. These vital areas are also worthy of scholarly exploration, and indeed have attracted it for several decades. But in other cases, these objects serve to palingenetically link certain environments with certain people in ways that invoke the "core themes" I enumerated previously: entitlement to land, naturalization of social forms, overvaluation of purity, and a willingness to entertain mass violence (if not perpetrate it). These themes (and the objects with which I pair them across the chapters) are not mutually exclusive, but different writers do reproduce some more energetically than others depending on context. All of them, to varying degrees, also inform (and are informed by) histories of racially, nationally, and environmentally motivated violence in times of apparent crisis. In this respect, they speak to a broader "apocalyptic disposition" that Betsy Hartmann argues has long shaped political rhetoric in the United States, mobilizing escalating forms of exclusion and violence to protect an ostensibly privileged nation and resurging in the twenty-first century in reaction to global climate changes.[93]

It is in this sense that I use the word *crisis* in the title of this book. The term denotes more than disruption, disaster, or even catastrophe. It refers to the sociopolitically uneven structures of reaction (discursive as well as material) that build up around them. For Kyle Whyte, a "crisis epistemology" is one according to which a suspension of "certain concerns about justice" becomes "defensible by real or perceived" emergencies (and one that, in the United States, finds its template in the settler-colonial contact zone).[94] Earnest threshold object narratives react to such scenarios by seeking to consolidate a given person or people's sense of purity and identity with nature in an effort to absolve them of complicity in ecological disruption and exempt them from its effects, even as they scapegoat others according to existing stratifications of social power. Worth noting, however, is the fact that for marginalized and especially Indigenous peoples, the line between apocalypse and everyday reality is and has long been quite thin. Conditions in the Americas have for centuries undergone drastic, irreversible, and life-threatening changes at the hands of extractive settler colonialism, its imperialist and neo-imperialist managers, and its casual beneficiaries. Only recently have its ongoing effects achieved sufficient scale for a critical mass of those beneficiaries themselves to recognize, care about, and respond to them—far too often in ways that resonate with Whyte's definition of crisis epistemology. Historically, Native and other marginalized writers and speakers have made sense of their changing worlds in quite different ways. For this reason, I do not limit my understanding of ecological disruption to the crisis epistemologies of threshold object narratives. Ecofascism, as a political genre, does not take shape in a vacuum. It emerges and exists in conversation and tension with other traditions and modes of representation.

For this reason, literary studies is a valuable avenue by which to approach ecofascism as, in part, a narrative process that unfolds across a multifaceted cultural landscape. Other approaches are important for different reasons. I do not seek to offer an intellectual history of ecofascism, as Biehl and Staudenmaier do in *Ecofascism Revisited* (2011). Nor do I focus exclusively on recent far-right movements or aim to forecast potential authoritarian futures, as Moore and Roberts do in *The Rise of Ecofascism* (2022) and Malm and the Zetkin Collective do in *White Skin, Black Fuel* (2021). And I do not come to the problem from the perspective of political theory or sociology, as so many scholars have come to fascism more broadly. All these angles offer invaluable insights to the study of ecofascism. Literary studies is particularly poised to consider its everyday dimensions in the form of speech acts that inconclusively yet potentially contribute to its momentum.

While literature itself might seem too "everyday" an object of study for a problem as potent as ecofascism, the methods of close reading and social history, pursued together, demonstrate how political genre seeps across contexts due to shared conditions and influences, as well as how the identities that genre articulates take shape and break down by virtue of their narrative construction. In this regard, literature's value is what Allison Carruth describes as its "facility with shifting from macroscopic to intimate scales of representation"—its ability, that is, "to shuttle between social and interpersonal registers and between symbolic and embodied expressions of power," revealing the extent to which everyday acts both stem from and contribute to broader cultural narratives and their effects.[95] But I also understand *narrative* broadly, as it refers to not just literary texts across genres but also patterns of representation across media. In early chapters, I read examples informed by the genuine convictions of their authors, as in Callenbach's *Ecotopia*. In later ones, I read works self-consciously composed in part to illuminate—and critique—the threshold object narrative's implications, as in Margaret Atwood's *The Year of the Flood* (2009). Many, but not all, are examples of speculative fiction, projecting utopian visions of ecological belonging or exploring more fully the implicit political violence on which such projects rely. Such texts offer rich readings for this project in their potential for juxtaposition: their capacity not only to imagine explicitly fascist regimes and figures but also to measure against them subtler, everyday activities that latently reproduce their narrative logic. What binds these diverse stories together is not just their shared interest in place-based identity, but also their fixation on individuals and communities who view modernity as a force that threatens to dislocate it, positioning them at the crossroads of radicalism and reaction (to use Staudenmaier's distinction) and ultimately dramatizing the second.

Though the chapters proceed more or less chronologically, I have organized them around different threshold objects because my emphasis is on the cultural work their consumption often performs, rather than on their genealogies. I understand these examples not as formative cases but as representative cultural sites that stand out for the specificity with which innocuous narrative elements have combined within them not only to purify a given person or people in a specific place but also to do so at the expense of impure, racialized others. I do not claim to be exhaustive. The book is neither a survey nor an argument for a niche canon of literature. Nor do I mean to impose a teleological tale onto this material, suggesting that certain stories inevitably lead to authoritarian outcomes. I am concerned with the implications of a recurring narrative logic that has shaped and might continue to shape certain attitudes about nation, race, and environment in the United States.

Throughout the book, I cover ground from the eighteenth century to the present, but I primarily focus on the past sixty years, beginning in the 1960s. While environmentalist appeals to racial purity, settler-colonial ownership, and "natural law" certainly pre-date recent decades, I concentrate on this relatively short contemporary period because its beginning marked a historical coincidence between two critical sociopolitical developments of the late twentieth century: first, the rise of the modern environmental movement and the ascension of ecological disruption to a matter of mainstream concern, and second, the reorganization of racial politics following the civil rights movement as a reflection of what Bonilla-Silva calls "color-blind racism."[96] Concepts of race, nation, and political belonging vary and shift over time. They did so dramatically over the past century. Interwar fascism itself contributed to these changes, as the Nazi genocide of European Jews prompted an uneven series of reckonings with various racisms around the world. This book really begins at an historical moment when ecological anxiety skyrocketed even as de jure white supremacy largely went underground, encouraging a "postracial" rhetoric that identifies racial chauvinism with explicit yet dwindling acts of overt brutality, but persisting in the form of implicit structural violence, making possible a scenario in which "color-blind" environmentalists negotiate their fears in ways that inadvertently sustain notions of ethnonational purity.

In chapter 1, "Land," I broadly (and by no means comprehensively) survey cultural narratives of land entitlement in the United States and consider the role they have played in explicit "blood-and-soil" acts of ecofascist violence, extending this Introduction by providing deeper historical background on intellectual, political, and rhetorical antecedents—namely, the principle of enclosure and appeals to natural law—that not only inform far-right movements and activities today but also animated early environmentalist thinking in the United States at large. In short, I trace discursive roots and ongoing interchanges between environmentalist and hypernationalist appeals to nature, which culminated to murderous effect in the El Paso and Buffalo shooters' accounts of environmental belonging, before turning in later chapters to contemporary, "nondeterministic" iterations of the same genre, some of which risk endorsing ecofascist violence themselves, some of which splinter into more liberatory alternatives, and some of which engage the genre in order to critique it altogether.

Chapter 2, "Tools," examines the persistence of narratives of land entitlement in environmentalist expressions of place-based belonging, as well as how they shore up in-group notions of purity in terms of race, nation or region, gender, and other social forms. Threads plucked in chapter 1 wove together in new ways at the dawn of the modern environmental movement, illustrating not only the extent to which blood-and-soil rhetoric might emerge on the left as well as the right but also the role the trope of consumption played in its resurgence at this historical juncture. In Callenbach's *Ecotopia,* a novel that has wielded sizable influence over sustainability activism since its publication, the acquisition and use of equipment for sustainable living revitalizes ideas about ethnonational purity and "natural" race, gender, and sex roles.

Chapter 3, "Food," pivots to consumption at perhaps its most literal—that is, ingestion—but draws similar conclusions. In it, I consider how food plays the threshold object role when one represents the consumption of local fare as a matter of regional self-indigenization. I specifically explore the prevalence of food motifs in writing from Appalachia, a landscape whose history and legacy of frontier mythology, resource extraction, and environmental injustice offers an exceptional case for the study of race, class, and place as intersecting social vectors. I focus on work by the gay poet Jeff Mann because his attention to sexuality and gender both bolsters and complicates an impulse toward self-indigenization common among progressive Appalachian writers of European descent. On the one hand, Mann represents consuming local food as a means of proving both one's ecological innocence and one's essential connection to place—like Callenbach, in ways that at least implicitly discredit both outsiders and certain residents. On the other hand, he gestures to the recipe—a representation of interpreting and preparing food rather than naturalizing or even eating it—as a form that typifies foodways, identity, and environmental action as ongoing, coalitional phenomena rather than exclusive, essentialist domains.

The last two chapters consider literary texts that incisively juxtapose explicit instances of ecofascist violence with implicit, everyday parallels rooted in suggestions of a sort made by Mann and Callenbach, whose works habitually prioritize strength (often in ableist and hypermasculine terms) as a prerequisite for environmental belonging. If bodily purity orients these figures, then psychic purity does the same for the subjects of chapter 4, "Drugs," in which I reckon with the twenty-first-century resurgence of organic psychedelics and their ostensible facilitation of ecological awareness through a reading of Atwood's MaddAddam trilogy (2003–2013). Atwood, a Canadian author, has long expressed an interest in sociocultural exchanges and parallels between the United States and its northern neighbor—and the rise of explicit ecofascist rhetoric, as well as interest in psychedelics as environmentalist conduits, has, in both contexts, deep roots in settler-colonial violence, appropriation, and erasure. The trilogy, situated in a near-future United States, features members of a religious sect who, like real-world counterparts, believe organic substances such as mescaline enable them to access a primitive, expansive psychic condition free of social mediation and melded with the earth. They not only present this reconciliation as tantamount to our species' survival, but also understand themselves as the enlightened few who possess the ability to achieve it, welcoming the death of unworthy others. Ultimately I contend that, in many contexts, recent psychedelic discourse differs from its countercultural precursors in that it has shifted from a radical aspiration to reimagine civilization to a reactionary prediction of its impending collapse.

Chapter 5, "Contagion," accordingly examines perspectives that treat global pandemics as catastrophic forces for environmental good. In such narratives, viruses, bacteria, and contagion in general emerge as threshold objects. From social media posts touting nature's "healing" during Covid-19 lockdowns to survivalist environmentalisms, various figures have not only argued that a pandemic's disruption of economic activity benefits the natural world but also framed viral contraction, death tolls, and even human extinction writ large as positive developments. Such arguments, however, often imply that the speaker's environmentalist virtue renders them immune: the appropriately "primitive" will inherit the earth. This romance of an earth unblemished by global capitalism risks glorifying ostensibly Indigenous lifeways while neglecting actual Native peoples who have tended to suffer most disproportionately from health crises like the Covid-19 pandemic. Adam Johnson's *Parasites Like Us* (2003) fictionalizes this exact sort of erasure, centering settler characters who romanticize paleolithic lifeways, inadvertently catalyze humans' viral annihilation, and emerge from the apocalypse unscathed to colonize earth using only ancient technology, even as the virus decimates a local reservation. It is through "natural" exposure to the contagion that they inoculate themselves, consuming trace amounts of the pathogen before it overtakes the earth. In so doing, they reflect a trend in immunity discourse that picked up speed in the 1980s and 1990s: a contention that "natural" immunity not only trumps vaccination but also proves which bodies are and are not fit to survive a polluted world. Louise Erdrich's *Future Home of the Living God* (2017) similarly chronicles the spread of a virus that "regresses" *Homo sapiens* as well as other species, in this case at the level of DNA. Erdrich, however, focuses more closely on networks of power that determine which populations emerge safely from global crises and why.

Throughout *Everyday Ecofascism,* I linger on various voices who insist that ableist, white-supremacist heteropatriarchy cannot sufficiently answer this question. In the book's Conclusion, I focus on one in particular: Kumeyaay poet and screenwriter Tommy Pico. In his Teebs tetralogy (2016–2019), Pico makes pervasive use of food motifs to juxtapose systemic historical erasures of Indigenous land, knowledge, and people, and his own experiences as a queer Indigenous man seeking love. Sex is also a kind of consumption, he suggests—and for many of the settler men he meets, Pico is doubly fulfilling, providing both sexual gratification and a sort of environmentalist exoneration. He ultimately pulls himself out of such relationships through a different mobilization of food motifs: the replacement of lost recipe traditions with new ones collaboratively designed with friends—an act of creation rather than consumption. Threshold object narratives center the incorporation of objects to access a state of purity—a perspective that essentializes and excludes. By contrast, the counternarratives that appear across this book—especially in two Interludes after the first and third chapters—approach identity quite differently and, despite their own diversity, consistently: as a process of accrual that gathers multiple forms of life, respects difference, and acknowledges the complexity of identity's material and narrative origins rather than denies it. In the Conclusion, I accordingly reflect on the catalog as a form that figures more equitable visions of human–environment relations, as well as the role played by marginalized writers in its mobilization. *Everyday Ecofascism* ends on the suggestion that perhaps the motif Pico offers—*making* rather than *consuming*—is one that might anchor justice-oriented instead of ecofascistic narratives, precisely because his perspective rejects the notion of purity altogether. The difficult work of environmental justice lies in building coalitions rather than eliminating other stakeholders: a project that gestures to the future without overdetermining or foreclosing a people or place's past—let alone purifying it.

« 1 »

Land

*Entitlement to Environment across
Settler-Colonial History and Partisan Lines*

It is fair to say that most people who anguish over the
population problem are trying to find a way to avoid
the evils of overpopulation without relinquishing any
of the privileges they now enjoy.
> —Garrett Hardin, "The Tragedy of the Commons"

In the case of US settler colonialism, land was the
primary commodity.
> —Roxanne Dunbar-Ortiz, *An Indigenous
> Peoples' History of the United States*

From one perspective, Garrett Hardin's words above could describe
the man who, in 2019, killed twenty-three people in El Paso, Texas,
given that he did so at a Walmart "If we can get rid of enough
people," the killer wrote in his manifesto, then our way of life can
become more sustainable." Both migrants and domestic people
of color, in his telling, behave as invasive species threatening an
endangered one. But he does not merely reverse the roles of colonizer and colonized, casting Mexicans (as well as Jewish, Black,
Muslim, and other Latinx Americans) as imperialists and Euro-
Americans as natives. Despite his ostensible environmentalism,
his choice of setting suggests almost that Walmart—as fitting a
symbol for unsustainable patterns of extraction, production, and
consumption as any—is itself an integral part of the future he aims
to save. If inevitable ecological catastrophe approaches the United
States, his solution is to cull its population of the wrong kind of

people—and to do so, in part, to maintain its consumption habits for the right kind. He is, in part, telling a story—one that observes the template I outlined in the Introduction. It proceeds in a seemingly antiestablishment mode, links a specific environment with specific people through appeals to nature and rebirth that reinforce existing patterns of power and inequality, and, traced to its logical conclusion, erupts in political violence. The man insinuates that resource extraction and consumption are the expected, exclusive, even *natural* behaviors of Euro-American settlers, privileged claimants to the land, its resources, and the economic systems that have secured them. Settler whites, by nature, productively consume. Others merely leech. The shooter nonetheless deemed them responsible for climatic and other ecological disruptions, resorting to an extreme defense of borders to safeguard these distinctions. And though his massacre repulsed many, the logic that informed it is widespread across conventional partisan lines. "Nature," the political scientist John Hultgren writes, "occupies an increasingly prominent position in the American immigration-restriction movement." It also does so, with mounting regularity, "in materials geared toward public consumption."[1]

Environmentalist support for immigration restriction is hardly a new phenomenon. Such alliances have formed in the United States (and varied widely) over the course of the past century and a half, from early twentieth-century eugenics to contemporary neo-Malthusian fears of population growth seemingly free of racial signifiers. Environment, Hultgren writes, is "increasingly . . . deployed as a form of *walling*—providing a subtle means of reinforcing 'traditional' territorial borders and national identities without having to revert to racial and cultural logics" that are "no longer socially acceptable within mainstream political discourse."[2] Immigration laws began, in the nineteenth century, explicitly as technologies for racial exclusion, designed to preserve the nation's imaginary whiteness. The mainstream political appeal of overt racial discrimination might have dwindled since then, but that trend has not stopped white-nationalist figures from organizing a revitalized (and largely successful) anti-immigrant movement that began in the 1970s—one that might never have thrived were it not for the support of environmentalists fixated on overpopulation. Calls for population control (and, implicitly if perhaps unintentionally, references to racial classifications that have historically underwritten it) have steadily intensified since.

Such arguments suffer from several inadequacies even on their face. The assumption that one can effectively gauge environmental health through nationally delimited metrics such as per capita CO_2 emissions, for example, not only naturalizes historically contingent borders but also neglects transnational patterns of extraction, trade, and consumption as well as the sheer fact that ecological change does not halt at geopolitical boundaries. This approach achieves little more than an arbitrary equation between ecological data points and absolute numbers, shifting attention from habits of consumption to the number of people consuming. It therefore also shores up the status quo: "Americans . . . are consumers," Hultgren writes, and more Americans "means more consumption."[3] It also perpetuates stereotypes, Neel Ahuja adds, about "how the world's poor mismanage resources," when in reality migrants most often arrive at borders in the Global North in the wake of displacement from agrarian lands and local commerce occasioned by the imposition (from the North) of energy and shipping infrastructures, the ecological changes and political conflict they've wrought, and transnational systems of labor and trade they've made compulsory.[4]

Progressive attempts to bolster sustainability by fortifying borders therefore function more like a bandage than an antibiotic, ignoring the mechanisms behind ecological crisis, targeting those who most experience its effects, and reinforcing exclusionary forms of political community—and lending support to more overtly chauvinistic projects—as they do. As such, they illustrate what Matthew Lyons means when he writes that nationalism in general and nativism in particular "*don't stand still.*"[5] Nationalism itself is a process, Daniel Woodley writes, that "forges identities through the rationalization of commonalities functional for the group in question."[6] And even if hard-core nativists like the El Paso shooter give the impression that "far rightists remain oriented toward classical fascism's vision of a strong state," many have in fact "abandoned this approach" in favor of political decentralism. This turn has occurred largely as a function of dwindling trust in authority at least since the Vietnam War, but also, Lyons adds, in part as a self-conscious effort "to tap into . . . Americans' aversion to big government and in some cases insulate far rightists against the charge of fascism."[7] An impulse toward decentralization has historically cut across conventional political borders in the United States, and crypto-fascists accordingly dangle it as a recruitment lure. And perhaps in no other arena has antiestablishment decentralism been a more obvious feature than in U.S. environmentalism, many forms of which (such as bioregionalism) strive to delimit political community at a scale far smaller than that of the nation-state—units that themselves might risk inviting their own forms of nativism.

Most of these movements indeed reject the racial overtones of nativist nationalism. "Theirs is not a crisis of national homogeneity threatened by cultural impurity," Hultgren writes, "but one of 'natural places' threatened by a hegemonic neoliberal ideology." But migration—conceived broadly, within national borders as well as across them—still routinely arouses opposition given "its alleged complicity with a neoliberal . . . economic agenda." In such cases, even the most progressive of environmentalists risks reifying normative, hierarchical ideals of national belonging and political sovereignty on spurious demographic grounds, shifting blame to racialized others rather than systems. Hultgren attributes this possibility to "something internal to environmental thought." Certain "ideals of nature," he writes, "themselves give rise to racialized iterations of sovereignty."[8]

Environmentalism and racialized sovereignty indeed share a deeply intertwined intellectual history in the United States, stretching from before the nation's founding into the twenty-first century. One element of that history is particularly relevant to ecofascism as a political genre: the idea of enclosure, the "walling" of land held in common as a matter of private ownership, a practice that has, historically, reinforced the notion that certain activities—and certain people—belong "naturally" within certain environs while others do not. It is also a principle that troubles the distinction between public and private. Public ownership of national parks established in the late nineteenth and early twentieth centuries, for example, founded U.S. environmentalism on the basis of a pristine nature held in trust by and for the people. Yet much of the discourse surrounding both the parks and the public said to own it revolved around eugenic notions of nature, race, and citizenship, determining exclusions at the level of both the nation and its natural environment.

Originating in European colonial ventures, the principle of enclosure became a cornerstone of Enlightenment natural law. And in the United States, it not only animated legal guarantees to property but also contributed to racialized perspectives on the land and certain relationships with it. As the example of national parks attests, appeals to natural law and attendant claims to land also underwrote the settler-colonial displacement of Native peoples. Unlike colonial outposts, Lorenzo Veracini writes, settler-colonial projects "claim both a special sovereign charge and a regenerative capacity." The goal is not simply wealth but "a better polity."[9] Palingenetic rebirth, in other words, is baked into settler colonialism from the beginning. It is for this reason that scholars such as Jack Forbes and Zak Cope suggest that fascism, as a "relative admixture" of authoritarianism, racism, and militarism on the part of political actors "on [their] own soil," can be read as "imperialist repression turned inward"—an experience Native and Black peoples, especially, have endured in U.S. territories for centuries.[10] If in Italy, for example, fascist violence was "brought home from the distant colonies," Rowland Keshena Robinson writes, in settler-colonial contexts "this violence . . . was perfected within the exceptional state of the expansion of the frontier, the clearing and civilizing of Indigenous People to make the land ripe for settlement, and the carceral continuum that has marked the Black experience on this land from chattel slavery."[11]

Land is a keyword in these relationships. As Patrick Wolfe writes, the "primary object of settler colonization is the land itself rather than the surplus value to be derived from mixing native labor with it," as in colonialism more broadly.[12] And settlers themselves are "unique migrants," as Veracini puts it: they are "*founders* of political orders and carry their sovereignty with them." Later migrants, by contrast, "can be seen as *appellants* facing a political order that is already constituted . . . [and] characterized by a defining lack of sovereign entitlement"—or as "invasive species" harassing an endangered one.[13] Several hundred years after the initial European settlement of the present United States, anti-immigrant attitudes proceed from an assumption that the nation in its present form "is natural," a "clearly demarcated entity with a uniform culture," despite its complex formation and constant renegotiation over time. In this context, abstract nature—and the concrete land to which the idea affixes—"functions as a . . . signifier" that "underscores . . . connections between blood and soil," such that "purity refers to the national culture as much as the natural environment."[14]

Environmentalist overpopulation discourse sits at precisely this nexus between the eugenic roots of U.S. preservationism and a broader cultural investment in enclosure and the sovereignties it has underwritten. Throughout this preliminary chapter, I follow both threads to the knot they tie in contemporary environmental rhetoric. My intention is to take stock of the intellectual, political, and social antecedents that have informed not only explicitly ecofascist individuals today but also environmentalist thinking in the United States more broadly. I pay particular attention to how the idea of enclosure and appeals to natural law have animated expressions of land entitlement, related arguments about effective environmental stewardship, and associated assumptions about "natural" patterns of inequality based on race, gender, and other social forms. (I acknowledge, however, that it would be impossible to be comprehensive. The settler-colonial project is uneven in its relation to the land that comprises the current United States and the people who have lived on and with it, as have been the narratives told about it. Settler colonialism, like fascism, is an ongoing process.) My purpose for this chapter, in short, is not necessarily for it to make a discrete argument of its own, but rather to preface the chapters that follow by tracing (in more detail than the Introduction) important dynamics among land, nature, consumption, and belonging across U.S. cultural history that have made possible distinctions such as the El Paso shooter's—that is, between "native" and "invasive" humans—which in fact inform environmental representation in a variety of contexts.

I begin by moving backward through nineteenth- and early twentieth-century eugenic race science to the philosophical justifications for settler-colonial conversion of common land to private property, before returning to the modern far right and the broad influence of postwar population panic on ideas about land ownership, sovereignty, and race. Entitlement to land (and the narratives about nature, race, and belonging with which it intersects) has both underwritten and proceeded from its consumption. Again, I use the word *consumption* somewhat loosely. The complex reality of land resists objectifications of it, and to speak uncritically of "consuming land" might indeed risk reproducing the logics of settler colonialism and unsustainable resource extraction. At the same time, attending to the ways different figures and narratives have themselves situated land in a framework of consumption offers insight into not only patterns of possession but also certain modes of identification and their effects. Identitarian entitlements to land have reproduced in subtle forms of land consumption at least since the dawn of the modern environmental movement (which emerged in the 1960s and 1970s chiefly on the left), beginning with the "commonplace notion of the natural world as a primordial dwelling place." Such an assumption, Taylor Eggan writes, not only "unmarks territory . . . relegating it to a literal state of nature that erases any preexisting"—or alternative—"ties or claims to a particular place," but also rests upon the violent and systematic expulsion of those ties to begin with.[15] I end this chapter, however, by turning, in an Interlude that follows, in an altogether different direction: to narrative as well as activist resistances to dominant conceptions of belonging to both land and people that flourish even in the borderlands that fascists like the El Paso shooter see fit to police. Native and women-of-color writers have for generations countered homogenous notions of ethnonational and ecological belonging, which have shored up power in ways that disadvantage or actively harm not only racialized populations but also women, queer people, and others. This book focuses chiefly on everyday iterations of ecofascist narrative logic, but it is with attention to counternarratives of ecological belonging that I immediately follow this chapter, not only to preface similar alternatives that appear later but also to acknowledge the foundational perspectives of Indigenous and women writers in all such efforts.

Land, Nature, and Race in the United States

On October 27, 2016, militarized police stormed a peaceful camp erected near the Standing Rock Reservation that straddles North and South Dakota, organized by water protectors consisting of Sioux, representatives from other nations across North America, and nonnative allies in protest of the Dakota Access Pipeline, which would shuttle crude oil through Sioux territory to the benefit of wealthy urban centers and at the expense of water safety and culturally significant landmarks. Police defended settler-colonial consumption of oil (and Native lands) with concussion grenades, batons, pepper spray, and the threat of sniper fire. "Ironically," Dina Gilio-Whitaker (Colville Confederated Tribes) writes, "the same day Ammon and Ryan Bundy were acquitted of charges in the armed takeover of the Malheur Wildlife Refuge" that January— the ranching family's second standoff with federal agents.[16] Law enforcement arrested the Bundys and fellow militiamen, who operated under the premise that the Bureau of Land Management has no constitutional authority to govern property that rightly belongs to state or private landowners, after four weeks of distant surveillance (and the death of one militant), during which time the ranchers teased the vandalism of Paiute artifacts on the site. Such threats are consistent with Ammon's attitude toward Indigenous peoples, whom he describes as having "lost their claim" to the land. Property, he and his associates are fond of repeating, rightly belongs to those who most effectively "claim, use, and defend" it.[17] (Cliven Bundy, Ammon's father, has on several occasions also suggested that Black Americans would be better off under conditions of slavery.) The man's attitude, Kyle Boggs writes, not only "positions him as an innocent beneficiary" but also "accommodates white nationalists who . . . clearly believe the 'current culture' is one characterized by white people."[18] But in the courtroom, his lawyer tacitly acknowledged that his claim required a certain performance: a reenactment of settler-colonial consumption of Native land through recognizable aesthetic tropes. "These men are cowboys," he argued, "and given that the jury will be assessing their authenticity . . . they should be able to present themselves in that manner."[19]

Such performances have long characterized the settler-colonial project in the United States, as well as more recent, overt calls to white supremacy and violence. Jake Angeli, the face-painted, headdress-adorned man who spearheaded a right-wing insurrection at the U.S. Capitol on January 6, 2021, staked his own performative claim to blood-and-soil belonging through a mode of self-representation Philip J. Deloria (Standing Rock Sioux) refers to as "playing Indian."[20] If Bundy asserted his ownership of land through a performance of its settler-colonial conquest, then Angeli intimated his identity with it through stereotypes of Native peoples' environmental purity—an identification his well-documented climate activism seems intended, in part, to reinforce.[21] Despite their shared affiliation with similar far-right movements, Angeli and the Bundys might at first appear at odds over the question of environmental protection. The family is representative of an influential antienvironmentalist strain in the western United States, according to which regulations enforced by the Bureau of Land Management and U.S. Forest Service inherently threaten the livelihood of ranchers, miners, and loggers. The issue for such figures is not so much land management as what James Pogue, an on-the-ground witness of the Malheur occupation, refers to as "the great American political position": a notion that collective goals are, by definition, never "as valid as the economic rights of the mostly white men who use the lands now, because they got there and claimed them."[22] Given their hostility toward environmentally motivated sacrifice of any sort, the Bundys don't quite qualify as ecofascists. Still, I turn to their example because they illustrate discursive themes in U.S. land politics that unite right-wing antienvironmentalists with environmentalists of various stripes, perhaps in surprising ways. The Bundys organized their protest to announce their rightful possession of a certain environment. Angeli staged his own, in part, on behalf of the environment's threatened integrity in the face of a changing climate—and he did so as part of an argument that he, and others like him, comprise the population most worthy of defining and defending that integrity, based on their privileged sense of identity with it.

Claims to nature and purity such as these belie the bloody political and discursive histories that make them possible. As the literary critic April Anson points out, the El Paso shooter's manifesto references "Native genocide as reinforcement for white settler sovereignty's blood and soil territory."[23] Despite the man's ecological anxieties, his actions read less as an indictment of the Anthropocene than a defense of what Kyle Keeler calls the *kleptocene*—the Anthropocene in terms of the colonial theft that underwrites extractive ecological despoliation.[24] One way to frame his screed, then, is as a declaration of a "settler state of emergency," which Anson describes as a narrative of impending danger that justifies unmitigated violence (consistent with what Kyle Whyte calls "crisis epistemology"). If "the function of a state of emergency is to protect a nation," it is, in practice, an inconsistently respected principle. Take, for example, the case of the Standing Rock Nation, whose attempts to protect itself from federal and corporate hostility met with state-sponsored violence. The Bundy posse concurrently received (for the most part) absolution. This "inconsistency," Anson argues, "is easily resolved once we acknowledge that the real function of the state of emergency is to mark racialized populations as perpetual threats"—threats, that is, to economic arrangements secured through imperialist violence— "through the same exceptionalist discourse that renders the terror of white conquest innocent."[25] In the eighteenth and nineteenth centuries, the federal government projected a constant Indian menace ahead of the westward frontier, despite the United States itself posing the actual existential danger to hundreds of Native peoples across the continent. As settler colonization endured, "the legal system not only made it impossible for Indians to defend their lands," Gilio-Whitaker writes, but also "portrayed them as violent predators . . . justifying state and federally funded genocidal campaigns against them."[26]

Environmentalism in the United States emerged in precisely this crucible of dispossession, nation building, and perceived crisis, foremost in the seizure of land designated as national parks beginning in the second half of the nineteenth century, largely after westward expansion ended. By the turn of the twentieth, figures such as President Theodore Roosevelt were vocalizing fears that industrialization (and the related mass migration from country to city) had produced or risked producing an "overcivilized man, who lost the great fighting, masterful virtues" that enabled settler colonization. Wilderness—nature ostensibly untouched by civilization—appeared, for these men, the bedrock of a particular American identity, one that naturalized aspects of Euro-American culture, disavowed their historical roots, and obscured the presence of Indigenous peoples in supposedly untouched milieus. This wilderness ideal emerged in tandem with a rise in populist nativism in the second half of the nineteenth century, spurred in part by the same socioeconomic anxieties that worried Roosevelt. As they promoted widespread opposition to immigration, nativist movements between the Civil War and World War II became "strongly associated with promoting Anglo-Saxon heritage"—a public project, the sociologist Dorceta Taylor writes, that "coincided with and influenced the emergence of pro-environmental thought and actions."[27]

This confluence of environmental sensibility with racial animus was no coincidence. "The invention of wilderness," Sarah Jaquette Ray writes, "was a reactionary *response* . . . to these social crises"—an architecture for national spaces "free of social deviants and groups thought to threaten America's image of itself, which linked moral purity to whiteness [and] cleanliness."[28] Many of conservation's and preservation's most ambitious proponents hailed from organizations dedicated to promoting eugenics, a supposed science that seeks to preserve the ostensibly superior qualities (and existing social status) of a particular race through means of selective breeding and, oftentimes, strict social control and even sterilization of putatively inferior others. The Save the Redwoods League, for example, involved itself in both eugenic and preservationist programs. Its members largely believed them inseparable. Madison Grant, a vice president of the Immigration Restriction League, considered the trees the fittest of all species, "the survivors of a master race" emblematic of white Anglo-Saxon Protestant America. Grant and his colleagues not only believed descendants of "Nordic" peoples naturally superior to others (and therefore worthier of survival and dominion) but also felt, for this reason, that various institutions must ensure, through targeted policy, that "the superior man's breeding habits" not culminate in white extinction by intermingling with "inferior stock."[29] Worth noting is the fact that, despite their presumed superiority, Grant's ilk considered intervention necessary. Far from emerging organically, the "natural law" of racial hierarchy must be constantly reestablished through active maintenance as well as social-Darwinist competition.

The eugenics movement regardless saw great success in the twentieth century, culminating in a trio of racially defined immigration acts as well as the widespread popularity of texts like Grant's *Passing of the Great Race,* which "crossed not only international waters, but political ones as well."[30] Grant praised the Nordic race's "vigor," drawing inspiration from nineteenth-century *völkisch* German political thinkers and later influencing Nazi elaborations on the same theories.[31] *Volkism* "affirmed the intimacy of entire peoples" a century before Nazism wielded it to develop its "all-important idea of the unified race," Sam Moore and Alex Roberts write. "In the *völkisch* telling, certain environments were the forges of robust peoples, whilst others were detrimental. Their view of nature, although locally holistic, was highly particularized," a type of Romantic vitalism.[32] By the time of Grant's writing, the "idea that human races evolved as a result of centuries of interaction with a specific natural environment was not new," Kimberly Smith notes. As early as the eighteenth century, "the belief that the physical environment determines the habits, dispositions, and the physical characteristics of national groups was commonplace." But again, proponents had continually to construct and reinforce their verdicts. For turn-of-the-century eugenicists, racial vitality was not "a matter of communing with nature's beauty," as it was for the Romantic poets, but one of "dominating a harsh natural environment (and other races)."[33] And for Nazism, "the German people, though inherently superior to others, were in mortal danger of disintegration," Walter Laqueur writes. "Therefore, the purity of their blood had to be preserved."[34] If Theodore Roosevelt and Adolf Hitler's anxieties seem homologous, it is because they proceeded from similar sources. Grant's writing strongly influenced the thinking (and policy) of both men. Eugenics, Nancy Ordover writes, has never been "solely the purview of the extreme right." And it has proven "extremely nimble," enjoying broad appeal for "its emphasis on individual and group 'failings' over analyses of systemic culprits" and "its protection of the status quo."[35]

For all these reasons, eugenicists like Grant are embraced as intellectual fountainheads by self-described ecofascists like the El Paso shooter. The essayist Shane Burley characterizes fascism broadly as an investment in or enforcement of "[i]nequality through mythological and essentialized identity"—in other words, through appeals to eugenic natural law. "Nature" in this context refers not just to environment. It also encompasses claims about human nature. And for "fascists across the board," Burley adds, "inequality . . . is critical, crucial, and correct."[36] Different people (and groups of people) express different characteristics that can and should be ranked in terms of bodily ability and morphology, athletic performance, and IQ tests, as well as more banal assumptions about race, gender, sexuality, nationality, and other social forms. Self-identified ecofascists more specifically mobilize "ecological themes to justify the necessity of . . . violence for survival," Anson adds—the social-Darwinist capabilities of those deemed fit and therefore natural enough to survive.[37] For example, the far-right Wolves of Vinland network justifies a doctrinal mix of "quasi-ecological tribalism" and "masculinist authoritarianism" through appeals to a nature they define as "a timeless hierarchical order and the alternative to modernity, whose multiculturalism, feminism, wealth, urbanism, and statist bureaucracy breeds decadence, weakness and inferiority."[38] For the Wolves, nature governs society, but has been obscured and betrayed by twin forces of neoliberal economics and social egalitarianism. Such groups do not so much transcend social politics as they do encode them, rhetorically reinforcing, through appeals to nature, hypermasculinity and white supremacy as matters of biological destiny while relegating other social forms to a pollutive cultural sphere.

But as I mentioned in the Introduction, distinctions between natural strength and cultural artifice are not limited to actors on the far right. Appeals to the "inherent cruelty and determinism of nature," Burley writes, have "permeated the extreme edges of the environmental movement for years," suffusing camps as diverse as animal liberation, bioregionalism, and Earth First!—a trend that perhaps could not have occurred had U.S. preservation and conservation not developed in the settler-colonial context, and its founding fathers not advocated the race science that retroactively justified it.[39] John Muir and Edward Abbey, two of the most beloved and influential literary environmentalists of the twentieth century, both refer to the presence of nonwhite peoples in the western United States as that of "foreigners."[40] Muir, instrumental to Roosevelt's decision to establish Yosemite as a federal national park in 1906, also disdained the Indigenous peoples who lived there. "The worst thing about them is their uncleanliness," he writes. "Nothing truly wild is unclean."[41] Muir and others paradoxically identified Native peoples with nature *and* its other, revealing the extent to which tenuous race science, rather than a willingness to learn from enduring sources of environmental knowledge, undergirded their concept of stewardship. If "Indians are seen as wild animals," Taylor points out, "the lands can be framed as areas untouched by human hands."[42]

The argument that Native peoples were and are poor stewards of the land indeed served as one of the most pervasive justifications for dispossession before and after the nation's founding. Despite a "history of commercial relations," Taylor writes, "whites and Indians had vastly different views and attitudes toward the land." By and large, Indigenous peoples "viewed themselves as custodians and stewards of the earth, not as masters with dominion over it," managing land in common. "By contrast, white settlers saw the land as a commercial product best suited for private ownership and exploitation," a perspective enshrined in the young United States' political theory.[43] Private property's value crystalized in Thomas Jefferson's ideal of the yeoman farmer, a linchpin trope of post-revolutionary democracy. Citizenship lay principally in property, and in *Notes on the State of Virginia* (1785) Jefferson makes an argument that only those who "perform the requisite labor" can "claim mastery" over land.[44] Interpreting the Enlightenment political philosopher John Locke, Jefferson argued that proper ownership of land consisted in the manner in which one used it. Anyone "had a natural right to resources, but . . . once an individual added his or her labor to bring about the improvement or development of a particular resource, then that person gained individual rights to it and can claim it as individual property."[45] Production, in this sense, becomes a matter of consumption as I used the word in the Introduction: as an act of incorporation by which the seizure and use of land becomes proof of emplaced identity and national belonging.

This perspective requires a willful ignorance of the sort of labor performed by Indigenous peoples themselves: collaborative efforts to "improve" land that often sought to safeguard not only individual livelihoods but also those of whole ecosystems. In his *Notes,* Jefferson first and most fully discusses Native peoples not in the chapter on "Aborigines," but in "Productions Mineral, Vegetable and Animal"—a detail that, for Jeffrey Myers, "underscores that in Jefferson's mind, the Indians are *productions* rather than *producers,* which is to say . . . that Indians have no special claim to any of the territory they inhabit." Despite centuries (even millennia) of meticulous land management practices involving controlled burning, agricultural experimentation, and complex irrigation (developed incrementally, to sometimes positive, sometimes negative ecological effect), Jefferson presented Native peoples as extensions of the landscape, requiring management of their own. The yeoman model also apparently precluded property claims by slaves of African descent, working land for white landowners such as Jefferson himself, who "goes to great lengths," Myers writes, "to intimate that blacks are incapable of the 'genuine virtue' of the agrarian ideal."[46]

In this respect, the historical relationship between land and race appears something of a self-fulfilling prophecy. Black slaves, because of their intrinsic inferiority, could not "genuinely" complete the labor that bestows ownership—and the fact that they couldn't in turn proved their inferiority. Native nations were and are, by contrast, exactly that: sovereign *nations* with a different relationship to the United States than populations falling under what is now the "protected class" of race. But Indigenous peoples were nonetheless in turn categorized (and their land further expropriated) as developmentally inferior according to nineteenth-century race science, a classification justified in part based on their inadequate commitment to private property. European colonizers and later U.S. nationals were, in general, "disdainful of the Indian custom of sharing . . . land" and "questioned the communal living arrangements" of many groups.[47] In holding land in common (and failing to sufficiently "improve" it in a way that accumulates capital), Native peoples forfeited their claim to it—a logic that helped engender, Myers writes, "a perception of the land . . . as naturally, even organically, the native land of white Americans."[48] Private labor became a transformative value. By it, land formerly held in common is both enclosed and constitutive of "natural" citizenship—but always in ways already circumscribed by existing assumptions about race.

Enclosure, Racialization, and the Labor of Belonging

Enclosure, as a social, political, and legal concept, constitutes one specific view or aspect of private property (and national as well as personal sovereignty) among many, but one with lasting influence on the politics of land in the United States, though it pre-dates the nation by a few hundred years. Roxanne Dunbar-Ortiz traces it to the development of capitalism and earlier periods of European colonization, especially by England, whose agents used the term "to denote the privatization of the commons," a conversion the nobility and merchant class had long mobilized to extract labor from peasants by rendering them reliant on landowners. Later, she adds, "this displaced population was available to serve as settlers in the North American British colonies, many of them as indentured servants, with the promise of land. After serving their terms of indenture, they were free to squat on Indigenous land and become farmers again."[49] Because Native peoples failed to enclose it, that land was allegedly empty—a notion that also reduced the people who inhabited it to inferior status. Jefferson declared in 1792 that the "Doctrine of Discovery" established in the scramble for territory among Christian European monarchies applied to the fledgling United States, and the Supreme Court's 1823 *Johnson v. McIntosh* decision all but codified it. It also did so, Gilio-Whitaker adds, in racialized terms, as a matter of "cultural superiority" that "gave the US the superior right of title to land . . . while Native nations merely possessed the right of occupation"—a claim enforced by subsequent legislation such as the 1830 Indian Removal Act (which relocated Natives over the Mississippi), the 1862 Homestead Act (which authorized military force to clear the Plains for white settlers), and the 1887 Dawes Allotment Act (which broke up Native land for private sale).[50]

Conquest itself functioned as a labor intended to "improve" the land—to prepare it for the system of private ownership that grounds democracy in the United States. "Reconciling empire and liberty . . . into a usable myth allowed for the emergence of an enduring populist imperialism," Dunbar-Ortiz writes, which she links to the 1820s articulation of Jacksonian settler democracy. "Land-poor white rural people saw [President Andrew] Jackson as the man who would save them, making land available . . . by ridding it of Indians," despite the fact that independent settlers most often lost their parcels to land companies, "thereby setting the pattern of the dance between poor and rich US Americans . . . under the guise of equality of opportunity."[51] In other words, it was (and is) never *just* labor writ large that granted entitlement to land (and created a polity), but also, more specifically, a labor of genocidal violence. (Jack Forbes refers to Jeffersonian and Jacksonian democracy as "Frontier Fascism" for this reason.[52]) Reconciliation between liberty and slaughter, that is, made possible a public acceptance of U.S. power at home and abroad.

Equations among enclosure, ownership, and natural right have indeed persisted across U.S. history, well into the twenty-first century. Daniel Martinez HoSang and Joseph Lowndes refer to this "usable myth" as "white producerism," a "vision . . . invested in a sovereign subject heroically reclaiming his autonomy."[53] As a system of political belief, producerism, Matthew Lyons adds, "draws a . . . distinction between good producers and evil parasites"—between the fit and the unfit—that itself functions as a powerful cultural narrative in the United States, a story template for what it means to be an admissible national subject. It is also one that has played a key role in the country's history of racial formation, often in antiestablishment terms. The Jacksonians, Lyons notes, "envisioned an alliance of 'productive' white farmers, artisans, planters, and entrepreneurs against 'parasitic' bankers, speculators, monopolists—and people of color." Similar distinctions animated a backlash that followed the 1960s civil rights movement, heralding the collapse of New Deal–era consensus. "Evoking the producerist tradition, right-wing populist initiatives accused liberal elites of giving special favors to communities of color, women, and poor people over 'hardworking' white men. Social welfare programs, taxes, and . . . government as a whole became scapegoats for . . . white people's economic woes," even though deregulation would largely be responsible in the coming decades. The effect in both contexts "was to bolster white supremacist violence, blur actual class divisions, and attack some elite groups while glorifying others."[54]

But producerism's subjects and objects have also changed over time, alongside the nation's ever-shifting socioeconomic conditions—a value displacement HoSang and Lowndes call "racial transposition." Coupled with the widespread economic precarity that has recently followed the prosperity of the postwar boom, the end of the civil rights movement—and the "concomitant (and contradictory) emergence of [its] broadly accepted moral authority"—especially shifted how producerism maps over racial hierarchies. As "claims to whiteness no longer protect many white people against charges of parasitism or dependence . . . a growing number of people of color have become valorized as the standard-bearers of a producerist and patriotic anti-statism," as well as of traditional, hierarchical models of heteropatriarchy, HoSang and Lowndes note. As sociopolitical and economic conditions in the United States shift, the producerist figure has also enabled a certain "plausible deniability of open racism" across the far right, even an embrace of recruits of color made possible by "a deepening commitment to racialized concepts that can, on their face, be denied to be racist."[55]

What I want to point out here, as I did in the Introduction, is the fact that such movements are largely reacting to the same conditions—economic insecurity, intensified securitization, cross-demographic political disenfranchisement, and the entrenched financial institutions and political arrangements that organize them—that animate the political left. At the same time, however,

just as Jacksonians embraced private landownership while rejecting its elites, so too do contemporary movements on the right
largely uphold neoliberalism's producerist ideals if not its institutions, mobilizing multiracial anger against socioeconomic dislocation and the individuals or populations perceived to be its
beneficiaries—including those at the bottom of the economic lad-
der as well as the top. Taking those ideals for granted buttresses
the economic system itself, the inequalities it exacerbates, and the
very elites such movements revile, even as producerism's grassroots appeal makes a distinction between phony producers who
outsource labor and real ones who actually do it—that is, real
(or "natural") American subjects. It ignores structural inequities
altogether.

This contradiction is on full display especially among the so-
called Patriot movements and other militia groups based chiefly in
the American West, which have in large part organized around the
producerist ideal in the Jeffersonian tradition, though not always
in explicitly white-nationalist terms. The Malheur occupation, for
example, played out largely as an exercise to "conjure and vener-
ate an autonomous and self-determined subject who makes his
living . . . by mixing his labor with the land." The Bundys staked
their claim, on one hand, against federal overreach—namely, environmental regulations and federal land ownership—which they
blame for regional economic decline. And they did so, on another,
by asserting their identity with the land itself, rooted in the family's tenure upon it. This appeal, however, requires the Bundys to
disavow, in performances of conquest and "improvement," the fact
that federally organized imperialism made possible their access to
land to begin with. It constitutes, in other words, another declaration of settler innocence in the face of an ongoing state of emergency in which peril has shifted from "Indians" to the state, based
on a logic of enclosure that the state itself seeded in the political
culture of the young nation. "This mythology, and the forgetting it
requires," HoSang and Lowndes point out, "continues to permeate
discourses of 'property rights'" in mainstream U.S. political culture
as well as militia activity, placing "profound constraints on the capacity of many people . . . to realize any viable responses to the conditions of precarity they now face." Militias like the Bundys' tend
to direct their ire toward environmental regulations yet ignore the
economic impact of corporate farming, mining, and energy inter-

ests that fund their fight to privatize land—parties that, unlike disaffected ranchers, stand to benefit from such exchanges. Economic depression in the Pacific Northwest owes a great deal to the timber industry itself: its uneven development between urban centers and a rural workforce, its global market shifts, and its patchwork withdrawal in the face of declining yields (in part a result of ecologically unsound practices driven by short-term profits). Indigenous nations have long addressed these challenges through decolonial advocacy. But the "producerist framework" favored by the Malheur occupiers "could not countenance or imagine . . . relationships of reciprocity" with regional Native peoples, let alone other individuals and populations impacted by industrial misuse, poor labor protections, neoliberal austerity, and carceral violence: "They were not dependent on anyone."[56]

The figure of the patriotic producer not only trades in the logic of ownership that largely spurs the political and economic anxieties of Bundy types to begin with, but also, doing so, makes and reinforces arguments for who does or does not belong in specific places, including the nation whose government they denounce. It functions, that is, as the sort of populist "political myth" that, for Daniel Woodley, "sustain[s] fascist movements." It operates not as an intellectually consistent system of belief but as a "commodified atemporal construct" that "defines a partial reality by suppressing autonomous identities and attachments." In the context of the United States, performances of rugged individualism paradoxically become a matter of cultural homogeneity. Only certain forms of labor and ownership—and relations to land—are recognized and, therefore, admissible.[57] This notion does not simply resonate with the fascist phenomena discussed in the Introduction. It is in part constitutive of them. Jason Stanley identifies producerist logic as one of classical fascist movements' most consistent strategies, often articulated in social-Darwinist terms: "'We' are hardworking, and have earned our . . . place by struggle and merit. 'They' are lazy." Those who "do not compete successfully do not deserve the goods and resources of society"—a perspective that ignores (even as it in part originates in) structural conditions and substitutes abstract national unity for actual forms of collaboration.[58]

My point is not that Patriot movements and related groups are, as Boggs puts it, "becoming fascist," but that their priorities focus existing cultural narratives in a way that conditions what I have

referred to as (eco)fascist effects. One is not born but rather becomes chosen, and for Patriots it is performative adherence to a
certain myth of rugged conquest and autonomy that grants one a
place: a literal slice of the land, "improved" and therefore owned.
One might say that the regional nativism of Patriot movements
takes shape as a racialization of ownership (continuing rather than
breaking from a long tradition of likewise defining citizenship in
the United States). To HoSang and Lowndes's point, post–civil
rights "racial transposition" has made possible a situation in which
far-right organizations sometimes welcome people of color who
share such perspectives. Multiracial Patriot movements have derived much of their energy (and gathered many recruits) not from
overt neo-Nazis but from the Wise Use movement that emerged in
the late 1980s, a loose coalition of ranchers, loggers, and sheriffs
sparring with federal officials over public land management and
political self-determination in general. Many of Bundy's followers,
Pogue writes, were in fact "very resistant to the idea that they were
antigovernment." We "believe," one occupier clarifies, "in government that people have a say in." At the same time, alliances with
other, more militant organizations—namely the Oath Keepers—
exposed faults (or, perhaps more accurately, continuities) between
"civil libertarian" and "authoritarian law-enforcement types." It
was "depressing," Pogue writes, that, rather than recognize "that
the same system that had almost managed to crush them also
crushes many thousands of other . . . mostly nonwhite families,"
many Bundy supporters, after Donald Trump's election, "suddenly
reimagined themselves as vigilantes in service of the same federal
government they'd so recently risen up against."[59] It's worth repeating that fascism is not a stable political theory but a process
that involves the circulation of cultural narratives across political
units. The issue for Patriots is not just self-determination but a
version whose premise is racialized ownership of land based on
imperial violence. For this reason, white nationalists often "see
their 'blood and soil' ideology at work" in Patriot activities, which
"tie identity to land." Their core values (and rejection of federal legitimacy) support other efforts, Boggs notes, "to sidestep . . . civil
rights laws by elevating local authority."[60] The logic of enclosure
is, in this respect, never as color-blind as it might appear, resting
as it does on existing assumptions about race, labor, and land that

coalesced in the nativism of eugenicists like Grant who continue to inform white nationalists today.

The producerist vision has, for this reason, helped to inspire not just backlash against liberal multiculturalism but also movements to establish secessionist ethnonations external to the United States. This trend is not necessarily recent. It builds on white-supremacist sentiment circulating at least since the Civil War, which burgeoned, in the mid-twentieth century, in movements organized against the New Deal consensus, many of which would later influence the proliferation of militias starting in the 1970s. "While earlier fascists had envisioned a revolutionary transforma-tion of US society as a whole," Lyons writes, "several groups now advocated a breakaway white homeland," signaling a broad shift in U.S. fascist thought from strong-state to decentralized ideology. But even though such figures frame their intentions as an escape from tyranny, "the smaller-scale political entities they envision are highly stratified and often profoundly authoritarian"—organized, that is, in terms of the appeals to eugenics and natural law I dis-cussed earlier, as well as more pedestrian assumptions about gen-der, sexual orientation, and other differences.[61] As Greg Johnson, editor of the white-nationalist *Counter-Currents,* puts it, the eth-nonationalist right strives for "a kind of organic society . . . that embraces a lot of critiques of class structure and capitalism and colonialism and imperialism that you find on the Left . . . but rec-ognizes that the best solution to that problem" is to "seek a world where every nation has its own sovereignty."[62]

Johnson's words speak to the fact that twenty-first-century far-right movements do not always advocate overt physical violence against racialized others per se. Instead, they promote segregation along nationalist lines—a stance many refer to as "Third Position-ism." Leaders of the "alt-right" that emerged around the 2016 presi-dential election, Burley writes, have "appropriated a caricature of leftist 'identity politics'" and in fact actively support them, given that "they want people to think of themselves *as* these identities rather than . . . of the ways that these identities exist in a matrix of experienced oppression." Many even support Black national-ism, for example, because it might achieve "the return of Africans to Africa, which would cleanse their territory of 'undesirables'" as well as "help white people to think of themselves *as a distinct people.*" Figures such as Johnson "argue their perspective is about *identity* before ideology, and that identity is rooted materially and spiritually in race"—and, as for Grant, his fellow eugenicists, and the Nazis, land. It is "*essential,* fixed," despite the complex history of racial whiteness itself. "By shifting language from an open advocacy of white supremacy . . . to 'Ethno-differentialism,'" Burley writes, far-right leaders appropriate and distort commitments, vocabularies, and appeals associated with the left.[63] (The Christchurch shooter identified himself as a Third Positionist after his deadly attack on a mosque, claiming to defend diversity, which, for him, is necessarily segregated.) This gradual adoption and contortion of progressive talking points—and tenuous deemphasis of racism—has, from the 1960s to the present, functioned in part as a strategic choice. As one Stormfront user writes, "Third Positionists are pro-environment and antiwar (the left is happy) yet they are anti-immigration and support traditional values (the right is happy)."[64] It's a far-right attempt to appeal to a wider audience already primed to respond by broader national—and environmental—myths about land, ownership, identity, and belonging in the United States.

Population Control and Environmental Protection since the 1960s

As a multifarious political program, environmentalism has a complex genealogy deriving from innumerable sources, some of them centuries (even millennia) old and others more recent, some originating in the Americas and others elsewhere, some more liberatory in direction and others more reactionary. Some sectors—such as environmental justice activism—stand on the shoulders not just of older campaigns for environmental protection but also, to a larger degree, labor and civil rights movements combatting the economic disposability of people as well as resources. By the same token, certain elements of conservationist and population discourse (both tremendously mixed fields in their own right) stem from less savory origins.

Ever since the advent of the modern, mainstream environmental movement in the late 1960s and 1970s, anxieties over resource consumption by a growing population have rendered immigration restriction and other forms of population control easy targets for partisan crossover. Paul Ehrlich's *The Population Bomb* (1968) functioned as an early lightning rod, condemning the ills of national and global overcrowding. Popular literary and nonliterary texts predominantly "envisioned" this phenomenon, Ursula K. Heise notes, "as an essentially urban condition" eliciting "serious . . . psychological and economic consequences."[65] Setting aside the fact that such accounts tended to neglect the ecological costs of food and water depletion outside the city (and the fact that people who reside in cities consume fewer resources per capita than those in suburbs and many rural areas in the United States), this emphasis on social degradation reencoded certain racial assumptions even as civil rights legislation presumed to lay them to rest. Writers like Ehrlich identified the grime and congestion of cities with its poorest residents, just as Roosevelt and Grant did decades before—and in similar, if subtler, racial and ethnonational terms. (Ehrlich wrote *The Population Bomb* after a trip to India, when Delhi's population was less than half that of his native New York.)

Ehrlich's book also brought together centrist environmentalists and white nationalists such that the latter influenced the former. Perhaps the most consequential of Ehrlich's readers was John Tanton, a Michigan conservation and family planning activist who would become the founder of dozens of anti-immigration organizations that have helped to spur the United States' broad rightward shift in the early twenty-first century. After Ehrlich installed Tanton as president of his own outfit, Zero Population Growth, in 1975, Tanton, having struggled initially to identify allies, began to partner and share fundraising with white-nationalist groups. In his correspondence with them, he not only turned from questions of global population reduction to U.S. immigration restriction, but also grew interested in eugenics—ideas he would soon share. Tanton targeted centrist liberals in his messaging, peddling a more palatable idiom of xenophobia, couched in environmentalist terms, than the sort offered by skinheads. "Eventually," Reece Jones writes, "prominent scientists"—including Ehrlich and the geneticist Garrett Hardin—"would find themselves rubbing elbows with white supremacists as their ties with John Tanton led them deeper and deeper into extreme views about immigrants."[66] It is impossible to overstate the impact these allies have had on mainstream environmental politics. In the 1980s and 1990s, nonpartisan NGOs began to focus on population in the Global South as a fundamental catalyst for global ecological disruptions, an emphasis that not only neglects structural economic and political factors related to poverty, population growth, consumption patterns, and migration but also perpetuates "a simmering racist metanarrative: the problem is really that brown people are too stupid and/or too sexual to control themselves."[67]

Perhaps no writer has better stoked Malthusian fears than Hardin, whose 1968 essay "The Tragedy of the Commons" has informed writers, activists, and policymakers as diverse as Earth First! monkeywrenchers, small-government champions of trickle-down economics, and advocates of immigration restriction across the political spectrum. The "tragedy" Hardin narrates concerns the fate of finite resources under pressure due to unchecked reproduction, which he presents in the form of a parable about common land. As more individuals seek to make use of land for their own ends, he argues, the commons inevitably collapses, to everyone's detriment. This inevitability (call it a state of emergency) anchored his argument: without intervention, the commons *will* collapse. "No system," he wrote in another essay, "can survive the effects of unopposed positive feedback. . . . The 'sanctity of life' must give way before the 'sanctity of the carrying capacity' "—an assertion that other scholars had already disproven long before his own writing, given its fixation on absolute numbers over vast disparities in resource distribution.[68] For the critic Rob Nixon, Hardin's "crucial move" is to supplement Thomas Malthus's already deeply ahistorical source material with "genetic and generic forces, creating a muscular tag team pulling for determinism."[69] He frames selfishness itself as inevitable: the tragedy delegitimates mutual aid or collaborative ownership, even though innumerable peoples worldwide have "manag[ed] common resources cooperatively for centuries" at a time, "successfully negotiating the tension between private gain and the public good."[70] In short, Hardin tied natural law to tenets of enclosure for a new, wider, less overtly racist audience.

The essay's bewildered ideological orientation arguably facilitates its uninterrupted appeal, evident in debates over migration and population growth within even that most orthodox bastion of environmentalism, the Sierra Club.[71] Hardin in fact appears to attribute the coming exhaustion of resources to a perspective typically identified with economic conservatism. "We can make little progress in working toward optimum population size," he writes,

"until we explicitly exorcize the spirit of . . . the 'invisible hand'"
and the related notion that self-interest promotes public interest.[72]
Hardin envisioned the opposite: the plurality of needs occasioned
by population growth "ultimately makes democracy impossible."
The sheer number of people vying for survival culminates in "the
acceptance of a totalitarian regime as the least of the evils available
to an overpopulated political unit."[73] On the one hand, Hardin's
warning would seem to presage the frantic admission by Sarah
Jaquette Ray's student audience member, mentioned in the Introduction, that submission to a green dictator might be prefera-
ble to ongoing climate crisis (itself often attributed to population
growth, largely because of Hardin's influence). But on the other,
because Hardin was writing against what he viewed as an *already*
unsustainable population, the admission seems to be his own: that
a suspension of democracy is the only solution to a growing population's strain on resources.

It might come as little surprise, then, that both critics and acolytes have identified Hardin himself as a prototypical ecofascist. The
conclusion he promotes is that new methods of checking human
population must be devised since traditional means no longer do.
If the "negative feedbacks of predation" and "parasitism" no longer suffice to curb growth, then "socially induced sterility and many
other factors that interfere with reproduction and favor death"
must be introduced—but not equally or voluntarily. Hardin suggests that "those who are biologically more fit to be the custodians
of property and power should legally inherit more."[74] The outwardly
anticapitalist thrust of his aversion to the concept of the "invisible
hand" is, as such, somewhat misleading. His objection is not to economic competition, but to the idea that all individuals are worthy or
capable of participating. Hardin, Nixon writes, "doesn't ask textured
historical questions"—questions that might consider enclosure a
motor of rather than panacea for resource depletion.[75] He distrib-
utes blame not across the shoulders of the institutions or people
most responsible for global and local ecological despoliation—
namely, the structures (and owners) of resource extraction (and
military intervention that enforces it) that undergird a financial
system housed in the Global North—but on those of populations
he deems incapable of a suitable relationship with land.

Hardin's problem, then, is not with the consumption of
resources—it's with consumption by *the wrong sort of people*. If

his words in the epigraph above apply to the El Paso shooter, they describe his own position just as well. In this respect, he is representative of a broader tendency—informed by his own work—to frame migrants as "trash": a rhetoric of disgust, Ray writes, that "masks the ways in which immigrants' bodily labor makes middle-class comforts for a vast majority of American citizens." Figures like Hardin cast nonwhite migrants "as a threat to nature and nation," even though migrants themselves "bear the cost . . . in the form of poor treatment of workers, reduced health and access to medical treatment, and . . . the risking of injury and death in the borderland."[76] It is environmentalism's "perceived function as a counter . . . to neoliberalism," John Hultgren argues, that has enabled arguments like Hardin's to successfully persuade activists on the left. On one hand, immigrant labor appears a symptom of a destructive economic order. On another, migrants might also seem to lack an attachment to place that nationals take for granted. From such a vantage, "steering the . . . relationship between nature and sovereignty in a sustainable direction requires a biopolitical intervention." The "fate of nature" becomes that "of the American nation."[77] But ideas about nature and nation did not simply develop alongside each other in the United States. They did so in a matrix in part delimited by standards of enclosure that have informed not only dominant modes of national belonging and the economic systems in which they take shape but also race and other social forms, drawing distinctions between "native" and "invasive" species all the while.

Modern Environmentalism, Purity Politics, and the Threshold of Consumption

Environmentalist laments over population that neglect economic systems, patterns of ownership, and cultural habits can be read in part as (perhaps unintentional) arguments for who should be able to consume and who should not, based on claims about who belongs within a given environment and who doesn't—a distinction that indexes people in terms of native and invasive species. Such arguments have proven persistent. Figures such as Hardin and Ehrlich not only anchored the rise of modern environmentalism in the 1960s and 1970s but also fixated on measures like coercive population control and the dismantling of the social safety net to conserve resources, specifically for those with existing access to them along national, economic, and implicitly racial lines. (Hardin referred to his work as his "case against helping the poor," largely ignoring extractive industries and risk-prone financial institutions.[78]) Perhaps unsurprisingly, then, writers like Hardin serve as frequent touchstones among today's self-styled ecofascists in online forums, who celebrate the "lifeboat ethics" proposed by such figures—a philosophy that rigid borders, indifference toward extranational events regardless of culpability, and expulsion of undesirable elements might lessen strain on (ethno)national resources and, somehow, protect the nation (and race) from global climate changes. Such solutions have less to do with mitigating resource consumption than with reserving it for a privileged few who already largely enjoy such exclusivity.[79]

Access and entitlement to those resources stems from the settler-colonial seizure of land to begin with, first as an arena for resource extraction and capital accumulation, then as a venue for reenactments of producerist individualism. To reiterate my framing in the Introduction, it was the consumption of land that occasioned racialized violence in the United States, as well as the producerist perspective that settlers were and are better stewards of it. Similar arguments about consumption, ownership, identity, and belonging animate claims to land entitlement such as the Bundys', based on (sometimes explicit, sometimes implicit) appeals to "blood and soil" that proceed "from the assumption that there was no 'before'"—no other ways of inhabiting and relating to the landscape, and no other peoples (or nonhuman others) who did and continue to do so. For this reason, Kyle Boggs notes, land entitlement is not merely "tied to identity." It "*has to* be narrated as part of the nation."[80] The sort of performance observed in the Bundys' occupation of the Malheur Refuge rehearses consumption of land: not just its violent seizure, telegraphed in a roughrider aesthetic, but also, through that recital of ownership, a claim to privileged possession and use of its resources. Such reenactments serve to rhetorically naturalize a particular identity position in terms of a certain environment while erasing others who challenge that relationship, laying groundwork for (further) violence toward them, if not advocating or effecting it outright.

These performances (and the narratives in which they participate) concern environmental representation regardless of the fact that the Bundys, at least, reject environmentalism as a big-tent political commitment. Various far-right environmentalists have seen "an ideological opportunity" in productions like the Bundys'. The "romanticized image of the rural rancher" not only resonates with the rebirth of a *Volk,* Boggs notes, but also readily informs a broader "environmental ethos . . . predicated on constructions of purity—racial and ecological—and performances of conquest situated in place."[81] Certainly the El Paso shooter sought to embody this ethos, narrating it in terms of national regeneration as he did so. Another way of framing this dynamic might be to say that, in the cultural field of ecofascism, one is not born but rather becomes pure, despite blood-and-soil appeals to natural law by figures across U.S. history. As the white-supremacist Patriot Front puts it, Native lands are "Not Stolen" but "Conquered."[82] The white race *worked* for its supremacy—its entitlement to land and innocence upon it—through conquest and social-Darwinist competition. A relationship between blood and soil is, in this vein, one that must be constantly reestablished through various stories told about it. That narration—a discursive consolidation of identity scripts distinguishing a natural, native *us* from an unnatural, invasive *them* along preexisting vectors of power—is thus also a prerequisite for ecofascism. In other words, it is not just existing ideologies of white supremacy that inform ecofascist rhetoric or violence in the United States. It is narratives about the consumption of land itself.

Blatant white-supremacist speech does not conventionally circulate in mainstream contexts in the twenty-first century, but these sorts of narratives can and do. For example, in an analysis of outdoor recreation advertisements and interviews with self-stated environmentalists, Samantha Senda-Cook and Danielle Endres found that participants most often spoke of recreation as an effort to find "a place of one's own . . . in the natural world." But even though "being alone was important," they write, "being away from unknown others was more." Participants' rhetoric simultaneously drew "boundaries between nature and culture" and "who can and cannot be in the area," or even within the sphere of nature itself. In this study, recreational consumption of the same lands from which U.S. imperialism removed Native peoples appears to be less about isolation than about drawing a distinction between who does and does not belong. Senda-Cook and Endres are not alone in their findings. Scholars of environment and race such as Dorceta Taylor and Carolyn Finney have arrived at similar conclusions, demonstrating how the discourse of wilderness recreation often marks natural spaces in terms of race and other social distinctions. But what I want to point out is that Senda-Cook and Endres's respondents did not necessarily view themselves as *inherently* belonging within ostensibly natural spaces. They unmistakably named what separates them from mere tourists: "challenge."[83] It takes *effort* to be sufficiently natural. One must do the proper consuming. These recreators might not have literally ingested the land, but they nonetheless incorporated it as a matter of identity—more specifically, as a matter of a privileged, naturalized belonging to place—through their recreational consumption of it.

It is the act of consuming—and of narrating that consumption—that rhetorically positions the speaker as a privileged subject within the sphere of "nature" (whether conceived of in terms of a specific bounded territory or not) rather than within an encroaching, pollutive modernity. As the following chapters demonstrate, such acts also often function to absolve the speaker of complicity in a variety of threats to ecological integrity. They function, in other words, as more-or-less casual acts of self-indigenization that implicitly cast others who have not participated in the same or similar activities as pollutants. But they also efface ongoing losses weathered by actual Indigenous peoples, as well as others who do not suitably consume. And some people might be ruled out of this vision of belonging in any case. Ray points out that environmentalist rhetoric that "promotes wilderness as the space of corporeal purification and ecological correctness" not only "requires that the retreat to nature be a physical challenge" but also ignores or dismisses "differences among people"—namely, people of color, historically barred from entering recreational spaces, and disabled folks unable to enter them regardless.[84]

It would be disingenuous (even irresponsible) to refer to everyday wilderness recreators, for example, as neo-Nazis. But the fact that they're *not* neo-Nazis is precisely what makes their rhetoric both pervasive and troubling. It reinforces and risks passing off frequently violent land entitlement as innocuous, even sensible. Depending on the stories told about it, recreation can function as a sort of proxy, indirectly staking a claim to ecological (and potentially ethnonational) purity and emplaced belonging, based on a different form of consumption of the same land whose settler absorption first established such entitlements. Euro-American expressions of outrage over the partition and sale of public lands don't just position settlers as victims of colonization while ignoring other, enduring inhabitants.[85] They also frequently reiterate divisions based on racialized histories of private and federal land ownership in the United States. James Pogue, chronicler of the Malheur occupation, "connected with Ammon" over shared resistance to a stacked political and economic deck—an important reminder that, however insurmountable present U.S. partisan divisions might seem, our shared socioeconomic conditions always contain within them a sometimes-surprising potential for solidarity. He gives the impression, however, that, for him, it is Bundy's investment in rugged individualist living—and an almost mystical connection between producerist owner and productive land—that links right-wing militant and left-wing observer. "[M]ost environmentalists and most angry Westerners . . . share the same basic sense that there's a way of being in the world that goes deeper . . . than anything our rampant, unfeeling, techno-capitalist society teaches us," he writes. "I tend to think that extremism in defense of an endangered species is no vice."[86] Pogue, a former monkey-wrencher, does mean actual endangered species, but he also means himself and even Bundy—that is, as long as the man starts to respect public lands as much as he does his own. They are, after all, a symbol of national as well as environmental identity.

This example merely illustrates the extent to which narratives of environmental protection get bound up with parallel narratives of producerist identity, even when, on the surface, a speaker remains critical of private ownership. Others in the ensuing chapters go further, conflating similar visions of identity and belonging with certain environments in ways that risk promoting violence against "invasive" others. This displacement of explicit narratives about land entitlement to more implicit expressions occurs in diverse ways. Jake Angeli, for example, does not derive his belief in his own purity from yeoman labor, resource use, wealth accumulation, or even specific landscapes. He locates proof elsewhere: in his consumption of organic foods, for instance, and even his resistance to Covid-19 mask mandates, in whose absence the virus might reduce the number of people placing strain on the earth while sparing those resilient enough to inherit it.[87] When I refer to *threshold objects* in the Introduction and later chapters, I have acts of consumption like these—and the aspirations behind them—in mind.

Beyond reinforcing and even creating racialized notions of ingroup supremacy, these sorts of narratives promote the idea that personal action furnishes the means to environmental purity, maintaining the neoliberal status quo despite the fact that many such narratives emerge, at least in part, in a spirit of challenge to it. In this respect (and as chapter 2 will address in more detail), the threshold object trope trades in the same assumptions that motivate "green consumerism" or "green capitalism," the idea that one can help save the planet by producing and/or purchasing ecologically "friendly" products. This notion permits consumers to "have a conscience without needing to revise their way of life," perpetuating the fantasy of endless economic growth that propels unsustainable ecological changes (and imperial violence) to begin with.[88] Advertisers have long appealed to environmentalist sensibilities to sell commodities, not only responding to changing attitudes toward nature and environment but also helping to shape them. Ray, however, cuts straight to the dilemma that green consumerism compounds: a "consumption-based model that is not paired with efforts to change the way corporations, industries, and governments produce, consume, and regulate" not only identifies environmentalism with personal habits instead of large-scale structural change but also "lulls us into equating bodily purity with environmental health," lending itself to the categorization of human individuals along the distinction she draws between "natural" ecological subjects and "polluting" ecological others.[89]

What these points lend support to, above all, is a notion I touched upon in the Introduction: that we might best understand (eco)fascism not as a stable ideology but as an authoritarian cultural and political phenomenon mustered to "'restore order' against a backdrop of economic collapse" that neglects to address—and, historically, often reinforces—the material systems that catalyze it.[90] Representations that prefigure this outcome circulate across partisan lines, broadly narrating the purity and belonging of certain individuals and populations, absolving them of complicity in ecological and economic crises at others' expense. In doing so, they "not only exclude people, but also . . . eschew competing imaginaries"—a key aspect not only of fascism but also of neoliberal capitalism itself, under which the individual subject assumes the burden of risk.[91] Such narratives, that is, devalue both people who do not or are unable to conform to them and other environmentalisms, especially movements organized by people of color that focus on matters of social as well as environmental justice. But such communally oriented politics are quite beside the point for frank ecofascists, who, despite their dissatisfaction with the environmental, political, and economic status quo, arguably behave in ways consistent with its mandate. In an environmentalist marketplace, what an ecofascist looks out for is not really the climate or the biosphere, but himself—and self-identity is always shot through with existing assumptions and narratives about place, race, and other social forms that determine who is and is not worthy of life in the United States, let alone on a changing planet.

Interlude I

Intertwined projects of racial subordination and land dispossession have performed a starring role in the articulation of the U.S. natural rights tradition over the past three centuries. And even if liberal multiculturalism became "the cutting edge of post-civil-rights-movement US history revisionism," as Roxanne Dunbar-Ortiz puts it, Native communities largely "had to be left out." As "treaty-based peoples . . . they did not fit the grid of multiculturalism but were included by transforming them into an inchoate oppressed racial group" rather than recognizing them as sovereign nations.[1] This failure of liberal universalism has, in some cases, in fact prompted a surprising "convergence of indigenist, bioregionalist, and far-right movements" due to shared (if radically different in terms of intent) grievances with neoliberal globalization, as demonstrated by the politics of, for example, the Tlingit activist Vince Rinehart, who has allied with white-nationalist organizations like Attack the System to promote a project of "tribal anarchism" in which "distinct tribes—not necessarily but potentially racial in nature—unite to bring down the imperialist United States government and corporations." Rinehart represents a perhaps unexpected bridge between Indigenous decolonial movements and right-wing Third Positionism.[2] Other proponents of cultural nationalism writ large have in fact more fully embraced the latter, parroting its characteristic appeals to natural strength, racial predispositions, and sex and gender roles, demonstrating how such rhetoric has reified the significance of "nature" in consistent yet flexible ways over time and for a variety of people, as evidenced by the haphazard embrace of Black and Latino men by various far-right organizations. Such examples speak not just to Daniel HoSang and Joseph Lowndes's observations about the racial malleability of far-right politics, but also to how appeals to nature can cohere across constituencies in complicated ways, often perpetuating assumptions and exclusions related to ability, gender, and sexuality as well as, in many if not all cases, claims to sovereignty based on land ownership.

Before moving on to the next chapters, I want to return briefly to the border between the U.S. Southwest and Mexico to acknowledge that it has chiefly been feminists of color who have combatted these tendencies since the 1960s, offering alternative accounts of belonging—with the land as well as with other people—that do not rely on claims to possession, acts of consumption, or appeals to ethnonational nature. Considering the U.S.–Mexico borderlands is especially useful in this context given the heterogeneous region's Chicana literary tradition, which has written back against not only U.S. settler colonialism and border politics but also the heteropatriarchy of the Chicano nationalism that emerged in the 1960s and 1970s to resist them. Gloria Anzaldúa, to name one such writer, interweaves environmentalist, feminist, and queer critiques of both nationalisms across her body of work, especially in her 1987 collection of essays and poetry *Borderlands/La Frontera: The New Mestiza*. Anzaldúa's work, like that of other queer Chicana writers, comprises a broadly decolonial project in which she also refuses to uncritically indulge the notion that nature, environmental and/or ethnonational, constitutes belonging. As a queer woman, she can't afford to. Mutually reinforcing ideas about shared nature and enclosed territory shore up identity in ways that rarely accommodate outliers or actively target them with physical violence. This is to suggest neither that queerness is unnatural nor that queer and women writers do not articulate their own grounded accounts of identity and belonging. It is, rather, to point out the degree to which such figures tend to scrutinize the material and narrative processes by which oppressive accounts of identity and belonging take shape, and to accordingly (if tentatively) "re-naturalize" their own on different terms. Anzaldúa, for one, does not advocate an outright dismissal of identity, sense of place, or even the concept of nature. She approaches these vectors instead as what Cary Wolfe describes as "ongoing acts of meaning-making" that rehearse "the complex logic of physical (and, specifically, biological) systems"—a complex constructivism "unfolding dynamically" in relation to nonhuman others and environments.[3]

As its title suggests, *Borderlands* is all about borders—and, more specifically, the way they overdetermine certain identities as well as ravage certain environments. Borders, Anzaldúa writes, "are set up to define the places that are safe and unsafe, to distinguish *us* from *them*."[4] A border*land* on the other hand, "is a vague and undetermined place created by the . . . boundary" that is "present wherever two or more cultures edge each other, where people of different races occupy the same territory, where under, lower, middle and upper classes touch" (25), as is certainly the case in a region where "colonial legacies . . . identify Chicana/os . . . as both colonizer and colonized," descendants (to varying degrees) of Spanish as well as Indigenous peoples.[5] It is "not a comfortable territory to live in" (19), Anzaldúa writes. "[A]nger and exploitation are the prominent features" when many U.S. citizens "consider the inhabitants of the borderlands transgressors" (25), despite the fact that modern borders cut through land historically occupied by Indigenous, Chicanx, and mestiza/o peoples whose homes pre-date them by centuries. In Anzaldúa's native Texas alone, the drawing of borders culminated in a mass land transfer from earlier inhabitants to Euro-American arrivals "by fraud, intimidation, violence, and force," delivering expanded ranching operations to white landowners and relegating Mexicans and others to low-wage work on land their communities tended for generations. These racialized distinctions not only continue today but have also fueled ejections from U.S. territory over the past two hundred years.[6]

Anzaldúa addresses both the environmental and identitarian aspects of these acts of settler-colonial enclosure, offering a brief lesson through a semiautobiographical lens. "*Los gringos* had not stopped at the border," she writes. "By the end of the nineteenth century, powerful landowners in Mexico, in partnership with US colonizing companies, had dispossessed millions of Indians of their lands," to the extent that Mexican citizens remain largely dependent on U.S.-owned factories today. On both sides of the border, "corporations hired gangs of *mexicanos* to pull out the brush, chaparral and cactus and to irrigate the desert" in the first decades of the twentieth century. "The land they toiled over had once belonged to many of them, or had been used communally by them." As a child, Anzaldúa herself "saw the end of dryland farming" and "witnessed the land cleared . . . cut up into thousands of neat rectangles" (31–2). By the early 1980s, Priscilla Solis Ybarra writes, "farming irrigation had depleted and polluted the Rio Grande. The promotion of South Texas as a farming region also motivated a trend to clear the land to make way for farms—some of which never materialized," resulting "in clear-cut lands that exposed top-soil to destructive erosion." The enclosure of the region was, in this respect, doubly destructive, maiming both ecological health and long-term residents' traditional livelihoods. In its rigid adherence to a particular understanding of appropriate land use, U.S. interests "rejected the knowledge Mexican Americans gained through generations of experience with the land in the new southwest United States," mounting "a literal alienation of Mexican Americans from land and the natural environment."[7]

Land repossession accordingly comprised a cornerstone of Chicano cultural nationalism of the 1960s and 1970s, which sought to reclaim land "to deterritorialize the colonizer," Ybarra adds. "But to what extent," she asks, has cultural nationalism (broadly conceived) "concerned itself with the dignity and respect of the land as much as with the sovereignty of the people who inhabit it?" This question is one that queer Chicana feminists such as Anzaldúa seek to address, especially given that, within the movement, conceptions of national sovereignty often rested on naturalized assumptions about gender and sex roles. For Ybarra, Anzaldúa and other queer women "challenge the patriarchy and homophobia of Chicana/o cultural nationalism" by contending in their work that such rigid hierarchy reinforces racial domination as well as environmental degradation. The playwright Cherríe Moraga, for instance, focuses much of her writing on Aztlán, the homeland of central significance to the Chicano movement, which she "cannot inhabit . . . unchanged as a biracial lesbian who refuses to endure male dominance," even if she, too, identifies with it. In her plays, Moraga reconfigures Aztlán as an "imaginary homeland" rather than one that "require[s] a material tangibility or possession" for the sake of nationalism. This "new Aztlán" to which Moraga and other Chicana writers appeal—a symbol of identification reflexively rooted in shared narrative—resists logics of enclosure and entitlement, conceived as it is not as land to be owned but as an idea to continually, creatively articulate on the basis of lived experience, including interdependencies with environment.[8] In the process, queer Chicana feminist writers refuse appeals to essentialized racial and gender identities, too.

Anzaldúa captures this form of belonging in *Borderlands,* critiquing rigid conceptions of race, nation, gender, and sexuality on both sides of the border. "Chicanos and other people of color suffer . . . for not acculturating," she writes (85). But for her part, it is impossible to fully "identify with . . . Anglo-American" *or* "Mexican cultural values. We are a synergy of two cultures" (77). Hybridity—as a refusal or inability to live up to cultural purity—invites scorn on both sides of the Rio Grande and within the Chicano movement itself. And notions of purity attach to a variety of cultural characteristics. "[V]arious Latinos," Anzaldúa writes, labeled her a "cultural traitor" for speaking English or Spanish in a Chicano dialect, "considered by the purist . . . a mutilation." But "Chicano Spanish," she adds, "is a living language," as "diverse linguistically as it is regionally." There is "no one Chicano language just as there is no one Chicano experience" (80–1). Nonetheless she finds the pressure debilitating in terms of her identity, her relationship to environment, and her writing: "The stress of living with cultural ambiguity both compels me to write and blocks me" (96). What benumbs her is the conflict between two putative totalities, the Anglo and the Mexican.

Cultural essentialism can offer a sense of belonging, but it also tends to foreclose other directions that tensions among multiple positions might reveal. For Anzaldúa, a "counterstance locks one into a duel of oppressor and oppressed" in which "both are reduced to a common denominator of violence." The liminal identity space of the "new *mestiza*" she proposes "operates in a pluralistic mode" and "turns the ambivalence into something . . . malleable" or adaptable, especially in the face of rapidly changing sociopolitical and ecological conditions (99–101). She connects this transformation to her writing, throughout *Borderlands* and elsewhere, as a matter of what she calls *compostura*: the way "one composes one's life" from "all the kinds of coincidental and random things" in it—including interdependencies with nonhuman others and environments (96).[9] Hers is a vision of social and ecological belonging that involves making, synthesizing, and articulating toward a consistent form rather than accessing something supposedly essential.

This is not to say that the concept of sovereignty dissolves altogether in Anzaldúa's vision or other accounts of social and environmental belonging that challenge fixed categorization. My aim is neither to celebrate national sovereignty nor to resist it uncritically, but simply to point out that marginalized writers have contested claims to national and natural essence. John Hultgren points out that, despite their variety, critics of environmentally motivated immigration restriction often propose "that sovereignty is inherently anthropocentric and exclusionary, whereas nature is an inherently borderless, emancipatory force."[10] Such strict opposition, however, does not account for Indigenous notions of sovereignty and territory, for example, that do not rest on privatization, extraction, and fixed conceptions of nature as foundations. Despite her own Indigenous ancestry, Anzaldúa in fact often worried, prior to her death in 2004, that her work risked "violating Indian cultural boundaries" and appropriating ongoing Native lifeways.[11] But her writing (and that of other queer Chicana feminists) reads more as an attempt to resist "succumbing to the allure of devising global-scale theories," as Ybarra puts it, that "forsake the value of knowledge found in specific cultures . . . caring for particular places, be those long-time or ephemeral homes."[12]

Those homes have indeed suffered under the global systems that self-identified ecofascists also decry. Numerous progressive critics have advocated solutions similar to some that right-wing figures propose, too. Ybarra, for one, suggests that the United States "and the planet, would . . . benefit from dismantling . . . trade deals" that "wreak havoc with national economies and . . . environmental protections. This would give potential immigrants to the United States the means to stay home, which I expect they would prefer to living in the United States, where they encounter racism and oppression." Her point is not that would-be migrants should "stay home" because they intrinsically belong there (as the radical right might have it), but that they likely might choose to do so simply because they do in fact live there and have in many cases already cultivated their own meaningful relationships with place and other people in those environments. "At the same time," she adds, the United States "would better invest its energies in reducing rates of consumption rather than building taller walls"—to say nothing of addressing the extractive logics that fuel such cultural habits, patterns of dispossession, and ecological disruptions to begin with.[13]

The distinction is not one between "borderless" nature and "anthropocentric" sovereignty, but rather one between two conceptions of environment and our belonging in and with it: "Is land really a *thing* over and on which different groups make claims, however unequally?" Or is it "a set of social, more-than-human political *relations* that entail normative obligations"?[14] In place of the "crisis epistemology" he suggests has governed U.S. settler colonialism,

Kyle Whyte offers an "epistemology of coordination," informed by Indigenous histories and narratives, that emphasizes "the importance of moral bonds—or kinship relations—for generating the (responsible) capacity to respond to constant change . . . without validating harm or violence."[15] As for Anzaldúa, this approach does not entail a dismissal of identity or normativity but an alternate articulation of both that challenges dominant (and fascist) narratives. But as the next chapter demonstrates, even good-faith efforts to formulate such an alternative can risk reinforcing existing hierarchies. It depends on mode of representation. In situations of ecological disruption, progressive writers, too, might naturalize existing patterns of violence according to the same narrative logic that has contributed to explicitly ecofascistic claims to land: by consuming certain objects in an effort to prove their privileged belonging on it.

« 2 »

Tools

*Circumscriptions of Territory across the
Communalist Counterculture and Its Markets*

[H]ere were the tools . . . of the alternative folk
economy to come, the tribal technology ready to be
ordered and put to work. When the cities collapsed (as
they were certain to do) and all the supply lines froze
up (which they might any day now) these would be
the means of cunning survival.
—Theodore Roszak, *From Satori to Silicon Valley*

If we are to survive as a species, it is beyond rational
argument that we must achieve sustainability. And
however twisted the path or painful the journey, when
we achieve it, I suspect it will in many ways resemble
Ecotopia.
—Malcolm Margolin, "Foreword" to *Ecotopia*

The neo-Malthusian anxiety seeded by figures like Garrett Hardin
and Paul Ehrlich informed the budding environmental movement
of the late 1960s and 1970s even as it inflamed the restrictionist
right. Concerns over population and resource management suf-
fused the intentional communities that flowed from the 1960s
counterculture, for example, troubling the status of the commons
for many of them. That concept nonetheless played a philosophically crucial role in their formation, as well as that of other, more
spontaneous projects. For example, in 1969 the Diggers, an anar-
chist group named for a seventeenth-century association of agrarian socialists, helped establish People's Park at the University of
California, Berkeley, by reclaiming and squatting on private land

set aside for development. In its early days, People's Park would exemplify the communalist philosophy of "open land" on which "anyone can settle for a season or, theoretically, a lifetime." According to its founder Lou Gottlieb, the Morning Star Ranch commune in Sonoma County, California, "constituted the first attempt to live on 'land-access-to-which-is-denied-no-one'"—offering, he adds in an interview, a "beacon" to residents seeking experiences in "voluntary primitivism." But he also describes it as having been "an attempt to solve the principal problem of communal organization, namely, who stays and who's gotta go, by letting the land choose its inhabitants thereby forming a tribe."[1] Even as he preaches a gospel of open land strongly rooted in libertarian-socialist notions of direct democracy, he glosses several important questions: Who belongs to the land? Why? And how, indeed, does the land "choose" its inhabitants? Gottlieb's own suggestion seems to be that only the sufficiently "primitive"—defined by arbiters such as himself—qualify.

This stipulation neatly illustrates what the cultural critic Susan Sontag described, in a 1975 essay, as a tendency she believed shared by leftist youth movements of the United States and the radical right in interwar Europe: the prevalence of uncritical appeals to and identifications with ostensibly authentic nature, inclusive of certain human characteristics as well as environments. Identifying with place does not itself fascism make, as I explained in the Introduction. It would be impossible in any case to divorce land from culture, and attempting to do so would risk reproducing the same reductive, instrumentalist views of land and resources that have fed genocidal colonialism the world over. But identifications with place take different forms—and have different effects—depending on the way they're articulated and enacted. For Sontag, seeds of fascist violence did not lie in identification with place, or even in the celebration of supposedly "primitive," antimodernist virtues, but in the neglect or refusal of critical perspectives *on* those virtues. Among the Nazis, it was "hardly . . . the intricacy and subtlety of primitive myth, social organization, or thinking that [was] being extolled," but a romantic ideal of a state of nature—one that, as the last chapter suggested, remains influential across U.S. political culture as well.[2] And in the 1960s and 1970s, aspects of that ideal were mobilizing in new ways as a romantic "back-to-the-land impulse that sweeps the country now and then," Timothy Miller writes, "was having one of its periodic resurgences," rehearsing "themes that had long danced across the American communal stage."[3]

Across U.S. history, changing social, political, and economic realities have often inspired not only feelings of material and existential alienation but also a spirit of rural idealism in reaction to them, a conviction that ostensibly natural lifeways facilitate social and personal rejuvenation—a "palingenetic," if not ultranationalist, gesture. Anarcho-socialist "sod brothers" at People's Park extolled such ideas rhetorically as well as philosophically, referring to themselves as "aboriginals." Among settler communalists, Native Americans especially have long represented a state of nature (human as well as ecological) vanishing under urban, (post)industrial, capitalist artifice.[4] Native peoples served, across the countercultural imagination, as a foil to technology and technocracy, which "made [people] slaves to work and . . . precipitated the environmental crisis"—an argument that prompted many young people "to step backward from modernity into a primitive past." This countercultural objective was (and is) exactly that: *countercultural* (or at least superficially antiestablishment), which is to say reducible neither to left nor right. This blurry, nonpartisan appeal opens a potentially generative field for the cross-cultural cultivation of less exploitative political forms, based in part on greater attention to and appreciation of not only human difference but also human interdependencies with nonhuman others. In the 1960s, mutually beneficial relationships indeed developed among numerous communes and nations (including at Morning Star) in light of so many Native peoples' emphasis on the deeply intertwined relationships between humans and their environments. Still, "even absent a direct local Indian connection, communards in many places lived in tepees, wore loincloths while hoeing their crops, and came together for peyote rituals"—symptoms of idolization rooted less in what Glen Coulthard calls the reflexive "grounded normativity" of Native lifeways than in romantic simplifications of them.[5] Similar reductions have manifested on the far right as well. Jake Angeli, the man who spearheaded the January 6, 2021, assault on the U.S. Capitol, bedecked himself in mock buffalo horns, coyote skins, and "war paint" that he intended not only to evoke Native trickster mythologies but also to represent his own authenticity and purity in the face of an alienating social, political, and economic regime.

Still, Angeli's reaction to perceived artifice is incompatible with neither technology nor capitalism. "On a now defunct website," one journalist reveals, the man "offered online courses on shamanism," among other mystical products and services.[6] Angeli did not just claim privileged access to environmental purity. He also sold it, hawking his wares in a techno-utopian idiom. This last detail, perhaps more than any other, makes manifest similar figures' admiration for classical fascist idealism. Despite their frequent appeals to the natural, it was not quite a pastoral idyll but more accurately "an alternative modernity that fascist regimes sought," Robert O. Paxton writes: "a technically advanced society in which modernity's strains and divisions had been smothered by fascism's powers of integration and control."[7] The Nazi emphasis on rebirth, though it did rest on a primitivist aesthetic, largely played out as a drama of lost harmony reachieved through modern capabilities in medicine, agriculture, architecture, warfare, and communication. It also illustrates the synthesis between seemingly incompatible strands of producerist individualism and nationalist organicism in historical fascist movements—as well as in U.S. political culture. Individual patriotic labor could help to establish one's organic unity with the nation. And even if it could not save one from ascribed racial characteristics in Germany, it often could in Italy, "which generally allowed those who showed the right values and conduct to join the nation."[8]

Sontag's warning, though pertinent, belies the fact that many U.S. counterculturalists of the 1960s and 1970s also embraced new technologies as well as free-market patterns of competition and consumption touted by economically libertarian thinkers as their enabling conditions—a sign not of political division, but of ongoing conversation among the left and right. Popular depictions tend to remember the broad counterculture as a reaction against conservative social norms and capitalist commodification, but members of both left-wing and conservative youth organizations, such as Students for a Democratic Society (SDS) and Young Americans for Freedom (YAF), in fact shared populist and antiestablishment sensibilities, born within a nonpartisan atmosphere of widespread political alienation, distrust of the federal government, and interest in decentralized alternatives.[9] Fiscal libertarians as well as anarcho-socialists contributed to an expanding public conversation surrounding questions of environmental conservation and resource sustainability, championing market-driven solutions through channels like Stewart Brand's serial *Whole Earth Catalog*—hardly a right-wing text, but one that widely promoted its creator's "enthusiasm for . . . unfettered capitalism" and "ambivalence about environmentalism as an ideology" (specifically its roots in collective action and execution via regulatory channels).[10] It did so chiefly by marketing "tools" that would foster the sort of self-sufficient, unalienated living that so many, on the right as well as the left, desired. Despite popular renderings of communal life in the era, the back-to-the-land movement embraced new technologies more often than it shunned them, and communes in fact functioned as "notable centers of innovation."[11] But *Whole Earth*'s tools included not only practical instruments for agriculture and home economics but also the sort of bastardized emblems sported recently by the likes of Angeli as well as New-Age progressives: symbols and styles that, for many, telegraph a deeper attunement to—and worthier presence in—the natural world.

This chapter carries on preceding treatment of explicit eco-fascist violence by beginning to examine how the discursive elements that shape it recombine in certain contexts. Specifically, it considers how, at the dawn of the modern environmental movement, back-to-the-land rejections of private ownership, resource extraction, and wealth inequality in fact toyed with new systems of politically exclusive land entitlement based in part on the same social, intellectual, and rhetorical foundations that have justified privatization and racialization in the United States since before its founding. Intertwined arguments for ecological protection and group belonging—and the purity of both the ecosystem and its inhabitants—bled across the political spectrum in the 1960s and 1970s. During this time, consumption—again, in terms of identity-building self-incorporation—and subsequent use of *Whole Earth*–style tools came to more subtly express one's privileged belonging in a given environment than direct, violent consumption of land itself. In other words, commodities—both practical and symbolic—came to function as threshold objects. In certain fiction and nonfiction of the era, the use of such tools to sustainably cultivate the land executed a fusion of environmentalist virtue with producerist entitlement, asserting innocence in matters of ecological crisis while reserving land through individualistic means that nonetheless promoted nationalistic organicism. In the process, ideas about "natural" forms of labor, strength, and competition stoked assumptions about other behaviors and characteristics, especially in terms of gender, sexuality, race, and ability—a point I illustrate chiefly through a reading of Ernest Callenbach's 1975 novel *Ecotopia*.

Back-to-the-land communalists dedicated to direct democracy, libertarian socialism, and ecological sustainability have celebrated *Ecotopia*—even treated it as a sort of handbook—since its publication. More recently, self-identified ecofascists involved in various white-supremacist organizations, militia movements, and other right-wing projects have similarly lauded the novel.[12] Its striking appeal across two seemingly disparate audiences is what renders it a compelling object of study. Its reception announces a link between environmentalisms of the left and right—one that offers insight into how cultural narratives that spur ecofascist violence might circulate in a diverse variety of contexts. A self-conscious turn to inclusive democracy was indeed the context in which Callenbach wrote *Ecotopia*. After the collapse of the stridently antifascist New Left in the late 1960s, intentional environmentalist communities, or "ecovillages," especially attracted former activists who aimed "to lead a sustainable lifestyle in harmony with each other, other living beings and the earth."[13] *Ecotopia* dramatizes and expands this intention to the scale of a sovereign nation, inspiring a number of real ecovillages worldwide, particularly in the Pacific Northwest—or the Cascadia bioregion—already home to the largest share of intentional communities in the 1960s and 1970s.[14] The novel presents an alternate twentieth-century version of the region, which, having seceded from the United States, has established itself as a global leader in renewable energy, sustainable agriculture and waste management, and social welfare. For this reason, it has galvanized numerous Cascadian bioregionalists, many of them real-world secessionists who "have sought to make this fictional ecotopia into reality." But as Blair Taylor notes, "the open parameters of place-based politics" in the "overwhelmingly" white region have also "created an opportunity for participation by right actors" who see in Cascadia a "natural place to create a white homeland."[15] They, too, find inspiration in Ecotopia, which surpasses other nations not only in green energy but also in munitions manufacturing, border militarization, and the training of a paramilitary population eager and prepared to defend the homeland against outsiders. Most remarkably, it also observes a racially segregated system of social organization.

It is not my intention to represent the novel or its author as examples of ecofascism as a coherent political theory, no matter how many real-life fascists have flocked to them. Nor, again, do I wish to demonize self-determined, place-based political movements tout court. Callenbach intended his work to serve progressive environmentalist goals, and there is indeed much to praise and learn from in his novel, including its bold celebration of the commons, couched within a broad vision of nonexploitative (even, at times, reciprocal) relations with environment. My aim is rather to consider how, despite or alongside these themes and possibilities, the novel also weaves together certain cultural threads—including rural romanticism, producerism, and existing ideas about race, nation, labor, and environment—into a narrative that in part reproduces the generic template I defined in the Introduction, at times reinforcing existing patterns of power—and even entertaining violence along these lines—as it does so.

Consumption plays an important (if not the only) role in this dynamic. It is not particularly notable that Ecotopians consume objects in general. Different cultures across time have prioritized different forms of consumption and values regarding the objects they consume, whether these be mercantile, gift-based, capitalistic, or otherwise, but the tendency for cultures to understand themselves and others as connected to particular artifacts is fairly universal.[16] My interest in this chapter (indeed in the book as a whole) is not in consumption alone, but in consumption yoked to a distinct set of historical conditions and narrative conventions. Ecotopia nominally secedes from capitalism as well as the United States, yet Ecotopians locate both their national and ecological belonging not just in their values, food, and other cultural pursuits but also to a large degree in commodity consumption and economic competition. Like many real-world eco-communalists, they appeal to anarcho-socialist ideals and pride themselves on more sustainable habits than their neighbors, but the fledgling nation nonetheless organizes around a marketplace of *Whole Earth*–style tools, which, in the novel, encourages the sort of nationalism and racialization that have manifested across U.S. (environmental) history. Working land renders one its rightful inhabitant (if not its owner), and doing so with these tools, in Ecotopia, renders one environmentally pure at the same time. In this respect, certain commodities perhaps clarify my suggestion in the preceding chapter that labor or production can themselves telegraph the consumption of land, by which I mean its assimilation, in an acquisitive register, as a matter of identity. The tools function as threshold objects, confirming their users' shared ecological innocence and, through it, national belonging threatened by impure others. This pattern in the novel brushes against the logic of enclosure without quite touching it. To describe it as enclosure would be to defy one of *Ecotopia*'s core themes: the restoration of the commons. For this reason, I provisionally refer to it instead as a process of *circumscription,* by which I mean the restriction of certain behaviors or characteristics within certain boundaries—a definition that captures an inchoate logic of fixity in *Ecotopia* and elsewhere (as opposed to the grounded yet reflexive adaptation articulated by, for example, Taiaiake Alfred or Kyle Whyte) that applies to social forms like gender and race as well as to geography. I use the word in this chapter, in other words, to specifically denote a producerist logic consistent with enclosure but broader: one of either common or private ownership that not only establishes boundaries but also naturalizes a privileged population within them according to existing social imbalances.

My goal is not simply to argue that environmentalism in this context became yoked to the market as a matter of individual habits. That critique is as old, at least, as the era itself (though still vital now). My aim is rather to consider how postwar interactions between environmentalism and free-market libertarianism revivified the social logic of enclosure—in the form of what I'm calling circumscription—which, in *Ecotopia,* at least, not only casts strong borders as a sovereign and ecological necessity but also feeds crypto-eugenic notions of race, gender, and ability. Even if all Ecotopian citizens consume the same sort of tools, Callenbach suggests that different people nonetheless engage with them differently and, in a state of nature, segregate accordingly—and in Ecotopia, these vaguely Third-Positionist variations sort primarily along preexisting, deterministic assumptions about race. Throughout this chapter, I focus on four cumulative details that develop across the novel, starting with (a) *Ecotopia*'s antiestablishment vision of an "organic society" of a sort typically associated with the communalist left and (b) the competitive veneration of "natural" strength—a tendency more frequently associated with the right—that emerges from it. Together, these ideals justify (c) segregation based on immutable natural difference and (d) strict social roles structured and enforced by state and citizen violence.

Ecotopia's Antiestablishment Environmentalism

Miller suggests that communes in the United States have typically understood themselves "as either arks or lighthouses." On one hand, "communitarians band together to protect themselves from the outside world—from environmental collapse . . . or other threats of disaster." On the other, they frequently "build communities as shining examples of just how wonderful the world could be if we would live in better ways." Ecocommunities, he notes, often seek to "embody both types."[17] In an "Epistle to the Ecotopians" published posthumously in the 2014 edition of *Ecotopia,* Callenbach indicated explicitly that he intended his fictional ecocommunity to strike a similar balance at a vast scale. "*Ecotopia* is a novel," he writes, "and secession its dominant metaphor: how would a relatively rational part of the country save itself ecologically . . . on its own?" Ecotopia "aspired to be a beacon for the rest of the world" in its fictive geo-political landscape, and he hoped it would play a similar role beyond its pages, too. But the extent of that intervention is a matter of national debate within the novel itself: over "whether 'Ecology in One Country' is possible, or whether Ecotopia's own survival hinges on the exporting of survivalist doctrines to the rest of the world"— active involvement and aid, that is, for outsiders. At the time of the novel's action—roughly twenty years after Ecotopia secedes from the United States in the 1970s—it is only a handful of "radicals" who take this second position, despite the fact that, "as ecocatastrophes overtake other countries with increasing frequency," militarized borders make for inadequate protection against dramatic change. Ecotopia walls itself off from the rest of the world behind "the forbidding Sierra Nevada," protecting its own even as it hopes the rest of the world will follow its example.[18]

Ecotopia, in other words, focuses on a sovereign nation formed and fortified on the basis of an ecological "state of emergency."

Its appeals to crisis share much in common with the rhetoric of settler-colonial entitlement discussed in the previous chapter, by way of the earliest preservation movements whose proponents, Dorceta Taylor notes, "employed . . . idioms of loss of nature" to guard wilderness spaces against outsiders, "conjur[ing] images of mass slaughters of animals" and "the logging of giant ancient trees."[19] That was the nineteenth century. In the second half of the twentieth, after the publication of ecological warnings such as Rachel Carson's 1962 *Silent Spring* and more alarmist forecasts like Paul Ehrlich's *Population Bomb,* environmentalist rhetoric turned to focus far more on humans' own survival in the face of anthropogenic threats—including, from Ehrlich's perspective, human reproduction.

In large part, *Ecotopia* responds, as Malcolm Margolin puts it in his Foreword to the 2014 edition, to "a widespread recognition that the earth could not possibly sustain an ever-increasing population or an ever-expanding economy."[20] Callenbach himself, however, remained slightly more critical of the overpopulation argument than many pundits. In the "Epistle," he writes that humans "are multiplying to the point where our needs and our wastes outweigh the capacities of the biosphere to produce and absorb them" (176). But in a 2009 interview, he added that the "problem . . . is not that we have too many people" but "too many rich people. Too many high consuming people." He also found preposterous the notion that nation-states—"dinosaurs that we have not yet recognized as dinosaurs"—constitute effective gauges for measuring ecological and population health. Regardless, population control remained one of his preferred solutions: "If we can continue to have populations in the industrial world decline, we'll be a lot better off."[21] Despite the fact that for Callenbach (unlike for Garrett Hardin), declension would most effectively occur not by coercion but through education, social welfare, and widely available birth control regulated by women (progressive forms of management present in *Ecotopia*), he largely targeted population itself rather than habits of consumption per se. And despite his ire, both of its objects— "consuming people" and the nation form—govern the situation of his novel to a large degree.

Still, Ecotopia has much to recommend it as a model for progressive social welfare and ecologically conscious design. Callenbach was, by his own admission, "trying to be very realistic. . . . I didn't want anybody to say 'Oh, that's cute but it's science fiction.'"[22] As one critic puts it, he "avoided impossible scenarios and technologies in building an alternative culture that he hoped would be used as a model for future cultural developments." His "solutions-based realism" has indeed inspired real-world applications, even if "these adoptions have been piecemeal rather than parts of systemic cultural overhauls," as they are in *Ecotopia*.[23] The detail with which Callenbach explains how the nation composts human waste and returns it to the soil in the form of fertilizer, for example, doubles as a template for readers. Citizens also "eat better food than any nation on earth, because," as one character puts it, "we grow it to be nutritious and taste good, not look good" (20). They eat meat, but only wild game or cattle, poultry, or swine that are "never concentrated in forced-feeding fattening lots" (58). The assistant minister of food explains that citizens "like to live in conditions approaching the natural. But not only for sentimental reasons. . . . [O]ur system is considerably cheaper than yours, if we add in *all* the costs," which the United States "passe[s] on through subterfuge to . . . the general public" in the form of poor nutrition, sanitation, labor conditions, and environmental quality. Factories are worker owned or automated, eschewing "the assembly-line principles generally thought essential to really efficient mass production" (17–8).

Even more labor, however, observes the "mania for 'doing it yourself'" that characterized the counterculture broadly and the back-to-the-land movement specifically—and which resources such as Brand's *Whole Earth Catalog* fueled (26). Callenbach explicitly situates himself in this milieu—with one caveat. "People expect me to be a back-to-the-lander," he noted in an interview, "but I came from the land and have no impulse to go back." The urban sociologist Jane Jacobs influenced *Ecotopia* at least as much as DIY merchants like Brand. Callenbach once mused that the novel "is really about . . . how our cities can be sustainable if we go about it right."[24] Ecotopia is both spatially and politically decentralized, prioritizing "strange new minicities" where residents live "in buildings that contain not only apartments but also nurseries, grocery stores, and restaurants" (24, 14). If Ecotopia represents, for Callenbach, a rebirth of civilization, it is one that unfolds along techno-utopian lines, despite its "challenge to the underlying national philosophy of America: ever-continuing progress" proven by a "rising Gross National Product" (4).

The story proceeds largely as a fictive ethnography as its narrator and protagonist, William Weston, tours the nation as the first U.S. guest invited within its borders since independence. (Its secession is chronicled in a 1981 sequel, *Ecotopia Emerging*.) As is common in utopian writing, it also plays out as a sort of education for Weston, who crosses the border as a skeptical reporter and ends up a convert.[25] The novel is epistolary in format, weaving the man's dispatches with private diary entries—a series of memos that, on the one hand, "objectively" report on Ecotopian culture, politics, and their perceived inadequacy for a public audience, and, on the other, trace Weston's acculturation into Ecotopian life. His personal discoveries gradually displace the portrait relayed in his columns, encouraging him, by the novel's end, to remain. Weston's ability to make such a decision illustrates the fact that, despite its strong borders, Ecotopia does not in fact refuse entry or even citizenship to outsiders. One can, indeed, "become" Ecotopian—the requirements for which, as I discuss at the end of this chapter, involve approaching an idiosyncratic state of nature. Upon dressing in his old clothes at the end of the narrative, Weston comments, "*I looked awful, I didn't look* human!" (164). Over the course of the novel, he discovers a truer, "natural" self under the veneer of artificial American accoutrements, and thus assimilates.

Part of that conversion involves joining the Ecotopians in their celebration of seemingly innate national characteristics he (and, through him, U.S. culture writ large) initially faults: namely, their capacity "to take their modest place in a seamless, stable-state web of living organisms" (43). Their homesteads initially strike him as "dingy and unprosperous." Ecotopia "*largely abandoned*" nonferrous metals as manufacturing materials: "*[O]nly iron, which rusts away in time, seems a 'natural' metal*" (21).[26] And though Weston insists that "no one can be utterly insensitive to the pleasures of the open road," Ecotopia's "primitive and underpowered vehicles . . . cannot satisfy the urge for speed and freedom which has been so well met by the American auto industry" (27). This final complaint is representative of his critique throughout, which overarchingly tends to naturalize U.S. cultural tastes, taking them for intrinsic, unquestionable qualities inherent to the body politic. Ecotopians themselves do not necessarily do differently. For the figures Weston interviews, the "primitive" is the point—as is, indeed, the commitment to the "natural," in terms of supposedly uniform ethnonational qualities as well as building materials. This is not to say that the characters of Callenbach's novels reiterate the arguments in defense of racial purity advanced by figures like Madison Grant. Ecotopians explicitly view the matter of "eugenic planning" with "great distaste" (66–7). But there is a sense, communicated frequently throughout the novel, that Ecotopia "works" because all its residents share an ostensibly stable core, whether a given speaker represents it in terms of essence or shared commitment. One character calls it the "root agreement": Ecotopians can only "afford" the heated political quarrels that dominate their evening news, he argues, because of it (31). The statement is, on the one hand, an affirmation of the principles of direct democracy that mobilized so many communalist arrangements in the 1960s and 1970s—a sense that no real conflict splits Ecotopians because they all had a direct hand in forging the consensus. "In order to observe the social goal of coming to terms with limits," Heinz Tschachler writes, Callenbach "takes recourse to the model of 'organic society'"—more specifically, to "communal or egalitarian variants of organic society rather than a hierarchical one" of the sort proposed by figures such as *Counter-Currents* editor Greg Johnson.[27] The stable state of renewable energy, Tschachler points out, is quite different from that of a police state. But on the other hand, the unity to which the novel constantly appeals verges on the mystical. Weston observes that the government's *"control over population seems to be primitive compared to ours"* (3). The comment would seem to confirm that Ecotopia has indeed escaped a carceral approach to dissent. But it also raises another possibility that I will explore in greater detail soon: that Ecotopia's citizens *naturally* obey its strictures due to some instinctive quality they believe themselves to share. By contrast, the United States is plagued by divisions rooted in "insane" and "unnatural" economic and political structures against which the Ecotopians measure the perceived naturalness of their own. They believe, in other words, that they *belong* within their borders in a way U.S. citizens, specifically, do not.

The novel's emphasis on economic dysfunction—and Ecotopia's secession in response to it—reflects the frustration that lies, as previous chapters explained, at the root of both far-right and leftist movements. It also dramatizes the extent to which that unrest is bound up with patterns of ongoing (settler) colonial activity. It was the economic imperatives in whose name wealthy nations occupied resource-rich ones that generated the domestic opportunities for rebellion on which Ecotopia's founding Survivalist Party seized. The United States "continued secret wars against [anticolonial] uprisings, and the burden of outlays . . . caused a profound long-term decline in the world competitiveness of American civilian industry. A slow drop in per capita income led to widespread misery, increased tension between rich and poor, and ended citizen confidence"—conditions that speak to anxieties fueling antineoliberal and antigovernment sentiment on the right as well as the left in the twenty-first century. Secessionists "*filched uranium fuel from power plants for the nuclear mines they claimed to have set in New York and Washington.*" But show of force alone would never have been enough, Weston suggests, were it not for "*the severity of the national economic crisis,*" which made violence attractive to enough people that a temporary suspension of the rule of law became viable (2). "The deadly novelty" that Ecotopian economists introduced in this context, Weston tells readers, "was to spread the point of view that economic disaster was not identical with survival disaster"—that collapse was inevitable under extractive capitalism in any case, and even desirable. The Survivalists outlawed oil, enacted legislation to penalize scientists' and politicians' acceptance of payments or favors, and shifted the tax burden from consumers to corporations and craftsmen. These changes, Weston reports, aimed to "avoid loopholes by wealth accumulation" (91). Small political units like cities levy taxes and distribute resources, including a universal basic income. Citizens want for nothing and, correspondingly, the Ecotopian legal apparatus removes incentives to manufacture more than the population needs to survive.

It is for all these reasons that Weston is taken aback by his discovery that a strident culture of commodity consumption *does* in fact exist in Ecotopia. "Despite their aversion to many modern devices," he notes, "Ecotopians have some that are even better than ours. Their picturephones, for instance . . . are far easier to use" and of higher quality (14). They also "use far more power than would be expected," although "both its sources and its uses tend to be diffused . . . and novel" (102). These advances serve ends other than social welfare, despite the nation's pretense to isolation. Weston's "informants admit . . . that there is a modest export trade in electric vehicles—the Ecotopians allow themselves to import just enough metal to replace what is used in the exported electric motors" (25).

Apart from a few "extremists," they use plastics if convenient (78). But it is not just the availability of consumer products Weston finds surprising. It is also the socioeconomic context in which the Ecotopians make, sell, and buy them. Almost all functions of government "are organized, strangely enough, on free-market principles," including education, agriculture, and public works (93). Despite the universal basic income, everywhere Weston turns he discovers forms of privatization and competition that he recognizes from home—even some that outperform economic and political systems in the United States, as if privatization were itself a matter of competition between the two nations.

Alienation and Authenticity across Left and Right

If the last two details I've highlighted—*Ecotopia*'s earnest dramatization of a communal search for authenticity and free-market ideas—seem unlikely bedfellows within a work of utopian fiction by a progressive environmentalist, they nonetheless aptly capture the mingled priorities of the left and right in the 1960s and 1970s. This is not to say that communalists of the era were not genuinely critical of patterns of consumption and ownership. Many were. As one put it, "We were particularly opposed to our government's military violence, to the competitive behaviors we felt were inherent in capitalism, and to the selfish male dominated non-cooperative values . . . wrongly engendered by the nuclear family," as well as to racial inequality.[28] But the years following the mid-1960s "saw substantial evolution in communal forms in large part because of social and environmental challenges that confronted . . . American society as a whole," Miller writes. Countercultural back-to-the-land communes and more systematic eco-communities, "salted with traditional American rural idealism," contributed just two multifaceted voices among many to a much broader cultural "questioning of Received Truth."[29]

This combination of dissent and idealism often translated as what we might call a sort of nature chauvinism, rooted in agrarian romance. "The literature of the alternative culture is awash with thundering critiques of the depravity of urban life," Miller writes. "The automobile, riots, pollution, the high cost of living, alienated work, widespread poverty, crime, political corruption, and a thousand other ills afflicted not only countercultural dropouts but just about everyone else"—a sentiment that echoed both the turn to nature and racial animus of the late nineteenth century.[30] For communalists, as for Theodore Roosevelt and other turn-of-the-century conservationists, cities exemplified the ills of contemporary civilization writ large. Back-to-the-landers broadly rejected established social, political, and economic norms, and sought to reflect their refusal through their activity and self-representation. "Their clothes are patched, befringed, and beaded," the cultural critic Theodore Roszak wrote at the time. Their "straggly hair streams free or is banded back Indian style." The purpose of such fashions, he adds, was not to merely appear but actually "*be* 'natural'" or "'organic'"—to effect "a principled rejection of antiseptic, upwardly mobile middle-class habits in favor of a return to folk origins and lost traditions" inspired in part by "the noble savage."[31]

To Susan Sontag's point, the youth movements of the postwar United States were in this respect not so different from those that precipitated the rise of German National Socialism: they comprised "a hodge-podge of countercultural elements, blending neo-Romanticism, Eastern philosophies, nature mysticism . . . and a strong communal impulse in a confused but no less ardent search for authentic, non-alienated social relations."[32] Walter Laqueur suggests that "two ways of revolt were open" to the German youth movement: "[T]hey could have pursued their radical critique," potentially developing a more complex understanding of race and economic power, but ultimately "chose the other form of protest against society—romanticism."[33] Similar judgments have dogged the U.S. New Left since it dissolved into the largely apolitical counterculture in the late 1960s. For Amitav Ghosh, such a foreclosure of substantive political and economic protest signals a broader "collapse of political alternatives" and "accompanying disempowerment" occasioned by an "ever-growing intrusion of the market"—all of which he fears "have also produced responses of another kind—nihilistic forms of extremism that employ methods of spectacular violence."[34] Manifestos penned by self-styled ecofascists in the twenty-first century arguably vindicate his point.

But in the United States, this market-driven breakdown has occurred in a sustained fashion since at least the 1960s, and has done so, in part, in the wake of the same energies that animated leftist revolt. Popular accounts often remember the era's commitments to unalienated authenticity as the province of the radical left, but at midcentury they transcended ideological lines, prompting young socialists, anarchists, and conservatives alike to declare themselves victims of political and economic colonialism at the hands of established institutions. These links appear perhaps most clearly in the tortuous relationship between two of the most influential youth organizations of the era: the leftist SDS—from whose fractured ranks, at the end of the 1960s, many back-to-the-land communalists emerged—and the conservative YAF. Both formed in 1960, and though their multi-issue platforms appear, on their face, almost diametrically opposed (the aggressively anticommunist YAF promoted free enterprise and frequently opposed SDS's raucous campus demonstrations and socialist tendencies), both proceeded from remarkably similar libertarian foundations. SDS largely disintegrated in the late 1960s, chiefly over political priorities and tactics and the matter of the counterculture—a friction, that is, between political and cultural solutions to social ills. YAF also splintered over conflict between libertarian and traditional conservative camps. But in the years before their collapse, members of each organization often broke bread over shared democratic principles and activist strategies.[35]

YAF's libertarian wing especially participated in vibrant ideological cross-pollination with SDS. Common distrust of the state formed the strongest glue binding these factions together. Like SDS's founding *Port Huron Statement* (1962), YAF's *Sharon Statement* (1960) largely proceeds as a critique of U.S. society in the 1950s, namely, its perceived social conformity and international and economic policy. "Abhorring submission to authority," the historian Rebecca E. Klatch writes, "both groups . . . shared a thrust toward populism, toward removal of power from hands above and its return to those below," despite radically different emphases and goals. This antiestablishment affinity is perhaps best illustrated by the fact that many members of SDS (a group commonly named the postwar standard-bearer of the radical left) supported the 1964 presidential candidacy of Barry Goldwater (a figure most often remembered as the champion of a budding new right). Goldwater's appeal among young voters stemmed from his rejection of the political status quo—for members of both SDS and YAF the source of state oppression of civil liberties and consequent repression of authentic individuals. (Dave Foreman, cofounder of Earth First!, campaigned for Goldwater.) YAF's distrust, like that of conservatives before them, chiefly targeted the New Deal welfare state. But while traditionalists tended to retain a sense of hawkish patriotism derived from their anticommunist zeal, the libertarian element began to cleave from older conservatives. Their suspicion "was not just of collectivism in government but extended to . . . *any kind of concentration of power*" by virtue of a pivotal investment "in the *sanctity of the individual*" shared with SDS (although economic libertarians broke with SDS's extension of critique to capitalism). As Klatch puts it, a "parallel process of disillusionment provoked the involvement of young people at either end of the political spectrum" according to relatively consistent values, if not proposed solutions.[36]

All of this is to say that, contrary to conventional depictions of the U.S. counterculture and associated political movements, free-market principles that championed competition and hierarchy were not as incompatible with anticapitalist radicalism in the 1960s as they might seem in the twenty-first century. In the crucible of the decade's youth movements, they both stemmed from a shared libertarian impulse: a romantic desire to access or create ostensibly authentic, unregulated forms of selfhood and society. While not considered traditional conservative values at the time, these principles came to shape the future of the Republican Party. Many YAF libertarians went on to orchestrate the free-market austerity measures of the Reagan administration—the deregulatory bedrock of neoliberal economics. And when the organization's traditionalists began to eject them, many even joined SDS amid its own disintegration.[37] Despite the conventional association of the U.S. counterculture with the left, free-market figures were neither external nor incidental to the radical movements that comprised it—including, as SDS fell apart, intentional communities. To the contrary, they actively participated in and helped to shape them.

Free-market libertarianism also built a surprising bridge between the right and specifically environmentalist intentional communities. (Several young conservatives were even involved in the promulgation of open-land ideals.) "The Left/Right politics of counterculture libertarians," Andrew G. Kirk writes, "coupled with thoughtful consumerism . . . and business acumen" to erect an argument "that environmentalism is best left to . . . the free market."[38] Chief among the values of YAF libertarians was entrepreneurial individualism, for which the back-to-the-land movement furnished a virtually untapped market. Organic farming, for instance, had "long been integral to the communal vision," as Miller notes. "Most of the new communards, however, were urban young people" who poorly understood how to sustainably accomplish it. Despite that fact (or because of it), numerous "handy guidebooks" offered themselves as market-based resources—and none more ubiquitously than Stewart Brand's National Book Award–winning *Whole Earth Catalog*.[39]

Selling and Consuming Utopia in the 1970s

It was specifically new technology that mediated between romantic and capitalist elements of the back-to-the-land movement. Roszak noted in 1986 that communes have always emphasized "hard work, fraternal sharing, and minimal consumption." And yet, despite their inclination toward the "primitive," their attitude is most often future-oriented: communalists often find "the cure for our industrial ills . . . not . . . in things past, but in Things To Come." On the one hand, many indeed embraced totems of ostensible authenticity, often derived from Native American stereotypes. But on the other, they supplemented these artifacts with new tools whose use would enable them to access that nature to begin with—a dynamic Roszak described as a "reversionary-technophiliac synthesis." For many back-to-the-land communalists, Roszak writes, "the result of high industrial technology would be something like a tribal democracy where the citizenry might still be dressed in buckskin and go berry-picking in the woods. The artificial environment made *more* artificial would somehow become more . . . natural."[40] So, too, would the people who lived within it. Consuming (and using) products in a marketplace of organic commodities would itself be one way to prove that one had been "chosen" by the land (as Lou Gottlieb puts it).

Despite the anticapitalist mindset of much of its communalist audience, the *Whole Earth Catalog* traded in appeals to market competition and consumer acuity as well as to self-sufficiency and authenticity. Brand's intention was to "help my friends . . . starting their own civilization hither and yon in the sticks"—an answer to Edward Abbey's coeval declaration in *Desert Solitaire* (1968) that the time had come for alienated environmentalists "to find another country or—in the name of Jefferson—to make another country."[41] In light of the last chapter, this reference to Jefferson stands out. Abbey frames his own movement back to the land in part as a producerist venture (and, accordingly, often distinguishes between his entitlement to the land and others' lack of it). The *Catalog* intimates a similar relationship (Abbey's ostensible and often exaggerated technophobia notwithstanding). Brand, Kirk writes, "captured a new alchemy of environmental concern, small-scale technological enthusiasm, design research, alternative lifestyles, and business savvy," invigorating a seemingly contradictory mix of "technology, nature, and consumption" that U.S. "tourists and outdoor recreationalists . . . have long embraced." As *Whole Earth*'s content and readership expanded with its reissues, "pragmatic environmentalism . . . became the dominant theme" in the form of "tools and articles that celebrated rural life." And its readers and contributors "used the publication as a forum for ideas about alternatives to the legislation- and regulation-driven environmental advocacy that achieved great gains during the twentieth century."[42] For Brand as for Abbey, a new, more natural nation needed to replace the old, clogged by both state management and extractive industry. The *Catalog*'s tools might help to circumscribe it.

In this respect, the *Catalog* illustrates how back-to-the-land environmentalism, despite its apparent rejection of ownership and the vocal anticapitalism of many of its participants, in fact constituted one part of a broader trend in which countercultural goals and business culture mutually informed each other, complicating the idea that, for this generation, "business was the monolithic bad guy who had caused America to become a place of . . . conformity and empty consumerism"—a "great symbolic foil against which . . . young rebels defined themselves," as Thomas Frank puts it. Such accounts, Frank argues, "assume quite naturally that the counterculture was what it said it was; that is, a fundamental opponent of the capitalist order." But capitalism itself, he writes, is "as dynamic a force in its own way as the revolutionary youth movements of the period." In the 1960s, rebellion "became central to the way American capitalism understood itself and explained itself to the public"—that is, as "a hip consumerism driven by disgust with mass society itself."[43]

Brand and his *Catalog* demonstrate how, for the new business landscape evolving across the 1970s and 1980s, "the solution to the problems of consumer society was—more consuming."[44] And

Brand's own involvement in the environmentalist communities to whom he sold the *Catalog*'s wares illuminates how this turn did not so much constitute "evidence of a liberal sellout" as it did "an example of the extent that hybrid Left/Right counterculture politics had always" guided "the countercultural sensibility," as Kirk puts it.[45] Brand united several apparently distant sectors of his time, including not only rebellious communalists but also firmly established research institutions (particularly in the field of ecology) and consumer industries, with contacts ranging from officials in the Department of Defense to corporate representatives from Shell Oil. "The proper role of government in this new environment," the historian Fred Turner writes, was to "deregulate the technology industries that were ostensibly leading the transformation, and, while they were at it, business in general."[46] Kirk refers to the *Catalog*'s sensibility, amid these transits, as that of a "hip right"—a "fusion" of "free minds and free markets" with "a strong environmental ethic." Figures like Brand, he adds, were in this respect "building on . . . deep western political tendencies: the search for new frontiers, utopian desire for a new beginning, individualism, escape, and distrust of the federal government as problem solver. They embraced individual agency and inventiveness above all" and "created a new and extremely marketable vision of western authenticity."[47]

In short, Brand's intervention functioned as an iteration of the producerist trope—one that, despite the contradictions inherent in ideals of frontier individualism, still wields great influence today. Blair Taylor points out that twenty-first-century Silicon Valley's "unique combination of ecology, neoliberalism, and techno-elitism" (a culture keenly informed by Brand's influence) has inherited a tendency to celebrate not cooperative solutions to ecological catastrophe but "heroic individuals using technology to solve ecological problems created by the unenlightened masses, either via technological fixes or escape"—men, that is, such as Jeff Bezos or Elon Musk, "walling themselves off from the teeming throngs or abandoning Earth altogether for the greener pastures of space" even as they benefit from the spoils of global ecological disruption.[48] James Lovelock, the originator of the Gaia hypothesis, once advocated for suspending representative democracy in favor of installing power in such a technocratic elite.[49] Others have promoted a similar role—what Sam Moore and Alex Roberts describe as a "turn to authoritarian means" to "confront the enormity of the climate crisis"—for "green capitalists."[50] In reference to the *Catalog*, Roszak wrote in 1986 that "one sees the same assumption brought into play: that the industrial process, pushed to its limit, generates its own best medicine."[51]

The partnership between environmentalism and capitalism that developed in the late 1960s, then, founded a libertarian branch of environmentalism opposed to government-mandated reform that also coexisted, fitfully and somewhat paradoxically, with anticapitalist sentiment. Roszak, for his part, maintained that primitivist values were worth fighting for. Even if "one discounts most . . . gestures [to the natural or authentic] as impractical whimsy," he writes, "they stand as a provocative assertion of justified discontent which reached out . . . toward organic values that our industrial culture has left far behind." Still, the reversionary-technophiliac synthesis "crumbled" quite quickly, he writes, given that the "technophiliac values . . . won out. They are, after all, the values of the mainstream." But he believed that "the reversionaries may be regarded as prophetical voices": "looking back with fondness, they also looked forward"—specifically to the "death," he writes, "of a civilization grown tragically estranged from the mothering Earth," and to a "wildness reclaiming its planetary preeminence, perhaps not gently."[52] Miller writes of Tolstoy Farm outside Spokane, Washington, that "many contemporary newspaper accounts . . . commented on the farm's run-down physical plant. . . . But the residents had a sense that those who had learned to live outside of the dominant culture's technological support systems would be better off for it when, as many believed, the time would come when world crisis might remove such systems" (a prospect I return to in chapters 4 and 5).[53] The Farm was an ark, not a beacon: an anarcho-socialist expression of Garrett Hardin's "lifeboat ethics" that (perhaps unintentionally) emphasized the salvation of only a privileged, ecologically purified few. Anticapitalist romanticism and free-market solutions joined forces in the premium they placed on individual ability, leaving systems of environmental and economic extraction free to operate as they would.

It is in this respect that reversionary-technophiliac consumption of tools not only reduced ecological politics to personal acts but would also enable, in the case of *Ecotopia* and beyond, a reinvestment in small-scale ethnonational borders. Communalists such as those at Tolstoy Farm often believed both that societal collapse was inevitable and that consumption of the proper tools made one capable—even *worthy*—of surviving, being a better steward of the land (indeed, a more "natural" person in general). It also distinguished those who were worthy from those who weren't. Commodity consumption, then, itself became a mechanism that would partly determine who did and did not belong on a certain parcel of earth (or on the earth at all).

Ecotopia's Circumscribed Social Ecology

Of all sectors of Ecotopian life, retail seems to be the one in which decentralization does not apply. The industry is almost entirely consolidated in *"those fantastic camping-supply stores they have,"* but for individual artisans scattered across the country (146). And Weston finds far more products than recreational equipment on offer. Ecotopians share the broad countercultural affinity for new technologies that the *Whole Earth Catalog* represents and Roszak later discussed. What I want to emphasize is not just that Ecotopians consume these objects in a privatized, free-market system. It is also that their efforts to distance themselves from the United States makes that consumption central to their identity as Ecotopians. The commodities in which they trade—*Whole Earth*–style tools—are more "natural" than those bought and sold in the United States, and Ecotopians themselves are more "natural" for using them than their neighbors over the border. "As far as personal goods are concerned," Weston notes, "Ecotopians possess or at least care about mainly things like knives and other tools . . . which they are concerned to have of the highest quality . . . prized by their owners as works of art" (40). Privately, he adds that *"mysteriously,"* they *"do not feel 'separate' from"* these technologies. *"They evidently feel a little as the Indians must have felt: that the horse and the teepee and the bow and arrow all sprang, like the human being, from the womb of nature, organically"* (47). It is not so much that Native peoples are, for the Ecotopians, "productions" rather than "producers," as they were for Thomas Jefferson. Rather, the novel celebrates a synthesis of these two accounts, asserting that it is the former quality that renders certain producers more natural than others, and, in turn, that certain "organic" modes of producing render one an earthly production in his or her own right. The same goes for the consumption of these products, whose use in turn facilitates such production. If this logic seems to resonate with the racialized "self-fulfilling prophecy" mentioned in the last chapter, that's because it does. The tautology naturalizes Ecotopian national culture.

Setting aside the comparison to Native peoples for the moment, there are two details about these "organic" technologies I want to highlight. First, Ecotopians understand the tools they buy much as Roszak explains those esteemed by "reversionary-technophiliacs": as threshold objects, whose consumption and use not only enables the subject's sustainable activity but also reconnects one to the "womb of nature"—proves, that is, one's innocence of ecological overdraft compared to alienated (and, in Ecotopia, *alien*) others, and therefore one's belonging to the soil of Ecotopia. Second, this dynamic defines Weston's understanding of Ecotopian national identity, as well as the Ecotopians' own. "Video sets are everywhere, but strangely enough I have seldom seen people sitting before them blotted out in the American manner," he writes. "Whether this is because of some mysterious national traits, or because of the programming being markedly different, or both, I cannot yet tell" (38). Weston's chicken-and-egg confusion misses the point. It is in part because of what and how they consume that Ecotopians understand themselves to share those "mysterious national traits"—a privileged, natural belonging to the land on which they live and work.

The Ecotopians view strong borders as a necessity as a result, but also engender a slew of exclusions and quiet forms of prejudice that extend beyond that of national belonging. Ecotopians might reject individual ownership of land, but collectively they perform Brand's Jeffersonian movement, a collaborative labor to not only "improve" it but also do so "organically." *Ecotopia,* in other words, dramatizes circumscription on the scale of the nation, if not enclosure on the scale of individual property. In *Ecotopia,* what you consume determines how you act upon the land, and how you act reflects how natural or unalienated a person you are. This account is indeed reflective of a great variety of environmentalist narratives, but its implications depend largely on other values and ideas with which it intersects. And in *Ecotopia,* it blends with a series of rigid expectations for other social forms. Because this emphasis on the natural defines the "organic" national population, it also determines who does and does not belong—and prescribes a whole suite of fixed behaviors as it does so.

Those behaviors largely revolve around the competitive use of those tools (as well as their consumption). The "general picture," Weston writes, "is one of almost anarchic decentralization, a jungle in which only the hardiest survive" (111). Callenbach articulates Ecotopia in terms that resonate with a conservative intellectual tradition linking superiority to uneven, social-Darwinist fields of competition, which informed eugenic perspectives on race, sexuality, and disability (and the imperial projects in which they took shape) as well as midcentury libertarianism. Historically, the "battlefield" has been "the natural proving ground of superiority," the political theorist Corey Robin writes. "With time, however, the conservative would find another proving ground in the marketplace."[54] That continuum is compressed in Ecotopia, in which citizens find numerous ways to prove one's naturalness. But it is ultimately competitive strength that characterizes the nation.

It is precisely because of this fact that Ecotopia's "organic society" seems so organic. Those who do not (or cannot) appropriately choose and use organic tools have left or (more forebodingly) seem to have vanished. Early in the novel, Weston witnesses a performance of ostensibly natural labor facilitated by the consumption of such tools (specifically hunting gear) and the corresponding demarcation between insiders and outsiders it effects. A group of hunters "*stopped near me for a rest—and also, I suspect, to allow people to admire their kill.*" It is not just hunting but the gear used to do it that separates the Ecotopians from Weston. The hunters "*looked savage enough (long knives, beards, rough clothes) but they were evidently quite ordinary citizens.*" One man "*caught my eye and must have seen the disgust in it*" (15). Weston, haunted by the interaction, later refers to himself as "*a homeless wanderer*" by comparison: "*to an Ecotopian, who always has a strong collective base to return to, a place and the people of that place, my existence must seem pathetically insecure*" (127). The notion of a "collective base" resonates across political projects (on the left as well as the right), often in generative, caregiving ways. What strikes me about these examples, however, is their suggestion that not only refusal but also inability to enact certain fixed performances of "natural" labor renders one inadmissible to Ecotopia. They also participate in a rhetorical tendency across U.S. literary environmentalism to reinforce physical ability and strength as signifiers of purity.[55]

Nowhere in the novel does this emphasis on able-bodied vigor play more of a role than in what the Ecotopians call the "war games." Weston describes the practice in his columns: "Two bands of young men had gathered." Each "had a large, dangerous spear, with a point of sharpened black stone. And each man was painting himself with colors, in primitive, fierce designs" (71). The "excitement we focus on our major sports has been entirely diverted" into these pageants (36). As Malcolm Margolin explains in his Foreword, "Aggression, rather than having been eliminated, is ritualized."[56] It is not at first clear how sport itself does not suitably "ritualize" aggression, but the novel does eventually address this question. According to the games' defenders, "it was essential to develop some kind of open civic expression for the physical competitiveness . . . inherent in man's biological programming" (74). Callenbach differentiates, that is, between artificial sport and natural bloodshed: "Young men . . . needed a chance to combat 'the others' . . . to test their comradeship, to put their beautiful resources of speed and strength to use" (74).

In the novel, this outlet enables Ecotopians to prove and express their unrepressed, superior incarnation of biological destiny. Teams organize by town to spar. When Weston asks a wounded combatant "what the fighting was about," the man responds, "It was us against them, of course"—a naturalization of arbitrary social circumstances by which citizens decentralized across the nation (72). But bloodshed between groups seems only to strengthen their sense of unity as nationals. Weston confirms his outsider status by comparison. In a dream, he grabs a spear, then hesitates when the fighting begins: "[S]uddenly they turn and look at me with amazement, realizing I am not one of them" (76). Marissa, a woman who later becomes his lover, chides him for being "squeamish about violence" and "[m]akes fun of American technology, claims we . . . can no long bear to just bayonet a man—have to spend $50,000 to avoid guilt, by zapping him from the stratosphere" (58–9). He does not, at first, measure up to the physical requirements of national membership, which are articulated here in terms of tools—the props of warfare. It is not violence itself that Marissa condemns, but its means.

Weston doesn't measure up to the Ecotopian definition of masculinity, either. It should be clear by now that the games reinforce gendered expectations. Women do not participate, choosing to compete instead "through rivalry over men to father their children" (74–5). The games offer an opportunity for "open civic expression" for this sort of "physical competitiveness" as well. At the landing of a "fatal blow" during the first match, "all hostilities miraculously ceased. . . . Some of the winning side went off with women into the bushes" (72). Sexual appetite appears to define "natural woman-hood" in Ecotopia just as bloodthirstiness does masculinity. Ecoto-pian women, Weston observes, "have totally escaped the dependent roles they still tend to play with us." But he also notices that they "still seem . . . feminine, with a relaxed air of their biological attractive-ness, even fertility" (33). The suggestion is that in cultivating more natural lives, Ecotopians have also recommitted to natural gender roles contested in the post-1960s United States. Weston's wife in New York "possesses the signs or signals that are supposed to mean sexuality and vitality," but "Marissa just has sexuality and vitality, so she doesn't need the signals" (107). The emphasis is, again, on natural authenticity as opposed to alienated artifice.

In many ways, the novel frames these roles themselves as the essence of national character. Tools facilitate certain forms of la-bor and performance—like the games—which help citizens to realize their "natural" biological destinies as men and women. When Weston finally participates, he feels suddenly "as if the whole American psychodrama between the sexes . . . has left my head" (54). And, as if promptly attuned to some instinct, he "suddenly . . . heard my own voice saying, 'I am going to stay in Ecotopia!'—startlingly loud and clear. . . . and I realized I must have been fighting off saying that for weeks." A self-deceptive screen has lifted, allowing access to the nature behind it. Almost immediately, Marissa, walking with him in a forest, comments that it's a "Good place to conceive a child" (164–5). The exchange—the culmination of Weston's acculturation to and self-discovery in Ecotopia—paints the national character in stringently heterosexist terms. It is passion for the opposite sex that inspires manly acts befitting natural Ecotopian character, and those acts themselves that clinch that character's consummation in reproduction—the preservation of the land and nation. The novel does hint at queer tolerance in Ecotopia (chiefly in references to group sex) but the fact that Callenbach frames this moment as the proper resolution of Weston's story "suggests," as Nicole

Seymour writes of environmentalist rhetoric in general, "that concern for . . . the planet can only emerge, or emerges most effectively, from white, heterosexual, familial reproductivity."[57] One can argue that an ecofeminist element governs this arrangement. Callenbach himself asserts that ecofeminism greatly influenced his writing. The "cooperation- and biology-oriented policies" of Ecotopia's government "are usually considered to be derived mainly from female attitudes" (83). (Citizens even refer to President Vera Allwen as their "Great Mother" in *Ecotopia Emerging*.) But Adeline Johns-Putra adds to Seymour's criticism that, ecofeminist or not, this particular ethic of care—one that proceeds from an investment in reproduction—has also long "informed historical patterns of women's oppression" (not to mention queer folks'). Its "identity biases . . . are part of its wider (mis)conceptualization of moral agency and identity"—including national and/or racial as well as gender and sexual identity—"as fixed."[58]

The circumscription facilitated in part by the consumption of certain commodities, that is, applies to gender and ability in the novel as well as to land. All these vectors bind together in Weston's experience of the war games. He is injured, but the *"dread of their advance was replaced by an unutterable feeling of strength which we all shared, and knew we shared"* (138). When he receives a blood transfusion, Marissa tells him, *"[N]ow you have a little Ecotopian blood in your veins!"* (140). The comment belies the fact that belonging to both land and nation in the novel inheres to a large degree in the sort of performances and acts of consumption I've been describing, even as it situates Ecotopia firmly within a blood-and-soil vision of national sovereignty. Marissa strikes Weston as organically, subjectively connected—even consubstantial—with the land, as if she exists *"in a contiguous state of immediate consciousness"* with it and its people (68).

Consumer accoutrements mediate the Ecotopians' performances of their biologistic and nationalistic organicism just as they do their labor. Paints and costumes anchor the war games as firmly as combat itself. These activities offer a blatant example of performative redface on the part of white settlers on Indigenous land—an instance of "playing Indian," to use Philip Deloria's phrase, as an expression of both individual and national authenticity "amidst the anxiety of urban industrial and postindustrial life."[59] Weston likens the spectacles to "the ritual wars of savage tribes"—even frames them as situations in which "savagery" is "restored" (75). Most Ecotopians are *"sentimental about Indians, and . . . envy the Indians their lost natural place in the American wilderness."* And Weston *"keep[s] hearing references to what Indians would or wouldn't do."* This romantic picture of Native peoples informs consumer habits across the nation. *"Some Ecotopian articles"* like *"clothing and baskets and personal ornamentation"* are *"perhaps directly Indian in inspiration."* Citizens wear *"a lot of embroidery and decorations made of small shells or feathers"* (29, 10). Despite occasional claims to purity of blood, Ecotopians implicitly locate their privileged belonging to nature in their consumption of such objects. The fact that characters (and the novel as a whole) treat Indigenous peoples as if they've completely vanished—Ecotopians believe "a proper population size would be the number of Indians who inhabited the territory before the Spaniards and Americans came" (63)—reinforces romantic myths of Native subjectivity while ignoring the continued existence of Indigenous lifeways and political, economic, and ecological concerns across Cascadia. Given this fact, it's worth mentioning that Ecotopians source their styles from other stereotypes, too. Many of them, Weston notes, *"look like oldtime westerners, Gold Rush characters come to life"* (10). It's as if the nation doesn't necessarily secede *from* the United States, but *to* a certain Western ideal of rugged, natural reality. In the marketplace of privileged belonging to the land, any existing trope will do, no matter if it appeals to Indigeneity or its forced displacement.

For this reason, the fact that Indigenous peoples and nations are conspicuously absent from Ecotopia reads a bit like an assertion that they were not competitive enough to remain on the land—a quieter, presumptive version of Ammon Bundy's perspective discussed in the previous chapter—especially given that the country subdivides itself into smaller units along racialized lines. Weston observes that there "are surprisingly few dark-skinned faces on San Francisco streets." It appears to him a nearly exclusively Euro-Ecotopian city. "After independence," he explains, "the principle of secession became a lively factor in Ecotopian political life. Thomas Jefferson and other early American patriots were quoted in its defense." The region's Black population, en masse, "joined in the general exultation when the great break with Washington came." Oakland, Chinatown, and other areas "were officially designated as city-states within Eco-topia" with "their own . . . police and courts, their own industries," their own "farms in the nearby countryside" (98).

Two references in these passages merit attention: the one to Jefferson and the other to the enclaves' "own industries." In the broader context of Ecotopia and its nation-building project, these racialized outposts seem to emerge according to a similar logic of circumscription as Ecotopia writ large. The production, consumption, and use of "organic" tools and other objects simultaneously proves the natural cohesion of a given community and facilitates a corresponding demarcation of land in relation if not to individuals then to particular populations—in this case, defined by racial cate-gorization. The Black Ecotopian city-state produces and consumes its own particular goods that others do not. The culture of "soul city" (the name Callenbach gives the enclave) "is different from that of Ecotopia generally. It is a heavy exporter of music and mu-sicians, novels and movies and poetry," all of which reinforce Eco-topian identity given their ostensibly spontaneous (i.e., "organic") composition by Black artists, just as the production of, say, hydro-electric power does elsewhere (99). But even as they contribute to a shared national character, these particular artisans also seem to set themselves apart. The novel places special emphasis on differ-ences in the use and creation of commodities as the defining factor in the circumscription of racialized enclaves. It is as if Ecotopia organizes around an understanding not only that its national char-acter derives from its consumption of certain products and use of them to steward the land, but also that different races of people consume and labor slightly differently and therefore must sort ac-cordingly. There's a chicken-and-egg question at play here, too. Do Ecotopians racialize and segregate people and city-states based on what they consume and make, or do they consume and make based on "natural" predispositions?

In the context of his political moment, Callenbach's representa-tions of race (coupled with his politics) read as a good-faith effort to acknowledge the efforts of cultural nationalisms across the United States to reject liberal universalism, establish self-determined communities, and generally defy the nation's white-supremacist and settler-colonial history. After independence, "black separat-ist parties grew up to dominate the ghettos of Oakland and San Francisco—having been strangled by the white suburbs earlier, the black population now wanted to control their own territory" (98). Movements such as the Black Panther Party and Black Power organized, to varying degrees and with myriad long-term goals, around principles of self-determination, establishing mutual-aid networks in low-income Black communities across the United States and rejecting the hope that legal and cultural frameworks would ever expand to address deep-seated economic and racial injustices. In the novel, the enclave arrangement, "though it satisfies many blacks, seems to others inherently unstable, and they argue for full independence as the only long-range solution," advocating for a complete secession of their own to establish total economic self-determination (98). Rumors circulate that domestic Latinx, Japanese, and Jewish communities also plan to "formalize" their enclaves as independent sovereign nations.

That Callenbach acknowledges that different individuals and communities have different relationships with environment might almost seem to presage the premises of the environmental justice movement (to say nothing of Indigenous decolonial movements). What is striking about *Ecotopia*'s situation, however, is not just that its people arrange in small communities—nor even, given the period of its composition, that they do so along racial lines— but that this partition is presented as a natural inevitability. Black Ecotopians are not forced to segregate. "Many . . . gave up on racial harmony and segregated themselves," Margolin writes in the Foreword—an exodus that "bodes ill," Weston informs readers, "for our own great metropolitan areas" (101).[60] His mention of U.S. cities is significant in more ways than one. Callenbach pointedly includes passages on Ecotopian crime in the chapter that details voluntary segregation. Criminal sentences for street mugging, for example, are severe, but, as if by magic, the rate of urban theft and violence has dropped precipitously since independence (99). The detail's inclusion in this particular chapter, rather than any other, not only upholds racist associations of Blackness with criminality, but also suggests that the decrease can be attributed not (or not only) to the uptick in social and economic welfare, but to racial segregation. Peace, the novel implies, requires that races do not mix—a position (a *Third* Position, even) that situates violence not within structures of socioeconomic inequality but within racial proximity itself, naturalizing normative differences among enclaves. The war games, in bringing together different "tribal" communities, seem only to reinforce these crypto-eugenic distinctions. Such naturalizations allow little room for difference within or across normative racial categories. They also ultimately rule out cooperative governance and ecological stewardship altogether.

Running through *Ecotopia* overall, in other words, is a tacit narrative in which practices of consumption with the aim of organically working the land not only circumscribe it but also naturalize certain assumptions about ability, gender, sexuality, race, and other social forms. To become more natural is, in Callenbach's telling, to do so across an existing sociocultural board. Subtle stratifications proliferate in the novel as a result, diversifying circumscriptions along these lines—and satisfying the dreams of white nationalists despite Callenbach's own affiliations.

But even in the novel, borders fail to offer protection: "*Ecotopian monitor systems, which seem to be extremely sophisticated for both nuclear and general pollution, have detected a sudden increase in the radiation level of air blowing in from the Pacific,*" Weston writes. Many citizens "*seem to think the Ecotopian government is too tolerant of pollution coming in from outside*" (66–7). The novel fails to address how arbitrary geopolitical borders are supposed to withstand diffuse ecological changes. All they deter is outsiders—even those suffering the effects of Ecotopia's own habits. The nation does indeed engage in foreign trade, and among its imports is "rubber . . . from Vietnam and Indonesia" (81). Callenbach's utopia has divested of its own technologies that propel carbon emissions and atmospheric pollution, but still takes advantage of other "dirty industries" in "poorer regions . . . winning environmental gains in one area, but not challenging business as usual, which simply continues elsewhere," as Hannah Holleman writes of U.S. environmental policy.[61] One wonders if, should dreams of an actual, sovereign Cascadia manifest, rubber farmers displaced by soil erosion would more successfully find welcome at its gates than "climate refugees" from the Global South at the U.S. border—or if existing assumptions about nation and nature would lock them out as tightly as Ecotopia's.

Even as *Ecotopia* extols the virtues of alternative and sustainable technologies, economic systems, and ways of living with the earth—denouncing the cultural supremacy of private property in favor of collective, collaborative forms of belonging and ownership—the narrative itself reifies interrelated logics of circumscription (if not enclosure), blood-and-soil national sovereignty, and racial classification more than it undermines them. It does so by foregrounding the naturalization of its citizens through their consumption and use of the sort of products Brand and other entrepreneurs marketed to back-to-the-landers: "tools" that, in some contexts, depending on mode of representation, functioned as what I have termed threshold objects, purportedly forging organic links between consumer and land. My point is not that acts of commodity consumption in and of themselves directly and inexorably generate ecofascist violence in other circumstances. It is that particular ways of *talking about* such objects prefigure such effects by reinforcing crypto-eugenic notions of natural strength, hardiness, and superiority as grounds for communal, if not individual, land ownership—an emphasis that not only justifies borders for safeguarding privileged residents but also might segregate them within.

« 3 »

Food

Naturalizations of Self and Strength in Appalachia's Extracted Landscapes and Culinary Literatures

> [G]ame is said to be a source of considerable meat in the Ecotopian diet; it is prized for its "spiritual" qualities!
>
> —Ernest Callenbach, *Ecotopia*

> Indigenous like corn, the mestiza is a product of crossbreeding. . . . With stone roller on metate, she grinds the corn, then grinds again. She kneads and molds the dough, pats the round balls into tortillas.
>
> —Gloria Anzaldúa, *Borderlands/La Frontera*

Consumption functions to link blood to soil and naturalize social behaviors on several registers in *Ecotopia*. The novel both features hunters who outfit themselves in gear that telegraphs their suitably "primitive" relationship to their local ecosystems and frames their prey in terms that reinforce this connection. As Weston suggests in the epigraph above, consuming the flesh of native animals proves one's national belonging. Eating indeed functioned as an emblem of environmental sensibility across the era's communalist experiments. Theodore Roszak "sensed that organic foods were a sort of talisman" akin to *Whole Earth*–style "reversionary-technophiliac" commodities: for many, ingesting locally sourced fare revivified a natural link between self and environment.[1] Such foods, that is, also function as threshold objects in a long tradition of environmental representation. They play a role in Gloria Anzaldúa's *Borderlands/La Frontera* as well, likewise as an example of the "subtle ways that we internalize identification."

For Anzaldúa, "food and certain smells are tied to my identity" and "my homeland."[2] Both elevate the importance of local foods as matters of place-based belonging, differentiating them from and even critiquing other foodways—namely, the industrial food system. Despite their complex, cross-cultural influences, "cuisines are, almost everywhere, markers of difference," the anthropologist David Graeber and archaeologist David Wengrow point out, and have been since the diffusion of "'micro-lithic' tool kits" including pottery and grinding instruments.[3] But the way one frames those customs also matters, and *Ecotopia* and *Borderlands* present two different examples of how such fare might mediate between place and identity. For Anzaldúa, identity resembles a recipe: like a tortilla, it is no less a creative act for the constraints imposed by social and ecological context. For Callenbach's characters, on the other hand, identity and its relationship to place is often framed in fixed terms, as either one thing or another—natural or artificial—and food at times functions as yet another totem for proving one's privileged belonging on the earth.

As matters of representation, these two aspects of food are by no means mutually exclusive. Both perspectives emerge, for example, in the work of the gay, West Virginia–born poet, essayist, and novelist Jeff Mann, for whom food, place, and identity are deeply interconnected. In *Loving Mountains, Loving Men*, a 2005 collection of autobiographical essays and poems, food is markedly present when he writes about his reluctance to come out to his extended relations, especially his grandmother, "the great transmitter of family tales," for fear of reprisal. "Those stories I tell to this day," he nonetheless reports, reflecting fondly on a dream in which the woman "cuts [him] a piece of pecan pie." Mann's anticipated excommunication exists in tension with the cooking traditions his grandmother shared with him—an encounter that informs much of his writing. In an apostrophe to young queers leaving the region, Mann offers respite: "Come here, and we'll feed you brown beans and cornbread, chowchow, wilted lettuce, new peas and potatoes, ramps and creecy greens, biscuits and gravy."[4] Food becomes the locus of a queer kinship that revolves around what Mann describes as an effort "to juggle a very deep-seated Appalachian identity and a very frank gay identity."[5] Perhaps more than any other motif, food resonates across the queer Appalachian literary landscape, and has done so for several decades. It grounds Dorothy

Allison's poetic explorations of gender and domesticity and conspicuously metonymizes the livelihoods of characters in novels by Fenton Johnson, Ann Pancake, Silas House, and countless others. A 2019 volume of *LGBTQ Fiction and Poetry from Appalachia,* edited by Mann and Julia Watts, features numerous poems that revolve around the preparation of local ingredients by a diverse cluster of queer writers. And perhaps more than any other of these instances, *Loving Mountains* investigates food as a site for queer Appalachian identity negotiation.

Despite recent inroads, queer cultural formation in Appalachia remains an underexplored field—one that offers an almost unparalleled opportunity for the consideration of class, race, place, environment, gender, and sexuality as intersecting social vectors in the twentieth- and twenty-first-century United States. It offers, that is, a rich study of how representations of environment and identity might trend in a variety of directions, including—in examples that recapitulate implicit arguments about "natural" or "organic" characteristics involving bodily strength, race, gender, and nation or region—the narrative pathways sketched by the political genre that, in the Introduction and chapter 1, I argued prefigures ecofascist violence. It is the question of belonging to place and people that Mann addresses in his work, to the extent that it navigates a double-bind in which queer Appalachians often profess to find themselves: on one hand, subjected to right-wing violence at home, and on the other, dismissed as regressive, coal-loving "white trash" by urban progressives. One might even "see the oppression that Appalachians and homosexuals have in common," Mann writes, "when you start to count all the queer jokes and hillbilly . . . jokes" (44). *Loving Mountains* fixates on a related conundrum. "Sometimes it feels as if my Appalachian roots and my desire for men are two lovers I vacillate between," he writes. "When I feel spurned by one, I take up with the other" (42). Such conflicts between home and sexuality are mainstays of queer writing, as are consequent movements from country to city. Mann's own essays follow him from West Virginia to Washington, D.C. Their ultimate trajectory, however, seeks a reconciliation.

As such, Mann takes a stance that Scott Herring calls "queer anti-urbanism," a rejection of the sort of "metronormativity" that Jack Halberstam argues forges compulsory links between (gay, white, middle-class, cisman) homonormativity and urban locales.[6] Scholars have increasingly chronicled the various ways rural queers have fostered identities, communities, and livelihoods alongside urban parallels, "offer[ing] and operat[ing] under specific social and cultural conditions that [have] shaped [them] as an alternative modernity."[7] Mann and many of his contemporaries see in food and its preparation a recipe for just such an "alternative modernity"—one that takes as its foundation not a spectacular urban movement but the mundane lifeways of the everyday. In *Loving Mountains,* food centers Mann's essays and especially his poems, many of which revolve around the "hillbilly" gustatory traditions—foraging, cooking, and sharing wild greens, roots, and fruits—that defined his childhood, detailing the location, growth, and preparation of ramps, creecy greens, new potatoes, and more. In effect, they constitute a series of lyric recipes, each fixated on a single provision.

Food motifs are unique to neither Appalachian nor queer contexts, but Mann and similar writers deploy them in contextually specific ways to address what one queer Appalachian describes as the two biggest issues facing people like them: "lack of community" and "history."[8] In terms of literary representation, food "is never merely nutrition," as Allison E. Carey writes of Watts's novels.[9] It often functions, across a variety of traditions, as a matrix through which "self-identity and place-identity are woven" together, especially given that acts of eating encourage a sense of direct interconnection with environment—a mingling of internal and external as nutrients interact with cells—and therefore food often emerges as a central figure in the identity negotiations undertaken by writers concerned with the contours of nation, region, and other social forms.[10] It is never "simply the 'what' of what one eats that matters," Kyla Wazana Tompkins writes. "It is the 'where' of where we eat and where food comes from; the 'when' of historically specific economic conditions and political pressures; the 'how' of how food is made; and the 'who' of who makes and who gets to eat it." Above all, it is "the many 'whys' of eating—the different imperatives of hunger, necessity, pleasure, nostalgia, and protest—that most determine its meaning." What might happen, she asks, if we shift our thinking "from the *what* of food to the *how*" of its consumption—as well as representations of it?[11]

I am interested in precisely this sort of question in this chapter, as well as the aesthetic roles played by *gathering* ingredients, *cooking* meals, and *sharing* victuals. I draw particular attention to these acts because Mann's essays and poems, as well as those of his colleagues, busy themselves not just with food itself but also with its preparation as well as ingestion. This chapter advances two intertwined arguments related to this tendency. First, Mann's sustained yet broad exploratory consideration of food illuminates both the promises and pitfalls of its value as a representational shorthand for the negotiation of numerous identity demands, whether queer, place based, or both.[12] On the one hand, as numerous scholars of food have argued, because the act of eating food troubles conventional material boundaries between self and other, it might offer opportunities to upend the social distinctions that separate them. But on the other hand, treating food as a communitarian signifier risks reiterating fundamentalist notions of nature and region, as well as boundaries and hierarchies that have historically excluded queer folks, people of color, and others. This second possibility is, in an environmentalist context, consistent with the other narratives I've been considering—and is precisely what is at stake when writers frame food as a threshold object. But I focus on Mann's work specifically because it instructively vacillates between these two extremes, rather than settles on one. Appalachia comprises an immense, demographically diverse swath of the United States, but Mann, like many commentators inside and outside the region, is not immune to a tendency to universalize it, as well as to shore up his own masculinity as a privileged aspect of environmental belonging in the region. That said, my second argument is that by focusing in other instances on the open-ended preparation of food rather than the product, his poems also typify foodways and (regional) identity as ongoing phenomena, despite other impulses in his work toward essentializing them.

In all cases, it is questions about *why* and *how* food is consumed and talked about that offer instructive lessons about its potential as a threshold object and the possible implications of stories told about it. Other examples involve explicitly fascistic appeals. The Euro-American history of local and/or organic farming and food cultures is bound up with the eugenic right, a fact illustrated by a recent farmers' market scandal in Bloomington, Indiana, where vendors affiliated with the American Identity Movement not only attracted protest but also prompted surprise at their blatant connection between white supremacy and "locavore" farming and eating, given the latter's association with the leftist counterculture since the 1960s.[13] But as the last chapter illustrates, connections between localism and appeals to blood and soil transcend conventional ideological divides, in part because of an existing affinity between them. That link encouraged organic farming among fascists and crypto-fascists across Europe in the twentieth century. As the historian Corinna Treitel notes, "[I]t was the Nazis who first elvated organics to the level of state action."[14] Both sides of this relationship—emplaced eating and blood-and-soil fascism—share "a reverence for rural areas, as against ever-growing industrialized cities," Michelle Niemann adds. Eugenic social theory propelled the link between "soil health and human health" a step further, "in the direction of racial health."[15] Current far-right environmentalists (Jake Angeli comes to mind) also frequently commit to an organic diet, both as proof of the connection between their blood and soil and as a celebration of the "natural" health, vitality, and strength of the (usually male) body. Such figures also deploy consumption of organic foods to buttress claims to "indigeneity," which form the cornerstone of the Third-Positionist "tribalism" discussed in previous chapters.

"Tribalism" has also offered surprising inroads to far-right politics for gay men, especially "as fascist philosophy," Shane Burley notes, "moves further away from traditional Christianity." Though "still viewed as suspect," men like Jack Donovan—a tribalist who, in his book *Androphilia* (2006), disavows the term "gay" in favor of describing himself as a "man attracted to men"—have offered ammunition to young men across the far right seeking quasi-intellectual justification for their uncritical exaltation of brash, brutal masculinity.[16] Such alliances, however, are not new. They represent merely the latest iteration of an often-overlooked history in which gay men self-consciously identify with white-supremacist movements, even with neo-Nazism. The National Socialist League, for example, was an openly gay far-right group active from the mid-1970s to late 1980s, a "homophile organization for the Gay American Nazi." Its "explicit goal," Blu Buchanan writes, "was to promote a nationalist orientation toward the United States, while simultaneously imagining white gay men's inclusion within a nation 'free' of non-white and feminine influences." Its membership argued that white gays should be spared right-wing violence because of "what they can contribute to the overall cause, the racial 'struggle for White survival,'" drawing on "hyper-masculine white figures to situate itself against the image of the effeminate, racialized 'street faggot.'" Such figures, from the National Socialist League to Donovan, seek "coalition building for white masculine supremacy," harmonizing the ethos of certain gay men with that of the far right by fixating on "natural" masculine strength, coupled with the corresponding notion that "other forms of nonconformity associated with gender, specifically femininity" and "non-white, 'impure' racial performance," contribute to national decline.[17] And because "degeneracy is such an unclear and changeable category," Sam Moore and Alex Roberts write, "only the most consistently maintained hyper-masculine stance will suffice as a defense."[18]

None of the above positions describes Jeff Mann. For one thing, it is unlikely that he would declare himself a locavore. More importantly, he is certainly no white supremacist. But he does self-consciously echo much of Donovan's perspective on masculinity, as this chapter will discuss. Mann, as a gay man, might reject heterosexist visions such as *Ecotopia*'s, but he nonetheless reifies notions of environmental purity, naturalizes masculinity and strength, and connects these values. He also expresses an acute fear of the United States' sharp rightward turn: "The day after the [2016] election, I was numb and fearful" for family of color as well as himself. He even names institutional fascism as the object of his alarm, recalling the presence of queers in Nazi camps.[19] I find Mann to be as rich an example for this book as I do food precisely because of this tension between his aversion to the radical right and his embrace of some of its most precious assumptions about nature. Far-right, masculinist "assertions of virility *sui generis* are ultimately, and conspicuously, shallow," Moore and Roberts note. "The body is involved in an exchange with the outside." As a result, it is often "control of this exchange around which many of the most conspiratorial aspects of far-right politics flow." For those who accept that "nature makes our bodies" and "degenerate nature makes degenerate people," then "concern for perfection and purity become . . . intimately related to the politics of the consumption of nature"—including food, which, as a technology to decontaminate the body, can perform a mildly palingenetic function.[20] One does not need to identify with the far right to feel or express concern regarding the effects of food on the body, especially in a nutritional era characterized by the ubiquity of factory farming. But depending on how it is communicated—and how it is tied to social matters such as gender expression—such apprehension can nonetheless resonate with fascist narratives, if not actively participate in them.

To reiterate a provision I make in other chapters, my intention is decidedly *not* to suggest that Mann is an ecofascist who purposively aligns with the far right. He is not and does not. Nor do I mean to demonize local and organic food movements tout court. Many legitimately advance the goals of both environmentalism and social justice, levying important critiques against a global economy in which, as the ethnobotanist and locavore Gary Paul Nabhan puts it, one can "pick and choose from the planetary supermarket without any contact with local fishermen or farmers, let alone any responsibility to them."[21] My goal is, as always, to demonstrate how particular ways of expressing certain ideas together (and, in this case, framing food) rehearse narrative patterns that, in other contexts, prefigure ecofascist violence. The question I am posing about Mann, then, is not *Is he an ecofascist?* (no, he is not), but *What conclusions does his way of representing the world arrive at that he might not intend?* Mann links certain environments with certain people in response to ecological (as well as homophobic) threats, and he does so in ways that sometimes endorse or justify notions of purity, forms of hierarchy, and even histories of racialized violence.

Reading his work overarchingly enables us to trace differences in what representations of food can signify depending on their mobilization. Mann's writing walks a line between reconciling *queer* and *Appalachian* as matters of fixed identity or of ongoing acts of kinship—a distinction that turns in large part on variable depictions of nourishment.[22] In the pages that follow, I first outline the political, economic, and environmental situation of Appalachia as a region, with particular attention to its relationship with food. I then define the form and content of Mann's recipe poems and situate them in a broader literary tradition toward which Mann himself gestures, before I consider how that same tradition opens questions around race, class, gender, and environment that Mann grapples with throughout his writing, in some cases drawing on food to naturalize his own, idiosyncratic experiences of place. But I also follow this chapter with another Interlude that returns to his recipe poems to consider how they disrupt narratives of fixed identity, offering instead an account of ongoing acts of queer kinship organized around regional lifeways. The extent to which Mann explores food as a motif is representative of broader strategies among queer writers of Appalachian origin and/or residence, but it is specifically the tension between his recipe poems and other references to food that renders a reading of his work valuable for considering the motif's implications, not only for Appalachian culture, but also for the role played by threshold objects in contemporary writing about place and environment.

Regional Exploitation, Environmental Disruption, and Local Foodways in Appalachia

It is not uncommon for social media users to flock online in the aftermath of U.S. elections to shake their heads at the benighted politics of red-leaning regions and states. As one Twitter post put it in 2018, "[A]gain, Florida proves that it prefers white supremacy to being above sea level."[23] Similar reactions haunted West Virginia's senate primaries, particularly the enthusiasm with which some voters greeted Don Blankenship, one-time Republican candidate and embattled former chairman and CEO of the Massey Energy Company. Mann finds motivation for his environmentalism in his outrage toward such figures and the "human and environmental costs of coal extraction" they represent: the forest dead zones and bodies of water poisoned by acid mine runoff and coal slurry whose effects choke local flora, displace indigenous fauna, and upend human subsistence.[24] He also views these ecological concerns as part of a larger constellation of social injustice in the region and nationwide. "As a liberal, an Appalachian, a gay man, and an environmentalist," he writes, "I'm angered by . . . what's going on in contemporary America, including rampant conservatism, mountaintop removal, and homophobia."[25] But Appalachia's "originary status in the United States energy economy" complicates its relationship with mainstream environmentalism, Matthew S. Henry writes.[26] Mann's irritation also derives in part from the scorn with which urban progressives frequently view mountain folks in bulk, which he (rightfully) finds unhelpful. Such condescension nonetheless characterizes commentary on both the left and right, which, despite widely different goals and politics, tend to share an inaccurate perception that denizens of coal country constitute a homogenous (white, working-class) unit that fully precipitates its own misfortunes.

In truth, the region hosts a long tradition of grassroots environmental justice organizing (which grows out of a once-robust union culture) and even militant monkeywrenching. Such movements have, for over a century, targeted surface mining and, more recently, mountaintop removal, as well as hydraulic fracturing and other methods of resource extraction that decimate human and nonhuman ecologies. Efforts to abolish strip mining have often organized locally, among farmers and other working-class residents. "Like their middle-class counterparts, these critics expressed dislike for stripping in aesthetic terms," the historian Chad Montrie writes. "But they were more likely to bemoan the damage done . . . to farmland and homesteads." It was not until the late 1970s, when the decade's economic recession and energy crisis presented an opportunity for coal industry agents to frame the matter in terms of a "mutually exclusive choice between jobs or the environment," that widespread radical opposition waned and regional politics began to shift rightward.[27] But rural, working-class opponents of the coal industry in Appalachia have indeed cited both environmental and social concerns for well over a century.

Surface mining strips everything—rock, soil, and vegetation—to access deposits beneath, causing widespread erosion especially in steep mountain environments and, as a result, increased runoff that carries with it the byproducts of mining activity, which in turn exacerbates flood risks, silts and poisons freshwater sources, and generally wrecks animal and plant habitat. In some cases, mine operators actively dump the same chemicals down the sides of mountains in the form of "spoil" left over from a dig. Such conditions have not only resulted in fatal and, in the case of small-town Appalachia, literally community-destroying landslides and floods, but also foreclosed the possibility of crop production in much of the region, especially for independent farmers without corporate resources. As the coal industry carved up the region in the nineteenth and twentieth centuries, land became scarcer and subsistence farming increasingly difficult. Holdouts often lost their farms regardless (industry agents possessed greater knowledge of, and control over, laws and courts). By the middle of the twentieth century, most families depended for work on the coal industry itself, even as it systematically undermined labor protections.

But concerted downsizing, cost-cutting automation, and westward migration to Rocky Mountain states with more resources and fewer unions reduced the West Virginia workforce fivefold from the 1950s to the early 2000s—the result of intentional shifts (and market competition from natural gas), not reduced production or heightened regulation (which remains paltry, not least because the industry retains influence over local and state policy to this day). Even though coal and natural gas corporations continue to fete the economic benefits of their presence, "most of the people of the region did not profit from the extractive industries," Montrie adds. Nor do they today. Tax arrangements ensure that a trifling share of the industries' gains returns to local communities.[28] As the Kentucky essayist and poet Wendell Berry writes, "[T]he enrichment of the coal interests . . . has always involved the impoverishment of the people." Strip mining might be "enriching . . . on the basis of an annual accounting," but the "public expenditure that supports this private profit is long-term."[29]

The economic and environmental means to produce food was a quiet yet important casualty of this process, even as other threats to Appalachian subsistence mobilized in the twentieth century. The rise of what Allison Carruth calls "US food power" augured radical agricultural and economic changes that affected even remote mountain families still tilling small farms (whether they retained legal title to land or not).[30] The dominance of corporate agribusiness (and government subsidies for it) has had lasting effects on independent farms nationwide—enough that it became a recurring theme in Appalachian literature starting in the 1970s, when Earl Butz, Richard Nixon's secretary of agriculture, began aggressively pushing "get big or get out" policies that bankrupted small farms across the country. Berry wrote in 1981 that "conditions for going into farming now are . . . prohibitive even for young people who know how to farm." Independent farmers "must pay usury to lenders, and buy equipment and supplies at costs rising much faster than the value of farm produce."[31] The effects have been environmental as well as socioeconomic. "Instead of asking the farmer to . . . be a good steward and trustee of his land," the nationwide economic premium placed on efficiency and surplus "puts irresistible pressures on him to produce more and more cheaply, thereby destroying the health of the land, the best traditions of husbandry, and the farm population itself."[32] Carruth suggests, however, that these same conditions also propelled environmentalist support for locally grown food. Globalization, she writes, "provide[d] the imaginative frameworks and material structures . . . to re-localize food" via education and communication as well.[33]

Given its particular environmental and agricultural history, Appalachia speaks doubly to this relatively new "dimension of the American national imaginary . . . according to which food and agriculture propel, rather than offer a retreat, from modernity."[34] On the one hand, the region is representative of the rise of agribusiness and its effects on small farmers. On the other, it is home to some of the most recognizable voices calling explicitly for that sort of "retreat." Berry would hardly label himself a locavore, given the term and movement's own modish flavor. It is precisely the sort of enabling technologies Carruth mentions that he distrusts. (Despite the fact that "Think Little," one of his most widely published essays to this day, first appeared in the pages of the 1971 *Last Whole Earth Catalog,* he has constantly disparaged the technophiliac "gadgets" the registry pitched to back-to-the-landers throughout his career.) For Berry, food bridges the perceived gap between culture and nature, but only when produced intimately: "We should subsist from our own land" to "secure . . . some stable, decent, rewarding connection to the land worked."[35] Subsistence, for Berry, is a means of recuperating the health of both land and steward and of forging a shared, place-based identity between them—not just in Appalachia but wherever small farmers tend their fields. The Appalachian novelist and essayist Barbara Kingsolver narrates the same sort of project in *Animal, Vegetable, Mineral* (2007), and numerous regional enterprises, such as the West Virginia Forest Farming Initiative, have emerged in the early twenty-first century to foster this kind of work, not only educating residents about local plants, their properties, and sustainable methods for foraging, cultivating, and harvesting them, but also connecting these practices to family and other communal histories.[36] In all these instances, food emerges as an important facet of Appalachian identity building and community organizing.

In many cases, such engagements aim to redress matters of dispossession and food security. But in others, such as the locavore movement writ large, they can often seem more concerned with pleasure and recreation than justice or necessity. White, middle-class, urban locavores, Carruth notes, frequently "overlook systemic inequities related to farm and restaurant labor as well as food access," given a general tendency in the movement to neglect the "histories of empire, territorial war, and slavery that define[d] food in the era before American agribusiness" and "continue in the era since."[37] Many Appalachian writers, especially Berry, do not fit in this category. But despite his capacious vision of national and global food systems, even Berry speaks to a tendency among Appalachian writers to elide certain conditions of their place-based identities. On the subject of absentee corporate land ownership, he writes that "people of rural America have been struggling with the realization that we are living in a colony," an "irony" he describes as "especially bitter for Americans," who, "having cast off the colonialism of England, . . . proceeded to impose a domestic colonialism on our own land"—a situation in which "most of the money made on the products that we produce . . . is made by other people in other places."[38] Kingsolver likewise writes that "rural regions have been treated . . . as colonial property of the cities."[39] Their critique of absentee ownership is both shrewd and necessary. Their use of the word "colony," however, complicates their place-based identities and the politics of food that grounds them.

Critics such as Stephen Pearson and Darryl Leroux describe this sort of claim as an example of settler self-indigenization that obscures the settler-colonial violence that enables it. For Pearson, this practice is especially widespread among Appalachians of European descent. Beginning in the 1950s and 1960s, and inspired by worldwide decolonial movements, mountain activists adopted rhetoric from struggles abroad to critique coal mining industries and "assert their indigeneity."[40] Both parties, Montrie notes, have generally framed their conflict as "a dispute between property owners over the legitimate use of privately held land and its resources." This tendency, for Montrie and others, demonstrates not just the centrality of ownership to U.S. "political consciousness" but also an even more robust Appalachian tradition of "propertied independence." The notion that Appalachia constitutes a repository for quintessentially "American" characteristics dates to the decades after the Civil War, when local color writers plugged "Appalachian America" as the residue of the Revolution, "the former having progressed little beyond the latter's level of civilization."[41] This romantic depiction captured a variety of postwar anxieties regarding citizenship and race—and it did so, as I discuss in further detail below, by framing Appalachia as an antimodern ideal. It has also found a receptive audience inside as well as outside the region, speaking, Pearson argues, to a broad lack of attention to Appalachian settler colonialism, despite the Euro-American population's "preservation of distinct frontier identities . . . as sites of their own resistance to capitalist exploitation." Claims to indigeneity in Appalachia are not quite examples of "playing Indian," as certain aspects of communes often are. Instead, they generally "code features of White Appalachian culture as traditional . . . and Indigenous in their own right."[42]

To the extent that local foodways counter corporate "colonialism," they remain bound up in larger conversations surrounding race, imperialism, land, ownership, and belonging. The image of timeless subsistence that often underwrites picturesque representations of Appalachia masks the brutal settlement of the mountains by Euro-American farming families themselves (which, to be clear, Berry acknowledges and actively seeks to redress). Themselves a product of British empire, enclosure, and displacement, the predominantly Scots-Irish immigrants to the region (of whose lineage Mann counts himself) "formed the shock troops of the 'westward movement' in North America."[43] Numerous settler Appalachian writers, such as the Ohio-born poet James Wright, have sought to reconcile their sense of place-based identity with this history in their work. But generally, for "supporters of the colonialism model," Pearson writes, "the presence . . . of Indigenous peoples their predecessors raped, massacred, and dispossessed as part of their colonization of the region threatens their claims to being a colonized people with an unproblematic, Indigenous claim to the land." Engagements with and representations of food as a means to establishing or reinforcing regional identity in the face of ecological and economic challenges must negotiate this problem, lest they, too, "support the narrative of peaceful settlement in an untouched wilderness."[44]

The Recipe as Literary Form, Content, and Tradition

Food conspicuously peppers the essays and poems of *Loving Mountains, Loving Men* (and Mann's other works). In the book's earliest essays, Mann mobilizes expressions of eating to retrospectively mediate between the experiences of his closeted teenage self and aspects of his environment with which he identified rather than those he feared. Instead of taking the "beautiful flesh" of classmates "into my mouth," he projects same-sex desire onto the nonhuman world: "the hard curves of their biceps were river-smooth stones, their moist body hair was dark orchard grass" (13). He locates his younger self's eroticism, "consigned by age" as well as regional context "to metaphor," in the mountain landscape itself, as if divorcing the place from the prohibitive social conditions that characterize it. He also articulates his access to that sexually liberated sphere in terms of eating, which functions, as Kyla Tompkins notes it often does across literary history, "as a metalanguage for genital pleasure and sexual desire."[45] For Mann, eating additionally appears inseparable from the region his family's local food comes from, whether gardened or foraged.

Frequently, however, representations of preparing and presenting food to others supersede concrete or metaphorical expressions of eating it in Mann's writing. *Loving Mountains* opens not just on a gay bed and breakfast in mountain Virginia, but specifically on its food, the "down-home specialties I grew up on" (xiii). His Appalachian studies students at Virginia Tech often "brought me homegrown or home-canned treat[s]," all of them "excited to have a teacher who honored their heritage, a teacher who waxed ecstatic over mountain cooking" of the sort they shared with him: "kudzu jelly, deer jerky, . . . corn relish," and other delights (43). In many cases, food fulfills two functions in his writing: it illustrates a local or regional foraging or cooking custom and marks occasions when queer folks have gathered in a rural context. And for Mann, representations of food can fulfill the same task. "When teaching literature," he writes elsewhere, "sometimes I feel as if I'm giving students much-needed food. It seems inevitable that a man like me, descended from a family of hearty mountain cooks and gourmands, would compare a poem to a biscuit, a short story to a big slab of country ham." For the purposes of his own survival in the region, work by Appalachians, gay men, and lesbians has especially "felt like nourishment."[46]

A number of Mann's poems—specifically a sequence of lyrics titled after single provisions, from "Turnip Greens," "Creecy Greens," and "Chowchow" to "Dilly Beans," "Tomato Stakes," and "Digging Potatoes"—bind these roles together in a relatively consistent series of features. The poem "Ramps" (184–5) offers a representative narrative form. The speaker (autobiographical in many if not all of the poems) begins with a memory of his grandmother prompted by the discovery of wild onions at a farmers' market. Lessons learned from relatives dominate the following stanzas as the speaker cleans the onions, trims their roots, and chops their stalks. After adding a few other ingredients to cook an unspecified dish, the speaker shifts to the first-person plural on behalf of an implicit guest, perhaps Mann's partner: "We love ramps because they're rare, only once a year," and because they "remember the wild asleep / beneath our skin, a rich green wild" (lines 20, 25–26). All the poems likewise fixate on a single staple. The dishes the speaker prepares remain fuzzily unclear, even unfinished. Many of the poems don't gesture toward meals at all. "Turnip Greens," for example, focuses almost entirely on the speaker's ascent up a mountain holler to gather the wild greens of the poem's title, enumerating the physical features of plants, soil, and stone in a manner typical of lyric poetry. The mountain, however, bleeds into the kitchen subtly, almost unnoticeably. The boundary between the two environments is not so much porous as it is reflective: mountain and kitchen are two sides of the same coin. Accordingly, the lyric shifts to the activity of cleaning, massaging, and seasoning the greens in the company of an onlooker (including the reader), with the eating itself left unconsummated.

I refer to these verses as Mann's "recipe poems" because they center food as part of a process, though they do so in a way that decenters meals themselves. Each poem is formally distinct, but almost every one organizes around three consistent narrative characteristics. First, it describes the act of foraging, picking, and/or otherwise preparing a single local foodstuff. Second, this crop prompts the speaker to draw some relationship between themself and the region, whether familial, ecological, or otherwise. And third, each poem involves the transmission of these knowledges to another individual, typically a lover or friend, or entails a tacit acknowledgement that the speaker already shares this insight with them. This final feature captures a second reason to characterize these poems as recipes. Mann's suggestion is that recipes offer more than just instructions for cooking, chiefly because recipes, once shared and practiced, do not go away. Even when thrown in the trash, a recipe can persist like an heirloom, persevering as a tradition binding those who participate in it. These recipes aren't for meals. They're for relations.

In this respect, the threefold structure of Mann's recipe poems positions them in a broader literary tradition. "Even the root of recipe—the Latin *recipere*—implies an exchange, a giver and a receiver," Susan J. Leonardi writes: "A recipe is, then, an embedded discourse, and like other embedded discourses, it can have a variety of relationships with its frame."[47] Leonardi argues that for this reason, cookbooks can be evaluated as literature to the extent that their writers construct authorial personae, attend to form and style, navigate their context, and cultivate responsive reading communities, as she suggests texts such as Irma S. Rombauer's *The Joy of Cooking* (1931) do. Rafia Zafar argues similarly of cookbooks by Black writers such as Vertamae Smart-Grosvenor's 1970 *Vibration Cooking* and Carole and Norma Jean Darden's 1978 *Spoonbread and Strawberry Wine*. Autobiographical vignettes throughout such texts, Zafar contends, "help us understand how a recipe collection functions as an articulation of a personal and/or communal identity. Each text works as autobiography *and* history in addition to engaging, obliquely or not, the linked issues of Black stereotyping and class."[48] Each might do so in its own distinct way, but all typically aim to recuperate a group identity fragmented by circumstance by foregrounding food's enmeshment with history alongside its creative potential. Stephen Vider points out that Lou Rand Hogan's 1965 *Gay Cookbook* attempted an analogous project for gay men by depicting the midcentury "gay home" as "a central stage for shaping individual lives and relationships, without necessarily conforming to the gender norms embedded within Cold War domestic culture."[49]

Mann adds place to this sort of project, mobilizing regional foodstuffs not only to cultivate group identity around shared experiences of desire and discrimination, but also to do so within a specifically rural rather than urban context. He also flips the script. Rather than package recipes as a literary genre, elements of that genre inform his literary work, placing his poems in a convergent tradition that he explicitly acknowledges. In one of his essays, Mann writes of his "painful vision of expatriate queer Appalachians in their tiny, overpriced apartments yearning for good biscuits, barbeque, and bowls of greens. . . . the sort of rough, filling, healthy, cheap food that poor people eat." Almost immediately, he ties access to local foods to access to poetic representation. "I want to read poems about greens," he tells the reader, and he indeed points to Lucille Clifton's "cutting greens" and Rita Dove's "Sunday Greens" as two examples (147). In this essay, Mann places his own poems in a literary tradition in which marginalized writers experiment with food's preparation as a representational strategy. As Clifton's speaker, for example, cuts her greens, she reflects on the relationship between her own body and "the bond of live things everywhere."[50] The verses highlight food's potential to destabilize boundaries as well as to reify them in new ways. The body relies on food, but food relies on intermediaries who prepare and share it. Family (hereditary or found) takes shape around these mundane acts of nourishment.

In this respect, representations of preparing and eating food can illuminate the articulation and construction of identity rather than express it wholesale. Eating, Elspeth Probyn writes, forces observers to confront various "interminglings of the cultural, the culinary and the corporeal."[51] On one hand, Tompkins adds, eating "threaten[s] the foundational fantasy of a contained autonomous self"—not to mention a national, regional, ethnic, and/or racial group—"because, as a function of its basic mechanics, eating transcend[s] the gap between subject and object." Still, on the other hand, representations of food and eating have often historically been "deployed in the service of . . . demarcating social barriers."[52] Even as eating foregrounds one's nutritional reliance on seemingly external objects whose assimilation troubles conventional lines between self and other, it can also shore up myths of the subject's secure place in the food chain (as well as hierarchies of authentic eating organized along lines of nation, region, and/or race). But if a poet such as Clifton intends to establish a consistent conception of group identity through imagery of shared gustatory traditions, they also articulate the extent to which that formation remains a process.

In other words, mode of representation matters. Intention, context, style, and tone have a considerable effect on the cultural work that food performs—as do other priorities on the part of the writer. It is for this reason that Mann furnishes such an excellent case study. Variations in his representations of food illustrate why the motif's prominence in the cultural formation of various communities (queer Appalachia among them) merits attention, if only to account for the diversity of meanings it might engender. Mann's own reflection on food as a literary trope demonstrates the ambiguity around its potential significance—as well as several of its pos-

sible directions. Shortly after praising Clifton and Dove, he poses
a question: "[W]hy don't white folks write about greens? Way past
time for a queer white boy to compose such a paean" (147). He immediately introduces a racial dimension to this tradition, cleaving
it into two camps—Appalachian and Black—even though Dove's
poem, among others, is situated in Appalachia. Naming and preserving different literary traditions, including along lines of race, is
quite often a laudable goal—indeed it formed a cornerstone of the
canon disruption reforming the intellectual establishment at the
time of Mann's writing, which aimed to recover and foster not only
those traditions themselves but also the broader project of multiracial democracy. On one hand, Mann seems interested in doing the
same for queer Appalachia (as well as for Black women), bridging
ostensible divides in a way other white writers have not, while still
respecting important differences in experience. In later writing, he
pointedly mentions his admiration for the work of the Affrilachian
Poets, a Black literary collective founded by the Kentuckian Frank X.
Walker, as well as the importance of Black Lives Matter to residents
of Appalachia, including members of his own family by marriage.
And cooking is a way he opens himself up to difference. "Sharing
good food," he writes, "can create community, gratitude, and cross-
cultural understanding, and . . . can banish the fear of the other"—
even in terms that critics such as Probyn or Tompkins might use:
"Meals remind us of . . . the ubiquity and recurrence of bodily appetite."[53] Time spent among his sister's in-laws reveals "how similar
black and white Appalachian cultures are"—and "the food," too, "is
the same, with a few exceptions" (120).

But these references to literary and alimentary traditions exist in strained relation to other tendencies and preoccupations in
Mann's writing—namely, his rhetoric surrounding the question
of regional typology and his arguably uncritical treatment (even
defense) of the Confederacy, both of which I consider in detail
shortly. Combined with these other features, his passing partition
of Black and Appalachian food cultures might also contribute to a
broader risk across his work as a whole: that of implicitly reinforcing a longstanding tendency, on the part of writers both urban and
rural, to configure Appalachia as a racial as well as a regional signifier, shoring up longstanding myths of the region's whiteness and
obscuring inhabitants of color, as well as their roles in shaping local
cultures. To be clear, I do not think this is Mann's intention—but

the narratives at play in his writing, taken together, can bolster this impression. My point, again, is that certain ways of talking about food can alter its valence, especially in the context of other, existing discourses of region, race, and environment, with implications for other social forms, such as gender and sexuality, too.

Naturalizing Race, Region, and Food in Appalachia

Food has long played a prominent role in prescriptive representations of Appalachia—namely, its association with poor eating habits, declining health, and reliance on government assistance—and points to how those depictions encode assumptions about race and class as well as region. As Katharina Vester points out, at least since the 1980s, federal studies of obesity as well as poverty (and press coverage of their results) "often use race as an indicator," framing matters in terms of cultural pathology rather than systemic economic, medical, or ecological constraints. Mainstream attitudes often "point to individual responsibility" when assessing health and, like similar studies of crime, continue to extrapolate medical data according to discredited theories of cultural deficiency.[54] On the right, the region (vaguely delimited) and its inhabitants (functioning more like strawmen than real people) emerge as wasteful, economically dependent freeloaders (a perspective reinvigorated by J. D. Vance's 2016 bestseller *Hillbilly Elegy*). On the left, the same specters powered the motor, fueled by regressive economic, religious, and environmental attitudes, driving the rise of Donald Trump and his ilk. These accounts converge on a monolithic conception of Appalachia's cultural pathology, reinforcing rather than challenging existing hierarchies and ignoring the presence of LGBTQIA+ and disabled folks, people of color, and others. This "white trash stereotype," Annalee Newitz and Matt Wray write, "serves as a useful way of blaming the poor for being poor" by racializing deprivation—or locating it in white racial deficiency.[55]

The very term *white trash* itself renders class and, in the case of Appalachia, region together a racial category that "marks out certain whites as a breed apart," as Newitz and Wray put it. The descriptor not only explicitly characterizes the European-descended settlers to which it affixes, but also implicitly circumscribes people of color, suggesting that those who are not white are trash to begin with. The descriptor emerged in the early nineteenth century

but proliferated after the Civil War—a progression, the historian
Carl A. Zimring argues, that speaks to a "growing conflation of race
and cleanliness" beginning in the mid-nineteenth century, inten-
sifying "along with worries about epidemic disease in cities and
insecurities about . . . racial hierarchy." The epithet "allowed the
wealthy plantation class to maintain contrasts with poor farmers
during Reconstruction. Adding the word 'trash' to an individual's
racial identity threatened to remove the power and privilege of
whiteness," which in turn "compelled poor whites to engage in the
rhetoric of white supremacy even in areas that did not have large
African American populations."[56] Daniel Martinez HoSang and
Joseph E. Lowndes point out that, while "[r]ace continues to structure the terms of political identity, mobilization, and responses to
economic vulnerability," processes of racialization shift over time.
As I mentioned in chapter 1, in a neoliberal era of vast wealth accumulation, liberal and conservative commentators alike often
"describe the white poor in language once reserved for people of
color—depicting them as socially disorganized, culturally deficient, and even genetically compromised."[57] The Appalachian hick
exemplifies this dynamic.

That figure has also functioned as a repository for urban environmentalist anxieties—often in deeply contradictory ways. Sarah
Jaquette Ray points out, for example, that for many locavores, "the
body becomes an indicator of one's environmental distinctions"
such that the "(increasingly obese) poor" become "environmentally suspect." Such attitudes neglect material conditions of food
insecurity and ecological health, assigning culpability for unsustainable habits to individuals rather than, in Appalachia's case, the
extractive industries whose practices have rendered local foodways
increasingly precarious (if not impossible). But the region also often
signifies a certain environmental purity (albeit a fallen one). On the
one hand, Appalachia functions as a symbol of neglect, corporate
greed, local indifference, and rampant environmental degradation.
On the other, its strange blend of nearness and isolation—its geographical proximity to the urban East Coast despite its mountain
terrain—has lent itself (as I mentioned before) to contemporary
rehearsals of the U.S. frontier myth and its projection of national
themes onto "wild" landscapes. The concept of untouched wilderness, Ray notes, "was not about nature so much as it was about
an imagined body politic," a population of self-reliant, rugged,

yet virtuous "ideal Americans" contrasted with "less privileged bodies . . . associated with—even blamed for—the toxicity, poor hygiene, and dirt that become associated with urbanization."[58] But Newitz adds that white trash "emerges as a distinct and visible racial identity when it can be identified as somehow primitive" in terms of "a kind of temporal discrepancy, where white Westerners exist in 'the present' and non-whites"—or deficient whites—"are living in a more savage, natural, and authentic past."[59] As Mann himself observes, commentary "from the 'local color' writers of the late 19th century to the well-intentioned 'War on Poverty' literature of the 1960s" has frequently "emphasized the exoticism, the otherness of the Appalachian people, as if the region were almost" a "remnant of frontier society frozen in time."[60] Even as this "perception of mountaineers as an isolated people of another time" demands their "badly needed modernization," as Montrie puts it, it also locates an untarnished, presumptively *American* authenticity in the mountain poor.[61] In other words, Appalachia sits at a strange junction in the discourse of racialized white trash as well as the U.S. environmental imagination: at once natural and unnatural, the site of pure authenticity yet also the scene of its violation.

In this respect, queer Appalachians might prove the rule rather than the exception, given enduring conservative attitudes regarding queer folks' ostensibly "unnatural" status. As Anthony Harkins has written of the "hillbilly" as a general cultural archetype, the Appalachian has "served the dual and seemingly contradictory purposes of allowing the 'mainstream,' or generally non-rural, middle-class white, American audience to imagine a romanticized past" while also "enabling the same audience to recommit itself to modernity by caricaturing the negative aspects of pre-modern, uncivilized society."[62] Carol Mason points out that accounts both sympathetic and condemnatory have also often figured such deviance in terms of sexuality, as has historically been the case for women and people of color as well: an aggressive, unruly, polymorphous perversity "that can be construed as comically or dangerously crossing the bounds of proper sexuality."[63] Mann, however, sees productive overlap in this tendency, as do many of his contemporaries. "So much of those histories" of queer and Appalachian life alike, he writes, "is about isolation and . . . hardscrabble survival, both physical and emotional" (137). Both "queer folk" and "mountain folk," he notes elsewhere, culturally circulate as "frequent objects of satire, hostility, and contempt," as well as experience pressure "to blend in 'for their own well-being.'"[64] As perennial others, the hick and the queer likewise experience the label of deficiency, and both in (re)productive terms.

LGBTQIA+ writers, activists, and organizations in the region increasingly draw upon this surprising yet perhaps organic alliance. Nancy Isenberg points out that identification with the *hick, hillbilly,* or *white trash* label pre-dates the 2010s and 2020s by over a century—a history in which queer constituencies have participated for decades. "Before the end of the 1890s," Isenberg writes, "'white trash' was rebranded as an ethnic identity, with its own readily identifiable cultural forms," including foodways. Appalachia "remained in the minds of many a lost island containing a purer breed of Anglo-Saxon."[65] This perspective might seem to resonate more with the "white identity politics" said to characterize the Trump era than with the artistic and activist endeavors undertaken by many Appalachian queers, which largely aim for coalitional environmental justice, healthcare, food security, and political access across lines of race, gender, sex, sexuality, and other social forms, based on shared context rather than nativism. In this regard, they preserve an often-neglected post-Stonewall tradition of "back-to-the-land gay liberationism" that scholars like Jason Ezell and Scott Herring trace through organizations and publications such as *RFD* and *Country Women,* which contested both white supremacy and a "group identity that appears exclusively gay, exclusively male," and "exclusively urban."[66] But in the process, Herring adds, they "embraced (or, perhaps, reappropriated) a 'hillbilly' working-class style" as a stance from which to critique heteropatriarchy, white supremacy, and metronormativity, despite its specific reference to white populations. Food played a starring role in this strategy, which Herring calls "critical rusticity."[67]

Mann similarly repudiates white supremacy, but at the same time renders certain qualities intrinsic to Appalachian people, and by extension certain queers (specifically rural gay men), in such a way that gestures toward the role food might play in such naturalizations. He believes his sister Amy's marriage to a Black man distances her from neighbors' approval as much as his own partnership with a man does him. But he and Amy also "love these mountains," "do for ourselves," and "regard mainstream . . . urban America, dubiously"—attitudes he derives from Loyal Jones's 1973

essay *Appalachian Values* and likewise articulates in terms of un-
alterable regional character (101). "We mountain people," Jones
writes, "are a traditional people, and in our rural setting we val-
ued the things of the past. More than most people, we avoided
mainstream life and thus became self-reliant." Later, he suggests
that European settlers gravitated specifically to the region's "great
natural beauty," which rendered it "ideal for a new way of life" de-
tached "from 'powers and principalities.'"[68] The essay establishes a
certain temporal primitivism as the region's chronotope: a purer,
untouched territory coexisting with modern neighbors but in an
anterior, more authentic condition. It would be a mistake to say
that Mann overarchingly romanticizes the idea of authentic nature
itself. Wilderness, he writes, "is emblematic of lives beyond convention, beyond society's pale," but he also, when young, "thought
of being discovered in this fairly isolated place by gay-bashers and
wondered what sort of violence might flare up" (129). In this line,
Mann claims an epistemological privilege for the Appalachian
queer: an inability to take for granted romantic conceptions of the
region (as well as nativist myths that often underwrite them). At
the same time, however, he understands the "bald-faced" injustices faced by queer and Appalachian folks alike specifically as an
affront to "that concept of individual freedom on which America
is based" and for which white-trash identity narratives often position Appalachia as repository (137).

In his essays, Mann deems the Appalachian personality the con-
genital custodian of that value and the rural gay man its inheritor.
His confidence in universal freedom not only trades in conventional
imagery of "the ideal American tested in the wilderness, show-
casing self-reliance as achievable through an encounter with raw
nature," but also identifies Appalachian and queer alike with that
very nature—specifically with its produce.[69] He praises the "beautiful, prickly blooms" of local flora: "Stubborn, able to survive the
harshest landscapes. An endurance I admire" (xi). That endurance,
however, is "tenuous" in the face of extraction and commercialization. "When I glare at the new McDonald's . . . or when I contem-
plate the environmental consequences of that modern blasphemy,
mountaintop removal," Mann writes, "it seems only logical that I,
like many southerners, would glamorize and idealize the past. . . .
mainstream culture has swamped the mountains, and I wonder
how long that native culture—that rich self-reliance that has taken

centuries to develop—will last in the face of such onslaught" (158). Despite his earnest promise to avoid romanticizing an ostensibly natural, even primitive past—as well as to historicize it as a "development"—these lines suggest that an unspoiled nature does in fact exist in the mountains. It has merely been buried under an "onslaught." It might potentially be recovered and preserved. That Mann takes his critique straight to McDonald's signals the centrality of food to this evocation of vanished authenticity. It also speaks to what Camille Bégin describes as a nationwide "sensory nostalgia for 'real' food."[70] Mann does not quite stage a critique of Allison Carruth's "food power," or even a more specific "fast-food power." Rather, he counterposes it against local fare as a conflict between artifice and authenticity, cuing a tendency in his writing to nativize foodways and, by extension, broadly prescribe the people who transmit and partake of them. That impulse inheres across his autobiographical writing and at times inflects his poems. "Digging Potatoes" (183), for example, concerns the unearthing of identity as well as tubers: "Today we are archaeologists, / psychoanalysts, digging the dark lobes / for something lost long ago to force" (lines 19–21). When read alongside those comments regarding the region's capitulation to commercial forces, the idiom of excavation that runs through the poem suggests that what Mann seeks to root up is not just taters but also an authentic Appalachian character buried beneath a corporate artifice.

Locally sourced food takes on the qualities of a threshold object: something that, when consumed, transmits or proves both a native belonging to the land and ostensibly pure, natural characteristics—environmental and otherwise. New potatoes and creecy greens not only "nourished mountaineers through the Great Depression, coal booms and busts, and mountain isolation," as Mark F. Sohn writes of cornbread (another Appalachian staple), but also reflect an intrinsic, "old-fashioned, brash mountain country spirit."[71] Foods themselves take on associations with rugged settler masculinity in the Appalachian kitchen. Mann invokes this connection in "Ramps," when its speaker and their companion "remember the wild asleep / beneath our skin" and specifically do so in the shadow of multinational corporations and pollutive fossil fuel extraction. Certainly such forces are deserving of critique. What I want to emphasize again, however, is that in Mann's writing this conflict largely plays out as a binary opposition between rural authenticity and encroaching urban artifice, rather than as a nuanced consideration both of competing accounts of what it means to be Appalachian and of socioeconomic realities concerning access to food and other resources. The hardy "weeds" on which the speaker of Mann's poems feasts counter the invasion of a soft, artificial civilization associated with not health but its decline. In such moments, Mann reclaims local foodways and their trashy associations—an act of "critical rusticity." But he also naturalizes them, reverencing Appalachian self-reliance in a rural-nativist idiom (a "rich green wild" counterposed against urban frailty) and in vaguely masculine terms. In other words, Mann preserves binary narratives framing white-trash Appalachia as the urban's primitive other. He simply shifts value from one side to the other, locating authenticity in the mountains and artifice elsewhere—and positioning local food as a threshold between them.

Naturalizing Desire, Gender, and Strength in *Loving Mountains, Loving Men*

In upholding (though revaluing) these aspects of the white trash stereotype, Mann's attitude in his essays seems to maintain rather than trouble associations between racialized others and supposedly primitive behaviors. The vogue for Southern foodways that began in the 1930s, Bégin writes, has often rested on certain "sensory stereotypes." Black cooks "were superior, more in touch with their senses," but because "smell and taste have always ranked low on the . . . sensory hierarchy," the skills in question aligned "with animalistic, 'primitive' needs."[72] Like all "traditional" foodways, Appalachia's cooking customs comprise a pastiche of ingredients and habits, adopted especially from displaced Indigenous inhabitants and Black adaptations and diversified by ingenuity during lean times—a fact that Mann acknowledges when he describes the kitchen's "many influences, including Native-American, English, Scottish, Irish, German, and African."[73] This comment, however, throws into sharper relief his treatment of local staples (if not cuisines created of them) as a threshold between the real and artificial. In many ways, Mann's naturalization of Appalachian produce, and use of it as a symbol for resonances between regional and queer identity, sits at the confluence of Appalachian self-indigenization and what Scott Lauria Morgensen calls "settler homonationalism."

Ezell notes that anticolonial rhetoric has circulated in *RFD* and other (largely white) queer rural networks over the past fifty years, given that many of them "imagined their own sanctuaries as parallel autonomous territories to the US state."[74] This rhetoric, however, has proven fraught. Numerous "mid-twentieth-century US sexual minority movements," Morgensen adds, formed "on normatively white and national terms, which could include reversing the discourses marking them as primitive and embracing a primitive or specifically Native sexual nature."[75]

It is in this respect that Mann's naturalization of Appalachian foodways and other customs leads to a naturalization of queer identity. In light of his substitution of sexual intimacy (expressed in terms of eating) with skin-to-earth contact in *Loving Mountains'* earliest essays, the "wild asleep / beneath our skin" that eating ramps awakens evokes what Dianne Chisholm calls "flows of desire that escape classical biology."[76] Mann deploys another eating metaphor to express such a goal, declaring his intention to emulate "a delicious paneroticism" inherited from the Romantic poets, a desire to "take nature as a lover" (30). At first glance, such statements trouble conventional sexual and even species boundaries. His "weird and compulsive communing with trees" (31)—hugging them and running his hands along their bark—facilitates a sense of intimacy with place as well as an experience of nonnormative sexuality. He also structurally positions these encounters against not only "the way the coal companies steal land, drive people away, rip up the landscape and leave what few residents are left to deal with the terrible environmental consequences" (119) but also, more generally, all those urban fixtures he sees not only invading Appalachia from afar but also simply existing.

But the rugged spirit of the "weeds" Mann consumes, and the rhetoric in which he couches his consumption, points more specifically to a naturalization of rural gay masculinity. He attributes his "love affair with masculinity" to growing up among—albeit rejecting—the "conservative faiths of the South," which "insist upon . . . traditional gender-role behavior." This proclivity, he writes, "caused me to admire and relate to conventional masculinity more than many queers, especially those who think of such manliness as dangerous and politically suspect"—an objection, he writes, in which he's "no more interested . . . than I am in a Baptist's disapproval of my sodomitic lust." This dismissal strikes me as one that almost willfully misses the point of such criticism, even as it exemplifies its target. Attraction to "conventional masculinity" does not seem to be, for Mann, a matter of preference or, more critically, of desire. (I'm a rural gay man myself, and predominantly attracted to the same sort of men that Mann is.) He writes, within the same breath, not only that he neither resembles nor finds himself attracted to "over-groomed . . . domesticated men," but also that he is "not, in other words, a fan of delicacy and artifice."[77]

Artifice seems here to be the keyword—one that crops up often in his most recent writing. In a 2019 interview, Mann commented that he "suspect[s] I'm way too country to count for much" not only in terms of the literary establishment but also in "the metronormative LGBTQ++++++ community (yes, there's an ironic eye roll in there)." Despite the alliance he fashions between the rural and the gay—as well as the vibrant presence of a range of sexualities and gender identities in Appalachia—his "ironic eye roll" consigns other facets of nonnormative sexuality and gender expression within the urban, away from Appalachia, away from authenticity. "Queer theory" and its "pronouns," he gripes, have "changed gay and lesbian politics in ways I deeply disapprove of."[78] Such comments might open an opportunity for a nuanced discussion of queer historiography, but for Mann, these terms seem only to operate according to the binary structure between rural and urban, authentic and invasive, that he flips. "After all the struggles and suffering that our generation endured," he complains, these implicitly non-Appalachian "brats are arguing about 'preferred gender pronouns?'"[79] A great deal of robust critical debate among queer folks continually considers the affordances and potential limitations of selective pronoun use, among other matters. But rather than take seriously such discussion (and apparently unconcerned that trans individuals face the greatest share of anti-LGBTQIA+ discrimination, violence, and other forms of "suffering" today), Mann opts to merely lump together a caricature of "young politically correct queers" that he can counterpose against his ideal of rugged Appalachian masculinity in terms of artifice versus nature.

If part of the point of pronoun politics is to achieve inclusion within contexts perceived as potentially hostile, Mann's goal of reconciling nonnormative sexuality with Appalachia hardly seems incompatible. It is the premium he places on this opposition—

and his own authenticity and strength—that renders it so. He speaks favorably of Jack Donovan's dislike of "gay culture" (even the term "gay" itself), mentioned briefly in the introduction to this chapter, though he adds that the avowedly antifeminist, male-supremacist, and white-nationalist "androphile" has "gotten way too conservative for me." Mann himself surely does not support the disenfranchisement of women, for example (as Donovan does). But reading Mann's 2019 *Endangered Species* alongside Donovan's *Androphilia,* one cannot help but notice the near interchangeability of their rhetoric when it comes to matters of masculinity, sexuality, rurality, and even spirituality—as well as, most importantly, assumptions about nature and strength in relation to contemporary political culture. Mann fluently speaks Donovan's idiom of masculine tribalism, and despite his aversion to the ethnocentric focus of right-wing movements organized under its banner, he also celebrates the Nordic iconography that often accompanies them. (Donovan once headed a chapter of the Wolves of Vinland, a white-nationalist group mentioned in chapter 1.) "I've expanded my interests to the mythologies of my bloodlines," Mann writes. "My patron deities are the Celtic Cernunnos, Horned God of forest and mountain, body hair and semen, and the Nordic Thor, Storm Lord of drunken feasts, fighting, and fucking." More playful than Donovan's, Mann's interest nonetheless captures his hyper-valuation of natural masculine strength, against which he sets anything—including queer politics—that does not match his personal standards of virility, exemplified by his unnecessarily hyperbolic comment that "valor should be honored, whatever the side, whatever the cause."[80]

If nothing else, this remark helps to explain his thoroughgoing defense of the Confederacy. His most recent works include several "violent, homoerotic Civil War novels" that not only further his efforts to navigate queer desire in hostile social environments but also speak to a "reverence for the Confederate experience and the Confederate flag." This posture is, for him, a mark not of white-supremacist sentiment but of respect for the everyday homesteads caught up in the war—that is, for poor farmers and other nonslave-holding families the Union Army decimated and often brutally abused. His critique is one of empire—and rightfully so. The advancing Union Army did indeed commit atrocities against women, especially, regardless of race. As such, Mann "understand[s] the fury evoked when . . . politically-correct outsiders try to take down Confederate monuments. Such attempts say to us: 'You're trash, your ancestors were trash, their struggles and losses meant nothing.'"[81] The idea that settler Appalachia comprises a colony under threat of political and corporate imperialism is on full display here. But Mann's critique of the relationship between class and power, common to analyses of the region's partisan history, remains potent. Most settlers indeed possessed no direct economic stake in chattel slavery themselves, but many died for it regardless, largely because of their position between two ruling regimes that did.

What Mann strangely omits is an equally avid critique of the Confederate States' own forms of empire.[82] What readers receive instead is something closer to an apologia for them (and by extension one for chattel slavery, regardless of his intention), as well as a demand: "[D]on't tell us what our symbols mean." This warning also seems to miss the point. Signs circulate within and across cultures. The meaning they carry is not reducible to Mann's preferences. His absurd claim that the "fact that many Confederate monuments were erected during the years of Jim Crow and segregation is irrelevant" is patently untrue. It neglects the power imbalances among Southern classes—to say nothing of racial inequities—as well as the meaning with which power invests its symbols.[83] His defense, such as it is, speaks less to the region's complex history of exploitation and oppression than it does to what Wendell Berry describes as the "false mythology" of "a 'regionalism' based upon pride" and "condescension," which he suggests exemplifies the South. The region "has been scarred by history," Berry acknowledges. "Shall we heal those scars by the establishment of a decent and preserving community" or "enshrine the scars and preserve *them* as monuments to the so-called glories of our history?"[84] Mann chooses here, at least, to tread the second path: to collapse class distinctions into an organic, quasi-vitalist regional identity and draw lines between insiders and outsiders based on their adherence to it.

I am less interested in countering Mann's attachment to such symbols than I am in pointing out his rationale for why he (or we) should respect them: sort of just *because*. "It seems to me that turning your back on your forebears and dishonoring your family history are . . . a special kind of betrayal, and deserve a special kind of hell," he writes.[85] It is as if he views neither identity nor the narratives that underwrite it as things to reflect upon, question, and revise. They simply are what they are, as natural to the region as the food he writes about. He quotes the (progressive) West Virginia–born commentator Joe Bageant in his defense: "After a lifetime of identity conflict, I have come to accept that these are my people—by blood . . . if not politically."[86] To attribute belonging (to place as well as to people) to blood, however, does not particularly allow for criticism of the categories by which one understands the world. Mann can "without confusion or conflict honor the heritage of African Americans and the heritage of Confederate soldiers, the two bloodlines that have converged to create my nephew," he writes. "Both cultural legacies should be honored; they aren't mutually exclusive. . . . Perhaps simple minds abhor complexity." He is surely correct that they are not mutually exclusive, yet complexity—in terms of gender and queer politics as well as place and belonging—does indeed seem to be what Mann abhors (though I would never do him the disservice of calling him simple). His anger at Dylann Roof, the young neo-Nazi who murdered nine Black churchgoers in 2015, turns swiftly to rage at others who question the narratives that informed the shooter. Instead of accounting for the power imbalances by which they might have done so, Mann marvels at the "effrontery and entitlement" of "Gen Z" for leading efforts to remove statues from public spaces. "This is the sort of solipsism, hypersensitivity, and . . . entitlement" he has "come to expect," and which he also likens to "the sanctimonious, outraged indignation that so often pervades the transgender community." Mann paints here with pretty broad strokes, despite the fact that, in the same essay, he accuses his foes of "thoughtless generalization." The charge reads almost as an instance of projection—though Mann also savors the notion that the "sinister Confederate battle flag . . . has so many fragile souls terrified these days."[87]

Absent a more robust explanation for Mann's own generalizations from the author himself, the reader is left to infer his rationale from the material he does offer. For him, "Gen Z" is weak, but *he* is strong; trans folks are weak, but cisgender men and women are strong; the urban is weak, but Appalachia is strong. He frames the region as a haven of sorts, safe from an abstract horde of weakness. And though, at this point, I have wandered far afield from the subject of food, I want to return to it to reiterate the fact that it plays an important role in this series of oppositions. Hearty

mountain food emplaces speakers like Mann—proves them rugged and natural enough to belong in those hills, as opposed not
only to industries that would extract them to rubble but also to
those "artificial" forces that threaten his sense of masculine nature.

At many points in Mann's writing, food plays the role of threshold object, offering just one potential solution in his effort to mediate between his sexuality and his home. Over a decade before he
published most of the essays in *Endangered Species*, he described his
taste in *Loving Mountains* as a "contradiction" wavering between
"lobster and paté" and "brown beans and cornbread," the *Gay &
Lesbian Review* and the *Journal of Appalachian Studies*. Though
these pairs "cannot be separated," they maintain a series of oppositions between queer and Appalachian, urban and rural, even mind
and body (xiv–xv). "When I decided to study both literature and
forestry," he writes, "perhaps even then I was unconsciously trying to balance the refined and the rough in my nature, the indoors
and the outdoors, the educated queer and the woodland-tramping
hillbilly" (51). But he also identifies the "educated queer" with what
he takes to be Appalachia's opposite. What, then, does the work
of reconciling the two accomplish? Gay "culture," he writes, is a
"delicious relief when one spends one's life entirely surrounded by
straight, mainstream culture" (xiii). But it appears that this mainstream (coded urban) culture also includes the changes to "gay and
lesbian politics" he decries. One must assume that what he finds
"delicious" is something more specific—something fixed: that Appalachian character, sexualized, gendered, at times even racialized.
By the same logic, anything else is trash.

Interlude II

I want to follow the last chapter by reiterating that mode of representation matters when it comes to food. In Jeff Mann's writing alone, threshold object is only one part that food plays—and when role changes, so too does rhetorical effect. His privileged naturalization of himself, his masculinity, and his sexuality in the soil of Appalachia (all while deriding the "artifice" of just about everything else) furnishes just one example of the everyday circulation of a genre that, in other circumstances, might prefigure ecofascist violence. But narratives of preparing food can communicate something altogether different than narratives of emplacing or eating it. Cooking and preparing are acts as dynamic and unfixed as eating and food itself, but the fact that recipes are subject to re-creation, interpretation, and variation renders them less open to consolidation. To examine the kitchen, Kyla Tompkins writes, is not to observe menu-picture meals tidily sorted into prescriptive categories, but to catalog "items only semi-formed on their way to the site of ingestion."[1] To effect and examine representations of preparation is to consider the processes and narratives that underwrite seemingly stable cultural traditions and, by extension, identity categories. Recipes, like identities, are malleable, prone to adaptation yet nonetheless meaningful in their consistency. They take shape and change through creative improvisations, revisions, additions, subtractions, and substitutions—a point that Mann, despite other tendencies in his writing, captures in his poetry. As for my reading of Gloria Anzaldúa, my point is not that Mann does or that one should seek to dismiss consistent forms of identity altogether. It is rather to highlight the difference between rooting identity in the soil as a matter of fixed characteristics, on the one hand, and attending more closely to its grounded, material conditions and processes of articulation—and creative possibilities—on the other. This latter approach not only holds the consolidation and complication of identity in tension but also arguably opens up human experience to nonhuman others to a far greater degree than the former.

The consistent threefold narrative structure of Mann's recipe poems in *Loving Mountains, Loving Men* offers a rather different account of (queer) Appalachian community than the instances of naturalization read throughout his essays or in isolated poetic lines. Each poem dramatizes the preparation of a single local provision, links that act to regional knowledge, and culminates in the transmission of that knowledge to a companion, lingering over the discovery and properties of the items rather than their consumption and emphasizing their potential combination with other ingredients rather than prescribing a finished meal. Preparation typifies similar poems by writers such as Lucille Clifton and Rita Dove as well. What Mann adds is, first, an emphasis on regional produce, making place central to the recipe in question, and second, the substitution of a finished product with the act of participatory knowledge transmission at each poem's end. Given that these recipes culminate not in a meal but in a relation, people as well as produce play the role of ingredients in these poems. Kinship itself *is* the recipe the poem represents. As such, *Loving Mountains* ultimately plays out almost as a dialogue between what Donna Haraway refers to as "final ends" and "mundane differences": grand categorical narratives of identity on the one hand and "worldly" processes and variations at the level of quotidian encounters on the other.[2]

Mann makes clear that food is central to kinship as he understands it (after the tradition of Loyal Jones's *Appalachian Values*), as is the skill required to locate, grow, harvest, and prepare it. In "Creecy Greens" (188–9), he credits his grandmother with imparting "how to live on weeds, how the wilderness feeds us / if we know which plants to pluck" (lines 34–5). The woman draws on foraged and hand-grown vegetables to endure harsh conditions in the mountains, bankrupted by energy corporations and global agribusiness. In acknowledging the greens' classification as a weed, Mann reclaims the trashy stereotypes that circle around his home. To forage and delight in such produce is to challenge the normative narratives that determine what constitutes a weed and what does not. From Mann's perspective, mainstream cultural narratives represent queer folks as nonnormative weeds just as they do Appalachians. But even if he weathers similar rural conditions and stereotypes as his grandmother, he additionally endures the right-wing dangers of his locale. Simply locating self-identity in existing kinship structures and traditions therefore does not appear to be enough to erect a bridge between his experiences as an Appalachian and a young gay man.

His response is to "re-create my family's home cooking for gay and lesbian friends," as he believes that for any Appalachian, including a queer one, "heritage is invaluable and can be lost if it is not carefully passed on" (85). It is the act of passing on that his recipes take as their subject, even more than home cooking itself. As a result, his poems become an exercise in experimenting with regional traditions to willfully craft nonnormative, open-ended kinship structures, rather than naturalizing those traditions as a matter of fixed Appalachian identity with the normative family at its center. For example, in "Gathering Green Tomatoes in the Rain" (35–6), the speaker guides his lover (and the reader) through the process of harvesting the titular tomatoes, mixing cornmeal with sugar and spices, and "heating up the sine qua non of / southern cooking, bacon grease" (lines 31–2). The activity is less about serving and eating and more about learning and practicing. Not only does the guest taste a fried green tomato for the first time, but also both participants enact a new relationship characterized by this culinary knowledge and their sexuality. The speaker has "waited years for this . . . Those years of waste are over" (lines 2, 44). These lines bookend the poem, announcing relation, in addition to tomatoes, as its subject. Relationship to place, too, takes shape in terms of concrete yet variable interaction rather than abstract yet permanent blood

These recipe poems encode a consistent tradition while leaving execution—and, as a result, the possible forms of queer Appalachian kinship built around it—open-ended. Mann finds in West Virginia's bars a "rich mix" of queer folks knitted together by "folklore" rather than by identity strictly conceived (139). Likewise, he recalls how one of his students "recognized me as a kindred soul and gave me such homemade treats as corn relish and such wild delicacies as creecy greens" (151). Food comes to function as a controlling metaphor for that "folklore" that, for him, "creates a kind of comforting group identity" capable of resonating with place and sexuality as ongoing processes rather than reconciling between them as stable types (138). Poems such as "Digging Potatoes" and

"Ramps" not only provide instruction on how to subsist in often unfriendly environs but also encourage creativity, despite the moments at which they seem to fixate on something more essential. "Chowchow" (190), a poem devoted to a relish whose composition varies widely depending on geographical and seasonal context, catalogs herbs, spices, and greens from Mann's garden, suggests how to combine them with homegrown beans and other foraged ingredients, and ends with a place setting: "a jar . . . brought up from the basement" (line 22). It is unclear, however, which ingredients come together for this particular batch. The poems all make certain suggestions for preparation, but ultimately leave the recipes and their accessory ingredients open-ended. Mann obeys only two rules: first, that food be made to endure, as when in "Tomato Stakes" (179) he jars a crop "to warm me through another bachelor winter" (line 19), but second, that it also ideally be shared, as in "Gathering Green Tomatoes." The food traditions in question remain consistent but undergo revision depending on context. All those elements—the people involved in the preparation and exchange, especially—influence the unwritten outcome of the recipe. Queer Appalachian folks themselves play the role of ingredients. The chowchow always turns out differently but serves the consistent function of representing an ad-hoc kinship cultivated among the folks who make it.

This narrative function also animates an alternative perspective on place-based identity to blood-and-soil nativism. Environmentalism writ large, Sarah Ensor writes, "typically predicates investment on health . . . and longevity"—the preservation of pristine, unblemished "nature."[3] This viewpoint, she adds, has historically been at odds with narratives of not only unreproductive, "unnatural" queer sex but also queer mortality. Having come out of both the closet and mountains during the AIDS/HIV epidemic, Mann associates a loss of friends with the erosion of environment, both cyclical, as "when the maple leaves turn red," and extractive, as in the case of mountaintop removal (37). His milieu in the late 1980s and 1990s, characterized by the mass death of gay men and mass departure of queer folks in general from a region perceived as both hostile to them and itself deeply ill, doubly comprised what Ensor describes as "communities whose unity—and sense of collective agency—is predicated . . . on shared terminality." But for Ensor, such communities "challenge the assumption that terminality is a condition of futurelessness." The "deathbed," she writes, is not only the "de facto setting of much of the queer literature written in the final decades of the twentieth century," but also a trope that "refute[s] the notion that nostalgic gestures of preservation . . . are the only acts that can be taken" in the face of change—including environmental change. For Ensor, such attitudes characterize mainstream environmental narratives that privilege preservation and more radical accounts (including explicit ecofascism) that champion biocentrism, often at the expense of the actual human subjects whose lives ecological disruption most affects. Emphasis on futurity, continuance, and unlimited prosperity, Ensor writes, "occludes the forms of action and relation that terminality itself can occasion." It is "nonreproductive" populations, she argues, that have most often offered "a set of practices" that observe not "crisis, rupture, and radical discontinuity" but "a kind of perpetuity or *steadiness*." These practices are "less salvific than reparative": concrete, pragmatic, and "cyclical" acts that maintain connections through "collective wisdom," such as tending gardens, brewing balms, and easing passings. They adapt rather than force heroic, technocratic, nostalgic, and/or reactionary solutions.[4] Queer environmentalists might contribute to the survival of human and other species not through reproduction but through folk transmission of environmental knowledge.

I want to suggest that such *steadiness* is precisely what Mann's poems come to tortuously articulate. "There is a timeless, ritual quality to garden work," Mann writes. "Often I feel like an outsider. . . . So it feels good to believe that I belong for a time, part of a long tradition of farming" (164). If Mann's poems succeed in evoking a sense of regional (queer) community that does not rely on prescriptive appeals to nature, race, gender, or region, they do so precisely because they focus on "garden work," which is to say the process of cultivating kinship as well as food through mundane, everyday interactions—the perceived banality of the rural—rather than rooting fixed, authentic identities out of the ground. As food scholars have pointed out, "the practice of cooking . . . sits at a blurred, ambiguous interface between tradition, innovation, and (re)production." Depending on taste, history, and prerogative, cooks exercise "considerable power and control over not just the food consumption practices of a household but, following food's important role in identity creation and maintenance, an important role in the creation of cultural identity itself."[5] As a genre, the recipe exists somewhere between process and product, recording relatively consistent instructions for preparation but ultimately yielding to the needs and whims of the cooks.

Mann's import of recipe elements to poetry announces his embrace of such agency on the part of not only the cook but also the poet. That he leaves most of his recipe poems open-ended, focused on scenes of cultivation and creative preparation rather than ingestion, signals how food might also lend itself to representations of community and identity as ongoing kinship projects, tethered to context and subject to mundane happenings that differently influence individuals and the narratives by which they ideate and express their relations with people and place. The tension between consuming "authentic" foodstuffs and creating open-ended meals that emerges in Mann's poems as such also parallels a tension between nativist environmental storytelling and other forms of everyday environmentalism, demonstrating how both proceed from engagement with the same sort of object but differ depending on how writers represent it. Both routes take seriously various stakeholders' felt attachment to place—just as environmentalisms as distinct as explicit ecofascism and environmental justice do—but the second offers room for revision while the first essentializes and excludes, too often along existing lines of social inequity. When they focus on foraging or cooking rather than finished meals or isolated foodstuffs and their consumption, Mann's poems illustrate how food motifs offer strategies to writers seeking to negotiate or complicate identity, its relationship to environment and place, and its attendant hierarchies, rather than shore them up.

« 4 »

Drugs

Purifications of Mind, Body, and Earth in
Contemporary Psychedelia and Its Prophecies

[I]t is possible to cut beyond ego-consciousness . . . to
become aware of the enormous treasury of ancient
racial knowledge welded into the nucleus of every cell
in your body.

> —Timothy Leary, Ralph Metzner, and
> Richard Alpert, *The Psychedelic Experience*

The people in the chaos cannot learn. They cannot
understand what they are doing to the sea and the
sky and the plants and the animals. They cannot
understand that they are killing them, and that they
will end by killing themselves. . . . And when you tell
them to stop, they don't hear you. So there is only one
thing left to do. Either most of them must be cleared
away while there is still an earth . . . or all must die
when there are none of those things left.

> —Margaret Atwood, *MaddAddam*

The tension between authentic eating and alternative, future-
oriented functions of food emerges in recent fiction as well as
nonfiction. For one critic, it's a thematic thread running through
Margaret Atwood's MaddAddam trilogy, especially as it follows
the God's Gardeners, a religious sect that worships God-as-nature,
preaches vegetarianism and animal rights, and eschews private
property, as well as a group of scientists with connections to it. On
the one hand, "Gardener produce was the real thing. It stank of authenticity."[1] Vegetarianism, for the Gardeners, purifies the soul as

well as the body. On the other hand, as they establish themselves on an earth recently purged of *Homo sapiens* (most of them, at least), "this tenuous community survives precisely because they imagine and reimagine themselves into the future, with food serving as both the physical means and symbol of their . . . sustainability."[2] But in the novels, humanity's demise also takes place in the name of sustainability. Crake, a biotechnical prodigy and titular figure in the trilogy's first installment, *Oryx and Crake* (2003), chemically culls the population to preempt further anthropogenic damage to the planet, concerned that it might one day totally foreclose the possibility of life writ large.

Crake is in this respect representative of a certain class of twenty-first-century pop-culture villain. Thanos, the antagonist of Marvel Studios' ridiculously popular *Avengers* films, makes a similar decision: to wipe out half the universe's population to conserve resources for the remainder. 001 of the Netflix program *Stranger Things* aspires to a comparable (if broader) goal: to wipe out human life altogether, taking the role of predator against a species that hubristically presumes to have transcended the status of prey—and echoing Garrett Hardin's comments about the utility of predation as "negative feedback" in the process. Critics both popular and academic have branded such figures—Thanos, especially—as archetypes of ecofascism, in that they advocate mass human death (tacitly excepting themselves) in the name of ostensibly natural balance.[3] Based on the broad definition I offered in the Introduction, one might refer to this sort of scheme as the purest form of ecofascism, in that the inequity it produces (or upholds) comes down to two basic figures: only those who truly appreciate nature—however the speaker defines it—deserve to survive. Everyone else does not. It is the sort of argument that declares all humans responsible for degradation, despite vast differences in contributions to and experiences of, for example, climate change. The fact that this logic appeals to a broad viewership seems only to confirm what Alexander Reid Ross refers to as the "creep" of fascism into everyday speech: "Thanos was right" is a slogan that appears not only in Marvel's Disney+ program *Hawkeye*, but also on message boards across the Internet.

Despite his more limited reach, Crake has received similar acclaim. "There are some people who are wearing buttons that say 'Go Crake,' like a diminution of the world population might be a good thing," Atwood mentions in a 2013 interview—doubtless, she adds, because he "improved humankind" and "eliminated the problems that got us into this great mess we're in."[4] In the novels, Crake's goal is to in fact replace what he considers the inherently selfish and destructive human species (evoking Hardin yet again) with a more docile, ecologically friendly race through a feat of genetic engineering. He's not quite Thanos—more like Thanos crossed with Elon Musk, informed by the sort of eugenic thinking that undergirded early U.S. environmentalism. For Crake, it is freedom from language, art, and culture that renders his "Crakers" the privileged inheritors of the earth. Biologically deterministic and supposedly lacking signifiers of difference, the humanoids mesh seamlessly with each other and the earth. Notably, the Gardeners salute the same virtues. Such lack is the mark of unity with both nature and God. In an attempt to achieve that condition themselves, the Gardeners regularly ingest psilocybin, a psychoactive compound produced by over two hundred species of mushroom, throughout the trilogy.

The conspicuous consumption of psychedelic plants and fungi in the MaddAddam novels speaks to not only their resurgent, even mainstream, popularity but also the fact that media interest overwhelmingly (and often favorably) frames their ingestion as an environmentalist activity.[5] "If everyone tripped on psychedelics, we'd do more about climate change," declares the headline of an article published by Vice Media. "Anyone who has tripped—especially outdoors—knows that psychedelics . . . can provoke sensations . . . that nature is a part of us, our bodies, our lives, and that we are a part of it," it explains. "Capturing that might lead people to *act* to protect the planet, since the planet is an extension of themselves."[6] The mere publication of Vice's numerous stories on the subject vindicates Jesse Jarnow's contention that psychedelics have transcended "the hairy, unchecked madness of the sixties," having become not just tolerable but even stylish. Because many such substances are administered by spiritual guides or medical professionals, their use even "seems to resist" the antiestablishment impulse associated with the Western psychedelic use of generations past.[7] Their technocratic dispensation, naturally occurring ingredients, and history of spiritual application help to explain their popularity among a wellness culture characterized by an eagerness "for things like mindfulness, detoxification, and organic produce."[8]

Still, proponents continue to highlight the ability of psychedelics to profoundly disrupt normative conceptions of self, environment, and society. In a 1999 testimonial, a woman reported that under the influence of ayahuasca, or *yajé*, a decoction of the *Banisteriopsis caapi* vine and *Psychotria viridis* leaf native to South America, she perceived a "fabric being woven" by herself and fellow psychonauts "as we all focused on our own and the Earth's healing." "Mother Earth herself" spoke to another participant. A third explicitly intended to "explore and heal my relationship with the Earth."[9]

Such phenomena—experiences of not only direct communication with a personified nature under anthropogenic assault but also even subjective unity with it—are common in representations of psychedelic plant compounds such as psilocybin, *N,N*-Dimethyltryptamine (DMT, ayahuasca's active ingredient), and mescaline (found in peyote and San Pedro cacti). Activists, scientists, public intellectuals, and other writers have long pondered the capacity for such substances to "expand" consciousness, inviting a renewed appreciation for our interconnected, interdependent ecological condition. Some even describe this experience as "more real than real."[10] As one proponent writes, "You are the hallucination; the 'you' is illusory; the self is a fiction."[11] For such writers, what organic psychedelics reveal to us is that the social identities we take for granted not only get in the way of understanding nature but also aren't part of nature to begin with. They are artificial.

This chapter expands *Everyday Ecofascism*'s catalog of threshold objects by considering the social significance of psychedelic plant compounds and their current vogue as "valid antidotes to environmental destruction."[12] My goal is not to provide a comprehensive cultural history of their many uses and meanings, to vilify their clinical benefits, nor even to thoroughly explore scientific or philosophical explanations for their effects (although I do touch on these details throughout). Over the past thirty years, medical research has indeed demonstrated psychedelics' remarkable potential for addressing or easing addictions, anxiety, depression, and other conditions, in addition to fostering some degree of ecological consciousness.[13] My intention here, however, is to examine a specific tendency among some proponents to assert that psychedelics don't merely foster more nuanced perception of ecological interconnection but more specifically revert one to an ostensibly more authentic psychic condition. As always, my interest is in how people *talk* about these substances—and how certain ways of talking indeed abide by narrative conventions that prefigure eco-fascist violence. Across psychedelic literature, plant compounds frequently function as threshold objects. If certain representations of consuming food aim, as the last chapter demonstrated, to telegraph the natural strength and emplacement of one's body, then, likewise, particular ways of representing psychedelic drugs aim to communicate the purity of one's psyche.

Reading Atwood's MaddAddam trilogy alongside earnest psychedelic literature clarifies this intention and its effects, given that, as I argue, the novels critically dramatize both. By mixing mushrooms in brews with other materials—"just a pinch" of muscaria to "crinkl[e] the window glass that separates the visible world from whatever lies behind it"—the Gardeners cobble together a knockoff ayahuasca, similar to real-world gurus Terence and Dennis McKenna's combination of fungi and *B. caapi* bark, "the closest approximation" to DMT "that we have found in nature."[14] For both Atwood's characters and their counterparts, it is ecological crisis at a global scale—and the economic regime that catalyzes it in multifarious ways—that inspires psychedelic consumption to begin with. Eastern cities have already drowned under rising sea levels and seasons no longer quite exist in a United States ravaged by intense year-round heat, although these changes are recent enough that characters remember a time before them. The trilogy's first novel, *Oryx and Crake,* traces the execution of Crake's plan against this backdrop of rapid ecological change. *The Year of the Flood* (2009), the second, considers the same calamity from the vantage of the Gardeners, who seek to cultivate radical awareness of their ecological belonging through psychedelics in response to the same upheavals that inspire Crake's solution. The final volume, *MaddAddam* (2013), follows the survivors of the first two novels as they take their place in a rapidly rewilding ecosystem.

The trilogy as such resonates not only with the renewal of psychedelic environmentalism, but also with the nascent yet explosive genre of climate fiction or "cli-fi." Axel Goodbody and Adeline Johns-Putra divide such narratives into two categories: "[T]he first type tends to be set in a recognizable, realist present (or very near future) and the second in a futuristic climate-changed world, which one could characterize as apocalyptic, post-apocalyptic, or dystopian."[15] MaddAddam plays out along both tracks. Half of it focuses through flashback on a moment that is more or less our present, a socioeconomically familiar United States in the early to mid-twenty-first century. But in the novels, our present is already past: the trilogy's present is a postcivilization future. Total apocalypse has always been a "fabulously textual" phenomenon, to borrow Jacques Derrida's observation on nuclear warfare: as a world system–ending event—as opposed to the status quo–preserving experience of nuclear violence and its ecological fallout by peoples in the Pacific, for example—it is "persistently present but only as so many models and imaginings." The disaster in question has only come to pass in text. Molly Wallace suggests, however, that unlike nuclear annihilation, climate change (as well as the localized nuclear violence I just mentioned) is also "absolutely material, a product of expert assessment, media presentation, political accord, and public reception, as much as it is an interaction of CO_2 and methane gas in the atmosphere." As slow yet concrete anthropogenic shifts in climate stability and ecological resilience have largely supplanted the swift but uncertain threat of nuclear Armageddon, disaster fiction has increasingly taken the "slow apocalypse's" distended climax as its subject, such that "the question shifts from a contemplation of one's future nonexistence to a contemplation of the nature of one's continued existence."[16]

The Gardeners elevate such contemplation to a matter of religious importance, prophesying a devastating yet ultimately regenerative "Waterless Flood" that will restore the earth as a "new Eden" after "cleansing" it of human abusers. They also assume they themselves will "float above" the calamity, even as it "sweep[s] away" everyone else (*YF* 45–7). As for real-world millennialist movements, such as the environmentalist Just Collapse platform, liberation, for the Gardeners, is a foregone conclusion: the Flood will deliver their Eden no matter what they do. They intend to prepare for it, not to bring it about. They are, in this respect, representative of evangelical—and biocentric—millennialism of the past fifty years. Cults, deep ecologists, and other doomsayers can hardly "be described as popular, in the sense of either populist or representative," writes Michael Trask. "But that is partly [the] point. . . . Members of these movements belong to an elect, either permanently outside the lifeworld of their fellows or a vanguard that might blaze a path for at best a handful of them." Such figures derive their "saving singularity . . . from a brutal eliminationism: either a Malthusian winnowing of the human surplus . . . or a divine culling"—or both.[17] If 1970s communes viewed themselves as lighthouses, the Gardeners view themselves exclusively as arks.

They also view psychedelics as the means to both spiritual and material self-purification, rendering them the privileged survivors of the calamities at hand. Plant compounds facilitate this benediction by opening what Terence McKenna calls lines of "direct communication" between human and ecosystem, and what Adam One, the Gardeners' prophet, refers to as *"feeling directly"* (*YF* 235). The Gardeners do not themselves bring about calamity, but their zealous anticipation of a Flood that eliminates future human activity but spares their own represents an extreme embrace of biocentric preservation at the expense of a justice-oriented environmentalism that understands human welfare as part of ecological resilience. Crake might be an explicit ecofascist, but the Gardeners implicitly share his perspective. Atwood, I argue, juxtaposes them for a reason: to tease out the often-subtle ways such ideas take shape.

Reading millennial psychedelia through Atwood enables one to trace narratives about such ideas to their conclusions in other, real-world contexts, suggesting that the malaise central to much environmentalist use has shifted from a mood of countercultural liberation to one of anticipation: from a desire to restructure civilization to a resignation regarding its impending collapse. To an extent, such anticipation is characteristic of, for example, contemporary ayahuasca pilgrims, many of whom, the journalist Ariel Levy writes, believe psychedelics "will heal not only [themselves] but civilization at large" under the looming threat of climate catastrophes induced by humanmade technologies.[18] As this chapter will illustrate, for many (but certainly not all) Western psychedelic gurus, this salvation comes in the form of individual consumption. One achieves purity through personal acts of subjective union with the earth, distinguishing oneself from other, insufficiently ecological minds. In such accounts, civilization is doomed regardless—it even deserves to die. But the enlightened elect will survive to create a new one. I do not mean to suggest that middle-class *ayahuasqueros* basking in Manhattan yoga studios yearn for the Atlantic to swallow their city. What I mean to argue is that certain narrative connections among environmentalism, psychedelics, and consciousness reify the cultural patterns that condition ecofascist logics by at least implicitly advocating palingenetic violence in an environmentalist mode.

Still, it's also my contention that the MaddAddam trilogy, at least, reflects unfavorably on these tendencies. Atwood's oeuvre, from her debut *Edible Woman* (1969) to her recent nonfiction, has long displayed a sensitivity to cultural trends that glorify one or another contrived aspect of "nature," a habit that makes notable her 2008 comment that psychedelics have lately enjoyed "a period of being thought, if not totally harmless, at least fashionable."[19] Even her casual attention to this topic signals a cautious attitude. And it is significant that she largely presents the Gardeners' philosophy and history through the perspective of Toby, a skeptic rescued by Adam who senses "no solid evidence" for the Gardeners' foretold apocalypse—an observation that drives home the extent to which they not only expect but actively desire their Flood to occur. Atwood, the critic Hope Jennings writes, is "one of contemporary literature's most rigorous demythologizers of the Apocalypse, while at the same time contributing to its tradition of prophetic warning."[20] At least one other reader has suggested that Atwood uses the trilogy to "preach" the Gardeners' gospel of "environmental stewardship, sustainable living practices, and reverence for the interconnectedness of all living things."[21] These priorities are doubtless important to Atwood, but this interpretation understates the extent to which she critiques how the Gardeners *express* them, offering, as she does so, "a cautionary tale *about* our cautionary tales."[22] Through Toby, she dramatizes and demystifies the uncritical romanticism that so often animates the rhetoric of both the Gardeners and real-world environmentalist proponents of psychedelics. For the Gardeners, psychedelics furnish a mode of reconciliation with a damaged planet by providing an ego-dissolving psychic experience that not only apprehends but also equates unalienated subjectivity with what Stacy Alaimo describes as the body's "trans-corporeality," "the interconnections, interchanges, and transits between human bodies and nonhuman natures."[23] Crake's virus, packaged as a pharmaceutical, literalizes that dissolution, reducing human bodies to decaying matter. Atwood's novels draw lines of affinity between psychic and physical dissolution in the figure of the drug, illustrating the logical limits of psychedelic romance for any environmentalism that takes continued human life as one of its aims.

Consciousness Expansion for the End of the World

The McKenna brothers are but two representatives of a cadre of ethnobotanists and psychiatrists who kept psychedelics alive in U.S. writing after the passage of postwar sanctions against clinical research, which did not recommence until a 1996 Johns Hopkins study on psilocybin. Since then, psychedelics have enjoyed an unprecedented renaissance, not least for their therapeutic promise. Devotees have especially emphasized plant compounds' "unique ability for humans to realize that they are part of a much larger imbrication with the environment."[24] Organic chemistry informs this appraisal: plants interact with their ecosystems via messenger molecules derived from compounds similar to human neurotransmitters, such as serotonin, which enables them to interfere directly with the experience of consciousness. Psychedelic effects result when such compounds interface with the neural axon, producing a variety of experiences linked by what the Johns Hopkins psychiatrist William Richards refers to as "a common core of characteristics," including sensations of transcendence, unity with the surrounding world, and ineffability.[25]

Chemistry explains the cause of psychedelic experience. Interpretation of the effect, on the other hand, has been a subject of debate since the first Western encounters with psychoactive plant compounds and their synthetic derivatives. "Of course, the drug does not produce the transcendent experience," wrote Timothy Leary, Ralph Metzner, and Richard Alpert (later known as Ram Dass) in *The Psychedelic Experience* (1964), a manual that helped to popularize the use of psychedelics across the U.S. counterculture. "It merely acts as a chemical key—it opens the mind, frees the nervous system of its ordinary patterns and structures."[26] For the authors, the function of plant compounds and their synthetic counterparts, such as lysergic acid diethylamide (LSD), was not just psychedelic—that is, "mind manifesting"—but specifically *entheogenic,* capable of revealing spiritual truths both internal and external. The science journalist Michael Pollan suggests that these experiences have generated two broad explanations. The first is a

"firmly materialist understanding of consciousness and spirituality, because the changes observed in the mind can be traced directly to the presence of a chemical." But on the other hand, "If
the experience of transcendence is mediated by molecules that
flow through both our brains and the natural world of plants and
fungi, then perhaps . . . 'Spirit,' however defined, exists *out there*."[27]
Metzner, long after his graduate study under Leary and Alpert,
continued to preach the latter view: "The ultimate expanded state is
the 'cosmic consciousness,' or mystical oneness with the Divine . . .
in which all separateness is dissolved," he wrote in 2015. Though
he admitted that "such states are transient," he felt the glimpses
of eternity they offered to be both real and crucial for addressing
twenty-first-century problems: "Our worldviews need to expand to
become eco-centric," he writes, "if our civilization is to survive the
impending collapse of the planetary environment."[28]

This perspective animated a great deal of psychedelic experimentation during its heyday in the 1960s. And Leary and Metzner
were not alone in touting its virtues. Stewart Brand's Whole Earth
Network—whose *Catalog* was a subject of chapter 2—also did for
psychedelics what it did for other new technologies. Theodore
Roszak wrote not long after of the "short cut to Satori" that organic
and synthetic compounds alike seemed to offer. Like other "tools,"
psychedelic substances "allie[d] . . . disciples with the ancient,
the primitive, the tribal."[29] From the outset of their vogue in the
United States, psychedelics fulfilled the role of threshold object—a
function facilitated (as I'll discuss in further detail shortly) by the
association between psychoactive plants and Indigenous American
peoples, many of whom incorporated cacti and mushrooms in
their cultural traditions for centuries (possibly even millennia)
before European settler colonization (and continue to do so). As
I noted in previous chapters, U.S. counterculturalists celebrated
Native peoples (or romantic stereotypes of them) for spiritual as
well as practical reasons—that is, for their perceived harmony
with the nonhuman world as well as techniques for living with it.
Communalists "were already familiar with the power of psychedelics, LSD especially," Pollan writes. "But LSD was a synthetic
chemical." Peyote and psilocybin (and, today, ayahuasca), on the
other hand, "represented a more organic, authentic, ancient, and
New World alternative, and one with an Indigenous pedigree."[30]
In the face of an alienating economic and political system, psy-

chedelics of all sorts, but especially organic compounds, offered a direct means to authenticity, just as *Whole Earth*'s tools offered the practical means. Even Albert Hofmann, the Swiss chemist who synthesized LSD in 1938, greeted the movement's enthusiasm "as an understandable response to the emptiness of . . . a materialistic, industrialized, and spiritually impoverished society that had lost its connection to nature."[31]

But the mystical imagery of much psychedelic testimony— the Indigenous, Eastern, even Christian visionary resonances of the trip—often conflates interpretation with essence. "Because Hofmann's experiences with LSD are the only ones we have that are uncontaminated by previous accounts," Pollan writes, "it's interesting to note they exhibit neither the Eastern nor the Christian flavorings that would soon become conventions of the genre."[32] Even more interesting is the fact that, when introduced to psilocybin several years later by R. Gordon Wasson, the first Westerner to sample it under the guidance of a traditional Mazatec healer in Mexico, Hofmann perceived that "the exterior world began to undergo a strange transformation. Everything assumed a Mexican character."[33] Clinical research suggests that psychedelic experience is highly impressionable. If an experienced user, such as Leary, impresses upon a neophyte, such as a reader of *The Psychedelic Experience*, the inherently Eastern character of an LSD trip, chances are that novice will enjoy an orientalist experience. Aldous Huxley, in *The Doors of Perception* (1954), was the first Westerner to link, in popular media, mescaline with Eastern iconography. Ever since, nonnative descriptions of its effects overwhelmingly do the same. These patterns speak to the importance of "set" and "setting" to psychedelic experiences—one's "interiorized feelings, hopes, fears, and expectations" and the "external situation in which the interior journey will take place."[34] It was in fact Leary, Metzner, and Alpert who elaborated the twin principles—vital even in clinical trials today—in *The Psychedelic Experience*. "If the manual is read several times before a session is attempted, and if a trusted person is there," they write, "consciousness will be freed from the games which comprise 'personality.'"[35] Despite their insistence on the essentially revelatory nature of the trip, they admit to their own hand in influencing the reader's interpretation of it.

Set and setting matter, that is, not just in terms of the individual's mindset and immediate surroundings, but also in terms of cultural context. And psychedelics' explosion in the tumultuous climate of the 1960s is no exception. Foundational manuals such as Leary and his collaborators' set the set and setting, so to speak, for generations of psychonauts after them—and that includes the rhetoric in which commentary situates psychedelic experience. And the fetish for authenticity as a response to economic and political instability that earlier chapters considered, and which, as I mentioned above, anchored countercultural interest in psychedelics, has persisted in writing about plant compounds through the decades of federal sanctions and into the era of renewed popularity, even in the clinical literature. "When we expand our consciousness we liberate ourselves from the slavery . . . inherent in all cultural and institutional systems," the psychologist Richard Louis Miller writes, taking the 1960s tack and denying the influence of cultural narratives as (or, perhaps more accurately, because) he does so.[36] Even William Richards, the Johns Hopkins psychiatrist, takes aim at "constructivists" who "have posited that the experiences people call revelatory or religious are significantly influenced . . . by the implicit suggestions inherent in one's community." He "does not deny that some experiences . . . are colored by expectations and suggestions." But at the same time, he insists on the fundamental reality of what he calls "a state of . . . pure 'is-ness' . . . or primal being"—an essence that persists beneath a grime of cultural forms.[37]

There is a neurological explanation for both this sensation of "is-ness" and the conflation of interpretation with essence. Clinical research since the 1990s suggests that these compounds function primarily by shutting down the brain's default mode network (DMN), the "higher order" processes that most recently evolved in primates, develop later in childhood, and play a chief role in organizing "the creation of mental constructs or projections, the most important of which is the construct we call the self." Like the ego of Freudian psychoanalysis, the DMN inhibits certain functions of the brain, including centers of emotion and memory we might refer to as unconscious, but also "helps regulate what is let into consciousness from the world outside," limiting perception chiefly to what is necessary for survival and daily performance and thereby functioning as what Huxley referred to in *The Doors of Perception* as a "reducing valve" that psychedelics help open. Psychedelic compounds bind with receptors involved in DMN functions, not only facilitating greater awareness of details and relationships in the world, but also weakening the brain's knee-jerk distinction between subject and object. "The gulf between self and world, that no-man's-land which in ordinary hours the ego so vigilantly patrols, closes down," Pollan writes, "allowing us to feel less separate and more connected."[38] In a collection gathered by Metzner, one ayahuasca user testifies to such an experience. In a purgative flush, the "familiar identity" of his ego "beg[an] to fragment."[39] This blurring of ontological lines, Pollan adds, might also "explain another feature of the mystical experience: the fact that the insights it sponsors are felt to be objectively true." Cognitive scientists who study the dynamics between the DMN and psychedelics speculate that "to judge an insight as merely subjective . . . you must first have a sense of subjectivity. Which is precisely what the mystic on psychedelics has lost."[40] This function arguably reinforces the narrative tradition in which enthusiasts often frame psychedelics: as a matter of accessing psychic nature in spite of sociocultural scrum.

These narratives take on renewed relevance—and urgency—in the era of climate anxiety. Beset by deteriorating ecological predictability—and mental health—psychedelics appear to offer a solution. "The wisdom of the earth and the mushrooms can return people to a healthy state, on all the levels of their being," writes the spiritualist Françoise Bourzat. "Perhaps the greatest gift expanded states of consciousness offer is the opportunity to reconnect with the aspect of our self that is always already whole. Beyond the wounds and belief systems exists an original, essential being" that is inclusive of a harmonious natural world.[41] Stephen Harrod Buhner, another advocate for psychedelically informed wellness, similarly celebrates plant compounds' "capacity to make more porous the boundary between self and other, to begin to lose the distinction between self and nonself." For Buhner, doing so is a matter of reconciliation with a damaged earth. "All organisms are, in fact, forms, or more accurately *transforms,* of environment themselves," he writes. Denying this interconnection "immediately creates an experiential and interpretational disjunct between self and world."[42] Human individuals unquestionably comprise recycled matter that exists in constant interchange with other organisms—the condition Alaimo refers to as "trans-corporeality." But for Buhner, such circumstances are not merely biophysical. He takes seriously the concept of Gaia—not just James Lovelock's hypothesis that the earth constitutes a self-regulating thermodynamic system but also the cult spirituality it inspired—and with it, a tendency to collapse all life into subjective as well as material totality. Many "philosophers and scientists," Bourzat writes, "propose that consciousness arises from the brain . . . as a result of chemical and electrical impulses responding to internal and external influences." But in "another view, the brain and nervous system serve as organic antennae, picking up information like a radio receiver as we move through an ocean of consciousness."[43] She and Buhner subscribe to this latter explanation, a hallmark of the New-Age transpersonal school of psychology.

Bourzat herself acknowledges, however, how far the New-Age pastiche of "dreamwork, cross-cultural myths and archetypes, Eastern wisdom practices, and indigenous healing traditions" has fallen from the anticapitalist countercultural tree.[44] The social ecologist Murray Bookchin wrote retrospectively, in 1984, that the counterculture's fixation on authentic "personalism" rendered it especially susceptible to mass commercialization, including in the form of "healing practices," Bourzat writes, that are now "sought after to the extent that they . . . have a capitalist sector of their own: the wellness industry."[45] Ayahuasca has skyrocketed in popularity ever since the União do Vegetal (Union of the Plants) church won a 2006 religious freedom case at the U.S. Supreme Court. (Federal agents appear to have ceased prosecution of import, possession, and use in the years since.) As psychedelic wellness and tourism boom, however, side effects proliferate. Shoddy product and charlatan "shamans" have instigated bad trips and in some cases even death. And as underground demand for peyote rises, Indigenous communities fear the purely recreational decimation of the few remaining wild populations of the culturally significant cactus (a fate that crowds of hippies visited upon them after the publication of Carlos Castaneda's 1968 *The Teachings of Don Juan*).[46]

Beyond these medical, ecological, and cultural impacts, it is also unclear what the individualistic wellness approach to psychedelia offers climate politics. After his post-psilocybin "integration," one of Bourzat's clients "focused on personal choices, as far as the pollutants he was using. He rethought detergents, recycling, and carpooling"—admirable lifestyle choices, of course, but ineffectual absent a more robust political framework.[47] Buhner goes so far as to mock collective action, locating the solution to climate change entirely in "a deep belief and trust in the individual" he inherited from the 1960s.[48] This premium on self-optimization seems primed to shore up the neoliberal status quo, not disrupt it. By "combining two separate civic religions—purification and consumerism"—the wellness industry, the science journalist Elanor Cummins writes, "has allowed people to purchase spiritual indulgences without modifying their behavior."[49]

The psychedelic trip is a profoundly individual experience—no two people will experience it quite the same way—no matter the supposedly universal and natural "is-ness" many enthusiasts claim it uncovers. But accessing that authentic, Gaian subjectivity itself becomes a matter of self-optimization in a great deal of psychedelic environmentalism. Some researchers even hypothesize that consumption of psychedelics imparts an evolutionary advantage. At least one suggests that "during times of rapid environmental change or crisis it may avail the survival of a group when a few of its members abandon their accustomed conditioned responses and experiment with some radically new and different behaviors." In this view, consciousness expansion functions as genetic mutation: "[M]ost of these novelties will prove disastrous," but some "might end up being useful, helping the individual, the group, and possibly the species to adapt to rapid changes in their environment." In an era of massive anthropogenic ecological change, "*Homo sapiens* might have arrived at one of those periods of crisis that calls for some mental and behavioral depatterning."[50] Buhner subscribes to this theory as well. "The restructuring of neural nets and the resetting of sensory gating . . . allow[s] more sophisticated responses to unforeseen environmental events," he writes.[51] Consuming psychedelics, he suggests, not only grants access to an expansive, authentic state of consciousness but also imparts a special capacity to survive and thrive in the face of extinction—not necessarily as a species but as an enlightened individual. As Appalachian foods do for Jeff Mann, psychedelics signify for spiritualists like Buhner a certain vitality or strength—one based on access to a condition of psychic purity.

MaddAddam's "Perfect Human Beings"

A subtle yet persistent emphasis on wellness and neoliberal self-fashioning runs through the novels of Atwood's MaddAddam trilogy. Jimmy, the protagonist of the first volume, writes copy for self-help manuals at a wellness corporation whose brand "min[es] arcane secrets from Wiccan moon-worshipers and from shamans deep in the . . . rainforests" (*MA* 249). Jimmy is no fool: "It wasn't these instructionals as such that generated the cash surplus," he notes, but "the equipment and the alternative medicines you needed in order to get the optimum effect" (*OC* 245). The God's Gardeners, too, are wise to the profit motive behind the wellness industry and the designer drugs it hawks, which they pass over in favor of all-natural DMT and psilocybin. These they associate with Gaian harmony—a "new Eden"—no less than the psychedelic gurus of the New Age. "There were mushrooms for eating, mushrooms for medicinal uses, and mushrooms for visions," the character Toby notes. Upon meeting her, the Gardener prophet Adam muses that she's "grown a callous and hard shell" after years of economic and sexual violence. "But that shell is not your true self." Later, after years of apprenticing with the sect's healer—and sampling, it is suggested, her mushrooms—Toby "breathe[s] herself in. . . . Her skin smelled like . . . earth" (*YF* 40, 100–1). Psychedelics facilitate her discovery of a "true" self beneath the "shell" of a false one—and she identifies that authentic self with the planet as a whole.

Gardener psychedelics perform an entheogenic function, enabling them to commune with the ecosystem writ large in conjunction with religious "Feasts" honoring environmentalist "saints" like "Dian the Martyr" and "Linnaeus of Biological Nomenclature." God serves as analogue for system: "Insofar as you do it unto the least of God's Creatures," Adam preaches, "you do it unto him." Members ritually give thanks to food before "joining its protein" to theirs (*YF* 53, 135). The two paths of psychedelic interpretation that Pollan mentions—the material and the transpersonal—unite in Gardener spirituality. Adam urges his flock to seek "the wisdom of *feeling directly,* as the serpent feels vibrations in the Earth" and "lives in immediacy, without the need for the elaborate intellectual frameworks Humankind is constructing for itself." The serpent's "Feast" arguably best captures the Gardener perspective on both spirituality and ecological materiality, as well as psychedelics. Who can tell, Adam asks, where a snake's "head ends and its body begins? . . . This then is the Serpent Wisdom we long for—this wholeness of Being. May we greet with joy the few moments when, through . . . the assistance of God's Botanicals, we are granted an apprehension of it" (*YF* 234–5). Their ideal is an unmediated state of psychic continuity with environment they ascribe to nonhuman animals—one that, due to its freedom from artificial human "frameworks," signifies a purity both spiritual and ecological—and psychedelics offer them a glimpse.

What is striking in the novels, however, is the extent to which the rhetoric of psychedelic self-fashioning resonates with Crake's project as well as the Gardeners' creed. One of the goals of psychedelic therapy, Bourzat writes, is to set concrete goals to manage what she and others refer to as "external chaos" in a way that improves how one's "environment affect[s] them energetically and emotionally."[52] In Jimmy's account to Crake's bioengineered "children," their creator's aim was the same at a grander scale. "In the chaos, everything was mixed together," he explains. "There were too many people . . . full of chaos themselves, and the chaos made them do bad things. They were killing other people all the time. And they were eating up all the Children of Oryx"—that is, animals. "Crake took the chaos, and he poured it away" (*OC* 103). If chaos is Crake's problem, eugenics is his solution. Something similar can be said for certain examples of psychedelic rhetoric as well. "Psychedelic medicine can facilitate our using the power of the mind to change our very genetic structure," Richard Miller writes. "We can change . . . outrageous genetic misfortune into a cupid's bow of a sculpted self."[53] Aspirational self-improvement emerges in the trilogy as a link joining psychedelic environmentalism with corporate biotechnology and Crake's eugenics. Even if the Gardeners locate themselves beyond the plot's neoliberal milieu, the novels emphasize the extent to which their narratives draw from similar assumptions about self-optimization, which leave the actors and systems most responsible for ecological disasters untouched.

Atwood herself, however, clearly recognizes the role played by socioeconomic conditions in both the planet's deteriorating ecological situation and Crake's turn to violence to solve it, in the context of both the trilogy and the real world she wrote it in. "Atwood is close enough to recent headlines," an NPR review remarks, "to make her invented universe believable."[54] The critic refers not just to the bioengineering breakthroughs depicted in the series, but also, in the wake of the U.S. Supreme Court's 2010 decision in *Citizens United v. FEC*, the fact that corporate power has totally usurped local and federal government authority in the novels, to say nothing of civilian oversight or civil rights and liberties. A corporate security force operates as both executive and legislature, serving business interests at the expense of citizen-consumers', spying on company employees, executing environmentalist and labor agitators for "treasonable crimes against society" and "hampering the dissemination of commercial products" (which are one and the same), and broadcasting punishments for additional revenue (OC 286). Critics customarily refer to this setting as dystopian, in keeping with Atwood's stated fascination with classical fascist regimes—that is, fascism in terms of a strong authoritarian state—in her earlier works, such as The Handmaid's Tale (1985). The critic Chris Vials suggests, however, that the trilogy invites readers to instead "imagine a capitalism that achieves . . . authoritarian ends without the intervention of a centralized state."[55] It dramatizes, that is, the sort of "fascist creep" (to again borrow Alexander Reid Ross's language) that I described in the Introduction: a slow, popular erosion of rights and liberties in reaction to economic dislocations occasioned by capitalist accumulation—one that targets racialized others rather than accumulation itself, thereby ultimately reinforcing the inequities it generates. Atwood dramatizes this exact sort of sequence. The novels constantly allude to global injustices involving labor and autonomy, as when a major coffee conglomerate aggressively expands into regions already characterized by imperialist monoculture, automates its operation, and renders workers and wages obsolete, forcing whole populations into poverty and sparking resistance that security forces mercilessly quell. Those wealthy enough to do so wall themselves off from the "pleeblands" they exploit in corporate "Compounds," racialize and demonize the penniless, disgruntled masses outside, and boost police violence for the sake of their own security and profits—a shot-for-shot allegory of Garrett Hardin's "lifeboat ethics." The trilogy's regimes of corporate malfeasance and racialized punishment of the poor, however extreme, reflect the conditions of our own world—the very same circumstances that inspire crypto-fascist movements in the twenty-first century.

Coupled with MaddAddam's climate crises, those conditions are, not incidentally, the same to which both Crake and the Gardeners respond. "As a species we're in deep trouble, worse than anyone's saying," Crake tells Jimmy. "Demand for resources has exceeded supply for decades in marginal geopolitical areas, hence the fam-

ines and droughts; but very soon, demand is going to exceed supply *for everyone*" (*OC* 295). The lifeboat ethics of the Compounds is
in part a reaction to the same situation—an example of what has
come to be called "climate security." In the novels as well as actual
U.S. media and federal defense reports, "climate refugees" loom
large as a driving force of ecological and economic destabilization
rather than as symptoms of them. "Alarm bells over the coming 'climate wars' find a powerful echo chamber in the military-industrial
complex," Betsy Hartmann notes. Such narratives "tap into and
reinforce racialized fears of the poor" inside as well as outside the
boundaries of the normative nation-state.[56] Crake represents an
extreme reaction to this prospect. The novels' socioeconomic context clearly drives both climate disruption and social violence, but
Crake—comfortable in his Compound, witnessing pleeblander
crime from afar—attributes them to biology. "*Homo sapiens*," he
argues, is "one of the few species that doesn't limit reproduction
in the face of dwindling resources," a problem he believes compounded by an innate selfishness he blames for all historical atrocities (*OC* 120). He neglects the fact that, as later novels dramatize,
pleeblander crime arises not from who the poor inherently are but
from patterns of systemic deregulation, privatization, and extreme
wealth inequality in which he participates. If Crake can be called a
fascist, it's because he targets people rather than structures and
does so in a way that reinforces his own power. *All* humans are
the problem because, for him, violence and ecological depletion are
matters of biology.

As such, his solution is mainly eugenic. To address "the biggest
problem of all, which was human beings," he determines to breed
out perceived defects in the next generation and murder everyone else (*YF* 305). Using corporate resources (and kidnapped scientists) he first creates and markets the BlyssPluss pill, which he
bills as a sexual enhancement supplement but privately describes
in overtly biopolitical terms: unbeknownst to consumers, it will
"act as a sure-fire one-time-does-it-all birth-control pill . . . thus
automatically lowering the population level" (*OC* 294). Forced
sterilization—specifically of Brown and poor populations—has
been a mainstay of eugenic population management. But Crake's
ambitions are even greater. The pill serves as the vector for an en-
hanced hemorrhagic virus that, once seeded, spreads rapidly, all
but wiping out *Homo sapiens* in a matter of weeks. Crake's "move,"

the critic Heather Sullivan writes, "is to carry out . . . genocide . . . thereby making slow violence 'fast.'"[57]

He also genetically engineers a new population to replace the old, borrowing characteristics from several animal and even plant species according to what he considers "efficient" for survival. The Crakers are "admirably proportioned," physically fit and universally sexually attractive, "each one naked, each one perfect" (*OC* 100, 8). They copulate only in heat: "there's no more . . . shadow between the desire and the act. . . . No more *No means yes*" (OC 165). Worth noting is the similarity between Crake's handiwork and Weston's impression of Marissa in *Ecotopia,* whose unbothered sexuality strikes him as an expression not only of her freedom from repression but also of natural womanhood. Crake doesn't make his choices in a vacuum. *Oryx and Crake* continually hints at the extent to which cultural assumptions organize his eugenic project (as they do *any* eugenic project). Compulsory heterosexuality isn't the only thing he hard-wires. He also inscribes normative gender roles. Craker men scent-mark and participate in deliberations with humans. Women, by contrast, "tak[e] no part in the conversation" (*YF* 411). He renders social differences true matters of biology, making a self-fulfilling prophecy of eugenic thinking. His ample exposure to pornography as a young man seems to have influenced him as much as zoobiology: "No ripples of fat" disturb the women's skin. "No body hair, no bushiness. They look like retouched fashion photos, or ads for a high-priced workout program" (*OC* 100).

Cultural assumptions and personal preference both play a role—an ironic detail, given that Crake's primary goal is to eliminate culture as such. *"Watch out for art,"* he warns Jimmy. As soon as the Crakers *"start doing art, we're in trouble.* Symbolic thinking of any kind would signal downfall. . . . Next they'd be inventing idols" and "kings, and then slavery and war" (*OC* 361). His obstruction of humanistic tendencies—art, religion, argument—manifests his desire to reduce the human to biology. Most ambitiously, he attempts to prohibit symbolic language, the entire concept of which confuses the Crakers. When Toby tries to teach one how to write his name, he responds, "That is not me. . . . It is only some marks" (*MA* 203). Despite their ability to speak, the Crakers struggle to comprehend the utility of a mediating system between idea and world. Crake believes he has eliminated their need to represent and even think about biological needs. Instead, they ostensibly communicate with each other (and other species) through the kind of direct, organic correspondence the Gardeners make central to their spirituality. He believes, in short, that he's wiped out the DMN, as psychedelics do in the short term.

Symbolic language, Crake reasons, lies at the root of all "the destructive features . . . responsible for the world's current illnesses" (OC 305). He's not alone in his distrust. Though they might seem strange bedfellows, a plethora of real-world anarcho-primitivist thinkers (to whom I return in the next chapter) similarly singled out not just capitalism—and not even just civilization writ large—but language itself as the root of both human depravity and environmental destruction in the second half of the twentieth century. Figures such as Kirkpatrick Sale and, more recently, John Zerzan have targeted specifically language's facilitation of abstract thought—a source, for both, of alienation from a state of nature. Blair Taylor points out the degree to which such thinking not only draws from "shared intellectual sources"—namely, Martin Heidegger—but even "mirrors Nazi discourse . . . identify[ing] Jews with the ills of abstraction and modernity."[58] (Zerzan, for his part, is not only a friend of Ted Kaczynski's but also a fixture on alt-right message boards.) Crake's thinking parallels these others', and, believing himself to have suppressed the Crakers' capacity for linguistic representation, he celebrates his creation of the "perfect human being" (YF 305).

The Gardeners likewise see language as the regrettable hallmark of human ontology. Their voluntary primitivism also resonates with the anarcho-primitivists' "palingenetic impulse coupled with romantic longing for a prelapsarian universe of authenticity and ecological harmony unsullied by the corruption of modernity."[59] The prophet Adam pontificates on the "multidimensional" Fall of Man: "The ancestral primates fell out of the trees; then they fell from vegetarianism into meat-eating . . . from instinct into reason, and thus into technology; from simple signals into complex grammar, and thus into humanity" (YF 88). Language, for Adam, marks a human disadvantage that distinguishes the species from other creatures. "Our appetites, our desires . . . Our Fall from the original Garden was a Fall from the innocent acting-out of such patterns and impulses," he preaches. "What commandment did we disobey? The commandment to live the Animal life in all simplicity" (YF 52). If language were stripped away, humans would be less distinguishable from other creatures and ostensibly behave less cruelly toward their kin.

Crake tries (and—spoiler alert—fails) to reverse this Fall into symbolic language not just by engineering the Crakers but also by making a human tabula rasa of earth (in a laboratory he nicknames "Paradice," no less). The world they inherit is to be a garden—an example of what Sullivan refers to as "dark pastoral," a "version of a damaged yet rejuvenating Earth" replete with "thriving, vibrant, and fecund realms of greenery" that "relies on an almost total obliteration of humanity."[60] In yet another conjunction with Crake, the Gardeners' faith anticipates this scenario: "Take comfort in the thought that" humans "will soon be swept away by the Waterless Flood"—an unspecified calamity, but one that accords with the Gardeners' Christian inspiration (which borrows elements from Genesis and Revelations) and their environmentalist definition of sin (*YF* 312). "We God's Gardeners are a plural Noah: we too have been . . . forewarned," Adam preaches. "We can feel the symptoms of coming disaster. We must be ready for the time when those who have broken trust . . . will be swept away" (*YF* 91).

The Gardeners, like Crake, in this respect also attribute eco-logical disruption to humanity writ large—except themselves, of course—at the expense of humans who most suffer not only its effects but also the profit motive that has historically induced it. When Adam notes that "some of our more radical former mem-bers" have demonstrated against the coffee monopoly I mentioned before, he adds that "[o]ther groups were protesting its treatment of indigenous workers, but those ex-Gardeners were protesting its anti-Bird policies" (*YF* 372). The line is quick but significant. It establishes clearly that social concerns lie beyond the Gardeners' interest, precisely because they so stringently divorce the social from the natural, the symbolic from the ecological. Such narrow biocentrism has, in the past, characterized movements like deep ecology and related organizations like Earth First!, both of which have attracted criticism not for their investment in the intrinsic worth of nonhuman life, or even for their argument that a long-term reduction in human population is necessary to protect it, but for their tendency, especially in the 1980s and 1990s, to recom-mend eugenic measures to accomplish that goal, such as steriliza-tion or disease. Such resonances sharpen the discursive connection between the Gardeners and Crake in the novels. Given the fact that the first two volumes feature scenes in which they trade in corporate secrets, the trilogy even leaves open the possibility that they collaborate—a link the final volume disproves. Crake works alone.

The Gardeners' Flood, then, seems less like a matter of insider knowledge than a function of Kyle Whyte's "crisis epistemology." Hartmann calls it the "America syndrome," an apocalyptic narrative tradition she argues has animated U.S. culture and politics—especially the notion of U.S. exceptionalism—since Puritan settlement. "Despite the official separation of church and state, religious axioms thread through the fabric of American political culture," she writes. "Pessimistically, we are headed toward a violent end. Optimistically, a golden millennium awaits us." Adam explicitly inherits this jeremiad tradition, having grown up in his father's evangelical church. Atwood's choice of the United States as setting is doubly precise in this sense: it foregrounds not just global capitalism but also apocalypticism. Across U.S. history—from settler-colonial expansion to the contemporary rise of the far right—that narrative has rhetorically functioned to sanction cruelty. "To reach our God-given destiny, war"—or plague—is "justified," Hartmann writes. "This land is our land, not yours or theirs. . . . Those who don't conform don't belong, and should be punished or banished." As a storytelling tradition, elements of this narrative circulate across conventional partisan lines, most recently in climate rhetoric. One of the "strongest legacies" of Al Gore's genre-defining 2006 documentary *An Inconvenient Truth* "was to make disaster imagery a . . . staple of our cultural imagination of climate change," not only enmeshing it with existing apocalyptic rhetoric in the United States but also translating it for the contemporary left. In many expressions of left millennialism, like those of the Just Collapse organization I mentioned previously, climate collapse will "redeem us of our sins. Those who embrace the radical apocalypse will be saved."[61]

For this reason, it is the *possibility* of collaboration between Crake and the Gardeners—the fact that their active involvement in humanity's genocide seems plausible—that is important. "All the real Gardeners believed the human race was overdue for a population crash," Adam's brother Zeb comments. "It would happen anyway, and maybe sooner was better" (*MA* 330). At the same time, the Gardeners fancy themselves "a plural Noah": "A massive die-off of the human race was impending, due to overpopulation

and wickedness, but the Gardeners exempted themselves: they intended to float above the Waterless Flood" (*YF* 91, 47). If the trilogy's Compounds are lifeboats, each individual Gardener is an ark:
"When the Waterless Waters rise . . . the people will try to save
themselves from drowning." If "you are clutched or even touched,
you too will drown" (*YF* 21). "This land," for the Gardeners, is the
planet itself, and those who "should be punished or banished" are
the insufficiently enlightened—the insufficiently ecological, in material as well as spiritual terms. The "perfect human beings" worthy
of survival are those stripped of cultural forms, "*feeling directly.*"
Happily, the Gardeners have a tool they believe can help them
achieve that condition themselves. According to the stories they—
and many real-world psychonauts—tell about them, psychedelic
plants and fungi furnish such threshold objects. For the Gardeners
as well as their counterparts, to consume a mushroom is to regur-
gitate Eve's apple: to make a "perfect human being" of oneself.

Psychedelic Dissolutions of Language, Self, and Society

Atwood's Gardeners indulge a charming idea, espoused foremost
by the McKenna brothers, that the consumption of DMT or mushrooms enables human and plant or fungus to converse. "If the plant
really is talking to the person, many people hear the same thing:
we are all one," Ariel Levy writes. "Some believe that the plants delivering this message are serving their own interests, because if
humans think we are one with everything we might be less prone
to trash the natural world. . . . But this sensation of harmony and
interconnection with the universe—what Freud described as the
'oceanic feeling'—is also a desirable high."[62] Levy's reference to
Sigmund Freud obliquely nods toward the striking abundance of
psychoanalytic terminology coursing through psychedelic discourse in both clinical and autobiographical literature—an influence that continues to animate Western gurus' ideas about self,
symbolic representation, and civilization itself.

Postwar psychotherapists such as Ralph Metzner believed that
psychedelics, coupled with "more or less standard interactions using a Freudian perspective," can "loosen" the patient's ego defenses
so that he or she might "become more vividly aware of his or her
previously unconscious emotional dynamics."[63] This perspective
was not limited to clinical trials, and the association persisted past

their retrenchment in the 1960s. What the McKennas term "the shamanic function" of ayahuasca healing "also includes a psycho-analytic capability," the enactment of a "participation therapy of the most sophisticated type."[64] The ego, Terence writes, "developed" from earlier forms of consciousness "as a necessary means of adapting to socialization." But it has also become such a detriment to ourselves and our environment that we must "reconnect" with "a globally conscious, ecologically sensitive . . . kind of consciousness that we can access only . . . through self-discipline, psychotherapy, [and] psychedelics."[65] Long before McKenna's writing, this ambitious "shift in the objective of psychedelic research from psychotherapy to cultural revolution" was, Pollan writes, "well under way."[66] The academic thrust of psychedelic research in the postwar era trended toward two applications scholars viewed as intimately related: the healing of neurotic minds and liberation of "normal" ones. DMT and psilocybin, McKenna argues, can unlock "the real power of the unconscious" lurking beneath a repressively civilized ego.[67] His call for psychic reorganization is a dual mandate for psychic and social liberation—a recovery of the repressed that would also resuscitate a lost, primitive mode of social organization—of a piece with the 1960s counterculture. In his introduction to *The Psychedelic Experience,* Daniel Pinchbeck notes that its authors also excoriate the "selfish . . . ego-game." "Apparently," he writes, "the tripper's nefarious ambitions to succeed in the game-worlds of modern life needed to be purged in the hallucinatory fire of the entheogenic encounter." Timothy Leary and his associates, Pinchbeck writes, "seem mired in a Puritanical and sin-stained conception of the individual."[68]

It does not take a cult, in other words, to situate psychedelic experience within apocalyptic narratives. Atwood may well have paired the two together in the MaddAddam trilogy due to their existing resonance. Proponents of psychedelics have long deployed a familiar story arc: that of a golden, precivilizational past, a disastrous present, and a future potentially glorious only insofar as it resembles the past. Civilization's inherent corruption (and inevitable fall) were mainstays of 1960s and 1970s countercultural utopianism. When filtered through a psychoanalytic idiom, such ideas made dissolving the ego, for some, appear not just an experiment but an ethical imperative: "Liberation is the nervous system devoid of mental-conceptual activity," Leary writes.[69] This idea has persisted in psychedelic literature ever since. "*Any* behavioral actions taken that are based on the mistaken experience that organisms are not environment," Stephen Buhner writes, "will disturb . . . the Gaian system." Thankfully, psychedelic plant compounds "regenerate . . . natural childlike feelings of empathy, the direct experience of the personhood of the nonhuman other, by altering sensory gating" such that "the boundaries between self and other thin" or "*disappear entirely.*"[70] Psychedelic utopianism is, in this respect, a palingenetic as well as structurally jeremiad discourse.

Given the dynamic between the DMN and psychedelics, clinical support indeed exists for the notion that they "return us to the psychological condition of the infant on its mother's breast, a stage when it has yet to develop a sense of itself as a separate and bounded individual."[71] But the cultural significance of this "regression" depends on the meaning with which people invest it, and Buhner's recommendation above participates in a long, predominant tradition in psychedelic literature that equates primordial infancy, undeveloped psyche, and nature. Richard Schultes and Albert Hofmann, in their 1979 primer *Plants of the Gods,* identify a "return to the maternal womb, to the source and origin of all things," as the true goal of ayahuasca ritual.[72] In a series of "yage letters" exchanged with William Burroughs, Allen Ginsberg describes "seeing or feeling what I thought was the Great Being, or some sense of It, approaching my mind like a big wet vagina."[73] Terence McKenna even tags the *Stropharia cubensis* mushroom as "the Ur plant, our umbilicus to the feminine mind of the planet." Through the reinvigoration of psychedelic ritual, we might resurrect a "preindustrial and preliterate . . . attitude toward community, substance use, and nature" that, for McKenna, survives in "feminine, foreign and exotic, and transcendental experiences."[74] For Buhner, "when we return to this world, something from the other remains inside us. It makes us truly barbarian, no longer civilized."[75]

Many of these writers evoke a litany of sliding associations among women, "exotic" racial others, infancy, and the land, bound up in a vision of lost psychic and social freedom. McKenna, among others, often pointed to Indigenous traditions to back up his claims, suggesting that Native peoples by default exemplify unrepressed, unmediated, infantile identification with environment.

"The natural world," for Bourzat, "is part of their psyche."[76] The psychiatrist Charles Grob notes that at "a time of psychoanalytic preeminence," shamanic healers "were judged to be mentally ill."[77] That "illness" is the point for psychedelics' most fervent devotees, who continue to embrace the notion that Native knowledge includes the psychedelic secret to "erasing established patterns of behavior by letting the ego melt under its influence."[78] Though celebratory, this interpretation of Indigenous lifeways not only homogenizes them but also perpetuates settler-colonial narratives that "uncivilized," infantilized peoples somehow exist outside of social forms, including cultural traditions of their own (such as the customs that make meaning of psychedelic use) as well as the devastating effects and legacies of settler colonialism.[79] Rather than recognize the central role played by ritual storytelling—or cultural mediation more generally—in Indigenous relations with environment and psychedelics, this Western narrative reduces complex histories and formations to a matter of essence. It plays out largely as an appropriative fantasy, a romantic celebration of feminized, primitive societies and their special botanical knowledge enabling subjective unity with the earth. "Underneath . . . human experience there is a deeper identity, one that all organisms on this planet share," Buhner writes. Under the influence of psychedelic compounds, "the particular view of the world that we have accepted from Western science, historical markers, family stories, our personal biography . . . are gone."[80] But one can only equate Indigenous Americans with the first of these conditions if one believes that non-Western peoples do not constitute cultures to begin with—and celebrating freedom from repression in the abstract also obscures the concrete realities of Native life in the United States, including lived conditions of environmental racism.

This collapse of cultural difference into a universal "deeper identity" speaks to the fact that "one of the many paradoxes of psychedelics" is "that these drugs can sponsor an ego-dissolving experience that in some people quickly leads to massive ego inflation," Pollan writes—a point that intersects with the apocalyptic narrative: "Having been let in on a great secret of the universe, the recipient of this knowledge is bound to feel special, chosen for great things."[81] Combined with the notion that psychedelics strip away a false, civilized self to reveal a truer, natural one, this tendency gives shape to the sort of apocalyptic distinctions Hartmann mentions: that there are also false and true people, those who do not belong and those who do. That "ego inflation" might have more banal effects as well—for example, on tone. Humans "need to transcend our consciousness—to go to the other side of cognition . . . as well as language," one self-styled guru recently wrote. "*You are the hallucination . . . the self is a fiction.* If that is too difficult for you to digest then I suggest that you stay clear of ayahuasca and DMT." Pompous self-importance aside, this spiritualist offers a representative example of the narratives surrounding what it is psychedelics *do* to strip away the fiction of the self. "[I]f you study Lacan then you would agree that language actually alienates us from phenomena," he writes. "Whatever you can formulate in words is not Real; words are mere symbolic and distant representations."[82] It's an accurate enough interpretation of Jacques Lacan's theory of psychoanalysis, although if you study Lacan, you also know that linguistic representation (oral and visual-symbolic) is not a condition one can escape—which is precisely what this writer claims psychedelics and spiritual traditions such as Advaita Vedanta can enable one to do (as if Advaita Vedanta were not itself an interpretive cultural frame).

Still, language seems to be the barrier between false self and true nonself that many gurus hope to transcend, although it stands in complicated relationship in these narratives to psychedelics themselves, alternately cast as the origin and bane of symbolic representation. Terence McKenna was the first to propose the infamous "stoned ape" theory, according to which prehistoric ingestion of fungi prompted a unique experience of synesthesia that, somehow, biologically imprinted in the form of linguistic capacity. Like consciousness, language itself seems, in the McKenna brothers' accounts, a transpersonal property of the universe. Tripping on *S. cubensis*, Dennis responded to a faint "buzzing" sound by trying "*to imitate these noises with my vocal cords.*" After a while, "*the sound and my voice locked onto each other and the sound was my voice.*" Language, the brothers suggest, is external to the human subject, a system in which individuals become implicated first through psychedelic experimentation and then through socialization. In the primeval human past, this prelinguistic humming "waveform" produced consciousness "holographically" by "encoding" sensory perception in the brain, though the resulting image "bears little resemblance to the object photographed."[83] The reference to Lacan above does seem relevant. The brothers' theories reflect the psychoanalyst's insistence on an incommensurability between human signification and the real objects it represents. They also evoke the Lacanian mirror stage, in which the ego forms in infancy as an imaginary image with which the subject identifies as an "I" within the symbolic order. All subsequent perception filters through the symbolic register. The McKennas, too, believe the human ego to be a construction predicated on symbolic language, generated by the transpersonal universe but nonetheless an obstacle to directly interfacing with it. If tryptamines gave rise to the conscious ego, however, they can also undo it by revealing and breaking down its construction, collapsing the distinction between symbol and referent and establishing "channels of direct communication with the Other."[84] By breaking down the chain of signification, psychedelics break apart the ego that is a product of that chain, enabling the brothers to better interface with their surroundings.

The God's Gardeners of Atwood's MaddAddam trilogy expect precisely this function from psychedelics as well, as a means of experiencing oneself as conterminous with the ecosystem by interfacing with plant matter at the neurological level. During her first psychedelic Vigil, Toby pays particular attention to what she perceives as nonhuman languages enunciated by the "crickets nearby, speaking in tongues." This perception gives way to soundless communion with a golden animal "with gentle green eyes and canine teeth" (YF 171). Toby's initial perception of diverse animal language bleeds into a vision of direct transference of information. As language dissolves during the trip, so too does the distinction between Toby and the golden animal. Toby nonetheless confronts the creature with chemical sensibility: "You are the effect of a carefully calibrated blend of plant toxins," she tells it. Other Gardeners, however, take the experience more literally, as a means to "feeling directly" in their everyday lives, like the individuals, Richard Miller writes, who "have already trained themselves to move through daily life and do critical thinking under the effects of large doses of LSD." Still, he adds, only traditional Indigenous "shamans function with volitional intention under the influence of ayahuasca"—the sort of plant compound the Gardeners prefer.[85] This exclusivity is, however, arguably the point for the characters, as well as for the sort of real-world psychonauts who romanticize Indigenous peoples' ostensible psychic continuity with environment at the expense of historical conditions. The Crakers, Jimmy notes, are "a whole new take on *indigenous*" (*OC* 97). Much later, another character speculates that Crake himself would "have seen the Crakers as indigenous people, no doubt . . . And *Homo sapiens sapiens* as the greedy, rapacious Conquistadores" (*MA* 140). If Crake hoped to re-create a romantic vision of primitive, prelinguistic indigeneity, the Gardeners aim to achieve it—to become indigenous to the earth, as it were. All other humans appear unworthy to survive the Flood by contrast.

But Toby's persistent skepticism signals that the trilogy, from the outset, reflects critically on the efficacy—let alone virtue—of the Gardeners' entheogenic commitments. On *The Year of the Flood*'s first page of prose, Toby reflects that she had "never been under the illusion that she can converse with birds," unlike her "more wild-eyed or possibly overdosed" colleagues (*YF* 4). She likens psychedelics' work to metaphor: "accessing my inner Pilar," the healer who trained her (*MA* 219). She sometimes finds her visions useful, but she never presumes to collect information from nature itself. She understands that culture mediates the effect. Psychedelic compounds do not impart meaning themselves. Individuals derive meaning out of the chemical reactions they experience after ingesting them, reinforcing the symbolic order they might seem to pulverize—a point dramatized by the fact that Toby's "golden animal" itself symbolizes the ecosystem writ large. How different, Pollan wonders, is such an experience, absent any critical reflection on interpretive framework, "from a psychological construct like the superego—an inner voice that recalls us to the moral and ethical strictures of our society?" In this scenario, "instead of undermining social norms," a psychedelic trip "actually reinforces them."[86]

Palingenetic Rebirth and Environmentalist Nihilism

Atwood herself does not in fact trust the idea of Eden, contrary to critics who claim the Gardeners function as a vessel for her values. "I don't believe in a perfect world," she stated in a 2010 interview. "I don't believe it's achievable . . . because purity tests set in. Are you ideologically pure enough to be allowed to live? Well, it turns out that very few people are, so you end up with a . . . mass killing scene."[87] That scene plays out not just for the impure masses in the MaddAddam trilogy but also for the Gardeners themselves, raising questions about the logical conclusions of psychedelic ecologism as well as its ecofascist resonances. The Gardeners' transpersonal outlook on consciousness takes on lethal significance in their celebration of death as the rebirth of recycled matter, "living on" in other creatures. *"Vultures are our friends,"* Toby recalls. *"They are God's necessary dark angels of bodily dissolution."* The "state sometimes called Death," Adam preaches, is "more rightly known as Renewed Life. . . . not a single atom that has ever existed is truly lost" (*YF* 4, 423). In a strictly materialist or biologistic spiritual view, God loves not man but matter.

Many ayahuasca users confess to perceiving just this sort of association during their trips. One woman claims to have heard a voice proclaim, "We are less than we think we are," heralding a sudden identification with her bodily matter and its eventual dispersal throughout the ecosystem after death as she "attained a liberating vision of light emerging from the death of form."[88] Allen Ginsberg, too, "faced . . . my death to come—everyone's death to come."[89] The initial horror of this sensation often gives way to placidity. One celebrant confesses to having experienced "a deep inner healing" in response to visions of frolicking seraphs that "incorporate[ed] death, disease, and other . . . horrors into their dance of transformation."[90] For some of Atwood's characters, this quiescence is a liability. Zeb, lost in the Canadian tundra, questions the practicality of consuming mushrooms in an environment actually devoid of human mediation: "That's all he'd need, an encounter with the 'shroom god" (*MA* 72). The line foregrounds Zeb's (and Toby's) perspective that psychedelics (and by extension their dismissal of a sense of discrete, personal agency) do not usefully contribute to survival in an "Edenic" landscape. But for other characters, death is the point. As a result, the lives and needs of living human individuals often escape the Gardeners' concern. Their worldview emphasizes the web at the expense of the people and peoples who comprise the flock.

To a certain extent, this particular Gardener gospel might also be said to consecrate the "flat ontology" advanced by some contemporary theoretical enterprises in speculative realism, the new materialisms, and other ventures. The endeavor to "eschew the distinction between organic and inorganic, or animate and inanimate" has inspired many writers in these areas to more broadly question where, if anywhere, to chart the boundaries between objects, including among humans.[91] The Gardeners' entheogenic biologism invites readers to consider at what point the material turn might venture into renewed mystical territory and reiterate holistic identifications within a Gaian ecosystem writ large. Many contributions to these traditions avoid such a totalizing perspective. As the critic Hannes Bergthaller points out, a flat ontology makes it difficult "to come up with a principled reason that any particular species or habitat ought to be protected," including human individuals, communities, or populations.[92] Other efforts in posthumanist philosophy, however, can trend toward rhetorical excess in their attention to matter's "generative flow of becoming" and "radical immanence," as in Rosi Braidotti's declaration that a "vitalist notion of death" not only "disintegrates the ego" but also "frees us into life."[93] Braidotti's words might provide some dismal reassurance in the face of mortality, but they might also justify an argument that death in general—or genocide in particular—is, from a biocentric perspective (or, more to the point, an ecofascist one), politically unobjectionable.

Likewise, at a certain point in *The Year of the Flood*—not to mention in the work of real-world psychedelic environmentalism—the line between psychic dissolution through psychedelics and physical dissolution through death becomes almost impossible to detect in the Gardeners' rhetoric. Atwood links the two phenomena in the figure of the chemical compound. DMT and psilocybin prompt the self-dissolution the Gardeners believe necessary to appreciate their interconnectedness. By comparison, Crake's BlyssPluss pill produces "hideous torments of . . . bodily dissolution" in its victims, whose corpses lie "evaporating like slow smoke . . . Their bones reverting to calcium; night predators hunting their dispersed flesh, transformed now into grasshoppers and mice" (*YF* 424, *MA* 313). As Buhner writes, "Gaia . . . understands death, for death is built into the system. . . . [E]very organism that emerges out of its matrix matters to the Earth . . . but it does not fear their passing." This perspective not only shrugs off questions of justice when it comes to rapid changes in conditions for human life and ecological consistency but also tacitly absolves those most responsible for them. The earth, Buhner writes, "does not need saving. . . . Gaia has been self-caretaking for a very long time . . . The belief that *we* must save the Earth—even if it is driven by deep concern for the damage that is occurring in natural ecosystems—is only another example of this hubris." On the one hand, this statement maintains the notion that certain people—those integrated with Gaia—might survive with her, even if other, less enlightened humans die. On the other, it basically amounts to a get-out-of-jail-free card for the most pollutive industries: "If you truly trust the Earth, you have to assume that the human species . . . is just the way it's supposed to be."[94] The implication is not only that Gaia will heal anyway but also that the purest among us might well enjoy it if corporations—or a figure like Crake—drive the rest of the species to extinction. The Gardeners, at least, actively celebrate that grisly fate.

But their dehumanization even of their own membership does not adhere when the Flood actually hits. Eden is ultimately something of a *"disappointment,"* Adam reluctantly admits. Most of the Gardeners do in fact survive the Flood, but their numbers quickly dwindle—not from disease but from predation. One of them, "via the conduit of a wild dog pack," makes "the ultimate Gift to her fellow Creatures," becoming "part of God's great dance of proteins" (YF 371, 404). The romanticized ecosystem they prayed for is what starts killing them off—*after* they survive. They get what they ask for: they experience nature, as in Adam's strict materialism, stripped of human culture writ large (including tools like modern medicine and other life-saving technologies). And they find they are not as prepared or privileged as they imagined. The novels tacitly condemn—even lampoon—such fantasies, in that the endgame of such a position, when taken seriously, would reduce the human to its biology to the extent that human lives do not matter except as food for predators and decomposers. The Gardener vision ultimately yields to nihilistic hopelessness: like extinct animals, they "must now witness the end of our Species" (YF 423).

The question of what does or should define the species—biology or culture—haunts the trilogy and Atwood's corpus as a whole. "When any civilization is dust and ashes," Jimmy argues in *Oryx and Crake,* human meaning survives in art, in "images, words, music." Crake rebuts that archaeologists are "just as interested in gnawed bones. . . . Sometimes more interested. They think human meaning is defined by those things too" (OC 167). Their debate foregrounds Atwood's preoccupation with the difference between defining the human biologically, in terms of material composition, and culturally, in terms of social construction and interpretation. The distinction has interested her at least since the 1972 publication of *Surfacing,* whose narrator comes to identify with the ecosystem writ large. But the novel ends with a chagrined admission that to claim a lasting and defensible sense of subjectivity, she will "have to live in the usual way, defining . . . love by its failures, power by its loss, its renunciation."[95] This vision of subjectivity is relational. The novel contends that identity is best conceived not as an expression of essence, which Atwood suggests always reduces to biologism, but as a series of constraints, experiences, affiliations, and choices.

She continues to take up and explore this idea in her work—including in the form of the Crakers. Supposedly limited to their biological functions, the "perfect human beings" nonetheless gravitate toward symbolic representation and cultural production. They constantly pester Toby for definitions and interpretations, displaying not linguistic ineptitude but an active interest in entering a symbolic order, like children learning to speak. "Crake thought he'd . . . eliminated what he called the G-spot in the brain," Jimmy notes. *"God is a cluster of neurons. . . .* It had been a difficult problem, though: take out too much in that area and you got a zombie or a psychopath. But these people are neither" (*OC* 157). Crake can't breed out the interpretive variation of the DMN, which is to say culture *as a facet of* human biology. In such moments, Atwood asserts that symbolic exchange and the creative production of meaning are crucial factors that resist attempts to reduce humans to other biological functions. In the process, she further lambasts the fact that the Gardeners' (and their real-world counterparts') belief in their own special belonging to Gaia itself relies on the narratives they tell themselves.

Atwood's violent demystification of the Gardeners' specific brand of palingenetic rebirth, and the novels' association of illusive with actual dissolution, informs the MaddAddam trilogy's critical attitude toward certain Western narratives of psychedelic practice as ultimately, though often unwittingly, nihilistic expressions of self-indulgent environmentalism. At a moment when psychedelics have grown extraordinarily popular as a means to psychic purity and a badge of ecological innocence, Atwood presents a narrative case for abandoning the Feast of McKenna for the hardheaded fare of Saint Toby: the conviction that cultural forms are not something to be jettisoned but finessed. The novels dramatize the importance of what Ursula Heise describes as "reimagining the nature of the future not as a return to the past or a realm apart from humans, but as nature reshaped by humans."[96] Looking backward, Atwood suggests, serves only to convince us that extinction is desirable—the logic that not only drives Crake to engineer his solution but also encourages countless readers to declare it necessary. "Do you think everyone has the potential to be fascist?" an interviewer asked Atwood in 2010. She responded with another question: "Does everyone have the potential to be a cannibal, if you were stuck on a lifeboat and your choice was dying or eating somebody else? . . . We do not know how we'd behave." But she nonetheless states her conviction that "a lot of people in this biosphere are in lifeboat situations right now."[97] Crake's plague dramatizes one possible reaction—one that chillingly resonates in casual rhetoric of the twenty-first century, from the psychedelic millennialism of New Age gurus to the banal praise heaped upon the supervillain Thanos. Was Crake "a lunatic," one of Atwood's characters asks, "or an intellectually honorable man who'd thought things through to their logical conclusion? And was there any difference?" (OC 343). No—because ecofascism is less a matter of coherent political theory than it is one of political genre: a series of narrative processes and potentially violent effects. The Gardeners' psychedelic investment in their purity treads the same path, illuminating how many real-world psychonauts risk doing so as well.

« 5 »

Contagion

*Inheritance of a Purified Earth in Viral Politics
and Apocalyptic Visions*

Coronavirus is Earth's vaccine. We're the virus.

—Thomas Schulz, Twitter user

[A] social system's internal contradictions should be
pushed to their limits in order to *encourage* rather than
overcome the system's *self-destructive tendencies.* This is
done to *hasten* the system's *collapse* or *demise.*

—The Base

There is a word for the Gardeners' keen anticipation of civilization's implosion, and for Crake's ambitions to expedite it: *accelerationism,* the thesis that one should not only "prepare for but also instigate system collapse."[1] It is an argument increasingly made among movements and groups on the far right, such as The Base (quoted in the epigraph above). It also features in the manifestos by the Christchurch, El Paso, and Buffalo shooters, who called on like-minded insurgents to catalyze widespread violence in the interest of scuttling society to pave the way for the white ethnostate(s) to follow. "As social and ecological dystopia feature ever more prominently in popular culture, the vision of stateless gangs living off the land in a brutal social Darwinian universe is already a familiar one," Blair Taylor writes. Extreme-right environmentalism "warns of this dystopian future while also embracing its potentiality, giving it a veneer of inevitability and desirability."[2] And its practitioners have found success recruiting from survivalist communities as a result, promoting a return to rural localism characterized by racial exclusivity and rigid hierarchy based on gender and ability.

Accelerationism is "essentially prepping," one leader notes. "You're decelerating your own life"—even as such figures encourage the intensification of conflict and collapse. (Ted Kaczynski, darling of the ecofascist right, was an accelerationist avant la lettre.) Mike Mahoney, founder of the ecofascist Pine Tree Party, puts the message succinctly: "ACCELERATE THE WORLD, DECELERATE YOUR TRIBE!"[3] As is typical of overtly fascist thought, such logic appears to break with the socioeconomic status quo, but in many respects represents its apotheosis. As Cedric Johnson notes, any "retreat from society and . . . creation of individual zones of safety and security for those who can afford to purchase them"—or to violently create and defend them—"constitute the logic of neoliberalism gone haywire."[4] But it also in many cases proceeds from what followers, as "Eco-Extremist[s] . . . focused on tearing down the system that exploits our land, animals, and people," understand as a genuinely antimodernist commitment to environment.[5]

I am not the first to point out that such sentiment found a milder, mainstream analog in the early months of the Covid-19 pandemic. Countless social media posts emerged (and themselves spread virally, online) in March and April of 2020 to declare that "nature is healing" as humans died by the tens of thousands, many of them service workers unable to isolate and/or members of marginalized communities without access to adequate healthcare. On Twitter, one post declaring that "we"—humans—are the true virus (and the coronavirus its vaccine) gathered roughly half a million likes by the end of April alone. One detects in the statement echoes of Garrett Hardin's lament that modern science has unduly limited "negative feedbacks of predation" and "parasitism," which, unchecked, would continue to cull the human population (and conserve resources for those who survive). As April Anson notes, the "universalist language" of such casual celebrations—and their misanthropic approval of human extinction on behalf of the biosphere—fails to account for the uneven distribution of blame for ecological disruption, not to mention the fact that, in the United States and worldwide, poor communities of color asymmetrically shoulder its burdens. Rather, it lumps these populations together with the same systems that disenfranchise them under a broad umbrella: the human virus.[6] It also remains mum on who does, will, or should survive, and at whose expense. Survivalists, at least, had their own response, especially amid widespread government inaction. In a neoliberal landscape, only the fittest have what it takes. But in a sense, the pandemic "has made 'preppers' of everyone," writes the journalist Alex Amend: it has "provided something of a dry run for how society will respond to disaster on the scale of the coming climate crisis."[7] As for previous examples, it would be alarmist and unfair to describe these casual accelerationists as overt ecofascists in their own right. But they do work within similar storytelling patterns, in response to similar conditions, and in light of similar attachments—in this case, if not distress about the health of a specific place, then anxiety concerning the future of a much larger one: the planet as a whole.

This chapter explores representations that treat global catastrophes—namely, pandemics—as forces for ecological good (as well as narratives that critique them), with an eye toward their implicit and perhaps unintentional arguments about who deserves to survive and why. It also considers in turn how a variety of actors have wielded disease as a metaphor for human activity as justification for their embrace of widespread human death—and how the gap between broadly misanthropic and narrowly genocidal expressions in this vein is much slimmer than it might at first seem. "It was an odd coincidence," Amend notes, that the far-right Finnish writer Pentti Linkola—an influence on the shooters mentioned above—died as global Covid-19 infections surpassed one million, after a long career spent arguing for an almost surgical intervention against the earth's "very own tumor," *Homo sapiens*.[8] But Linkola was not the first to use such metaphors to refer to our species writ large. Nor have they only recently transcended ideological lines. Lynn Margulis, coauthor with James Lovelock of early works on the Gaia hypothesis, once wrote of humanity as a "pandemic" that manifests in deforestation, desertification, and other such symptoms. But these inflammations are, "for Gaia, only petty activities. . . . *Homo sapiens,* she shrugs, soon will either change its wayward ways, or, like other plague species, will terminate with a whimper."[9]

This perspective has characterized the writing of numerous biocentric thinkers at least since Arne Næss developed the concept of deep ecology in the 1970s. Philosophers such as J. Baird Callicott, William Ophuls, and Paul W. Taylor took up the same line of thinking, inspiring radical movements in the intervening years between the rise of the modern environmental movement and the Covid-19 pandemic, from the Church of Euthanasia, which infamously entreated people to "Save the planet, kill yourself," to Earth First!, some of whose members applauded the AIDS/HIV epidemic's crescendo in the late 1980s and early 1990s. "Miss Ann Thropy," writing in *Earth First Journal*, declared that if "radical environmentalists were to invent a disease to bring the human population back to ecological sanity, it would probably be something like AIDS."[10] On their face, these pleas for extinction might appear a "graphic example of the ability of environmental ethics to transcend human self-interest," as Roderick Nash puts it. "But as biocentric philosophers were quick to explain, individual self-interest was indistinguishable . . . from the interest of the whole because the self . . . has no being outside the environmental context."[11] For critics such as Murray Bookchin, Tom Regan, and Robert Pois, such rhetoric nonetheless exemplified "a fundamental deprecation of humans *vis-à-vis* nature," in which the well-being of certain individuals or groups is separate from and subordinate to that of a privileged whole, that they read among "most Nazi ideologues."[12] Though this critique has struck other scholars as extreme, it is nonetheless true that numerous Earth First!ers have become or once were involved with neo-Nazi groups in the United States.[13]

For such figures, their own survival is rarely in question. They are sufficiently natural. It is *other* humans who constitute a blight on the earth. Perhaps it is also unsurprising, then, that many "nature is healing" memes in the early days of the Covid-19 pandemic originated with white-supremacist groups, in some cases in mockery of leftist environmentalists but in others out of genuine ecofascist commitment.[14] But origin is beside the point. What matters is how widely other social media users took up the call. (Even Inger Andersen, executive director of the United Nations Environment Program, weighed in.) A "nature is healing" post might not announce itself as an ethnonationalist declaration, but it still raises the question of what segments of the population remain sufficiently natural to count as part of Gaia and which constitute the disease. In what circumstances and to what extent do such messages, regardless of partisan affiliation, position the speaker as part of an ecologically privileged in-group in ways that center whiteness and other social forms at the expense of others? Or implicitly, if unintentionally, welcome their extinction? This chapter explores such questions. From social media posts touting nature's "healing" during Covid-19 lockdowns to anti-vaxxer environmentalisms, a variety of platforms not only argue that a virus's disruption of human activity benefits the nonhuman world but also, for this reason, frame viral contraction, death tolls, and even human annihilation as positive developments not just for the earth but also for an environmentalist elect.

My argument in this chapter is that in certain cultural narratives, viruses, bacteria, other microbes, and contagion in general function as threshold objects, in most cases wiping out massive swaths of the human species, but in others inoculating a deserving few. I am shifting in this final chapter, that is, to a consideration of consumption on the scale of whole populations rather than of individuals. Admittedly, my use of the word *consumption* is most stretched in this chapter. One does not "consume" disease as one consumes food, plant compounds, or even commodities. To suggest as much might even be to render bacteria, viruses, and other microbial organisms passive, reproducing distorted assumptions about ostensibly inert nonhuman others. But I do wish to retain the connotation I proposed in the Introduction: that of self-incorporation. What interests me is the extent to which certain actors themselves frame engagement with a given object (or life-form) as a matter of assimilation, as well as the extent to which this enterprise functions as a locus for a whole suite of behaviors and values oriented toward proving one's belonging—or one's mettle—relative to a specific environment or even the planet writ large. In the case of pandemics, huge numbers of people interact with the same organisms. But for some environmentalists—mainstream as well as radical—ongoing health indicates that certain modes or conditions of viral contact render them more fit to survive. Such representations rest on an implicit suggestion that one's environmentalist virtue grants immunity: the appropriately "primitive" will inherit the earth. In what follows, I read contemporary narratives of infection, inoculation, physical fitness, survivalism, and the legacy of the so-called Pleistocene paradigm alongside each other to show how certain ways of talking about contagion not only welcome apocalypse but also reify crypto-eugenic ideas about purity in terms of race, Indigeneity, gender, sexuality, ability, and environment in a way that makes an argument about what sorts of people should and should not survive catastrophe.

To do so, I read two examples of "cli-fi" that take contagion as one of their central devices: Adam Johnson's *Parasites Like Us* (2003) and the Ojibwe novelist Louise Erdrich's *Future Home of the Living God* (2017). Adam Trexler notes that many early examples of the cli-fi genre are, if not invested in ideas about identitarian purity, "distinctly chauvinist" and "parochial in their concern, describing the collapse of the global economy and a return to village localism."[15] In many such narratives, that "return" is predicated on the notion that the people and place in question are, for one reason or another, ecologically innocent. But mode of representation matters when it comes to localism as well as identity. Johnson and Erdrich furnish rich examples because, together, they critically juxtapose several perspectives on both. Johnson focuses on one that romanticizes an earth unblemished by global capitalism and glorifies ostensibly paleolithic lifeways of the Americas, even as Native peoples die in a pandemic that claims the rest of the human species and, indirectly, many others—a result, the narrator believes, of inherent human rapacity. In other words, *Parasites Like Us* foregrounds the conviction that "we're the virus." *Future Home of the Living God* also chronicles the spread of what one character muses "could be a new kind of virus. Maybe bacteria. From the permafrost"—one that mutates *Homo sapiens* and other species in unpredictable ways.[16] Two distinct responses to this situation— and articulations of place and identity—emerge over the course of the novel: a Christian fundamentalist regime that seizes pregnant women to maintain its power and a Native reclamation of ancestral lands that organizes around mutual aid.

Both novels feature pandemics that, for the characters, represent *regression*. In the case of *Parasites*, that regression is primarily social—an opportunity for primitivists to revert to a simpler, more authentic way of living. In *Future Home*, it is both social and biological, speaking to national anxieties about racial purity across U.S. history. The novels tell different stories about the notion of regression, but through them I trace common themes in contemporary cultural narratives about identity, survival, and socio-ecological belonging. In *Parasites*, contagion comes to function as a threshold object. Characters develop "natural" immunity to the plague by exposing themselves to trace amounts—a method that anti-vaxxers and others believe not only superior to vaccination but also indicative of who is and is not fit to survive in a polluted world. This fixation on bodily optimization appears in *Future*

Home, too. In this case, however, it is genetic integrity that renders one and one's family fit to inherit the earth. For the Christofascist state, whiteness is a prerequisite. But for other (Euro-American) characters, it is Native ancestry, prized for its supposedly intrinsic closeness to the earth, that conveys such privilege. It is my contention that Erdrich, like Margaret Atwood, juxtaposes these overtly fascist and everyday iterations of purity for a reason: to critically explore how the same cultural assumptions and narrative patterns that promote political violence can animate quotidian expressions of place, identity, and belonging as well—and to comparative, if not identical, effect in terms of the reinforcement of existing hierarchies. Across the two novels, contagion and bodies themselves emerge as threshold objects—a representational trend the authors critique, but also one with acute material implications amid ongoing public health crises and mounting legal threats to Native sovereignty.

Contagion, Inoculation, and the Natural Body

Anson describes the "nature is healing" phenomenon as a "storytelling strain . . . built on a long tradition tied less to . . . fickle political affiliations than to the circulation of a narrative tradition where violence is part of the 'natural' order, of people and planet"—a tradition that this book has in part sought to trace, beginning with its consolidation in the eugenic preservationism of the late nineteenth and early twentieth centuries.[17] In 2020, that legacy manifested in expected ways across the far right. Survivalists and accelerationists clapped themselves on the back, and evangelical leaders heralded a chance to put an end to the nation's mounting decadence—the exact sort of rally, scholars such as Roger Griffin note, that characterized classical fascist movements. According to Doug Wilson, the Christian Reconstructionist pastor of Christ Church in Moscow, Idaho, Covid-19 presented "an opportunity to reinstate . . . Christian order if things collapse." Cautioning against a postpandemic "return to normal," he added that in "mid-May we will be just days away from Pride month. . . . [I]s that what we mean by back to normal?"[18] Plague, by virtue of its disruption, became for such figures a fascist instrument in and of itself. It also, in the late 1980s and early 1990s, constructed an unexpected bridge between evangelicals and certain radical environmentalists. During the AIDS/HIV epidemic as well as Covid-19, contagion cleansed the earth of the ostensibly unnatural, in terms of both sexual identity and environmental overdraft. The nature-is-healing "storytelling strain," then, does not merely suggest "that human relationships to nature are essentially combative," as many have argued, but also that "natural" orders of people deserve to live while discursively manufactured, often marginalized, "unnatural" others do not.[19]

The period around the AIDS epidemic also ushered in changes to the way people generally understood and talked about contagion, infection, and immunity in such a way that made possible what the feminist critic and ACT UP demonstrator Emily Martin referred to, at the time, as a "new incarnation of social Darwinism that allows people of different 'quality' to be distinguished from each other," with implications for environmentalist rhetoric that persist today. Environment has always been central to conceptions of immunity, which fundamentally concerns the relationship between the body and its surroundings. *Reader's Digest* magazine first introduced the notion of an immune system to a wide audience in the 1950s, and in the decades after, mainstream publications relied on a consistent arsenal of metaphors to render it comprehensible: figurations that cast immunity as "warfare against an external enemy" on behalf of a "defended nation-state" and drew a rigid boundary between a beleaguered self and hostile world beyond it—framing that belies and oversimplifies the constant, complex, and crucial interplay between the human body and other organisms. In the last decades of the century, AIDS activists critiqued this "military" messaging, arguing that it "only supports everyone's homophobia" and "xenophobia" (not to mention shallow understandings of ecology and human microbiology).[20]

But those decades also comprised an era of self-optimization in personal wellness and other cultural sectors, for reasons previous chapters have explored. Widespread social panic over the destabilization of bodily boundaries occasioned by the AIDS epidemic did not necessarily disturb the notion that, as one young man put it, some people "have a stronger immune system than others, just because of the way they're made up." The ascension of neoliberal economics and its attendant cultural logics revised that assumption, promoting an idea that one "can develop an immune system more able to survive threats" through "practice and training"—perhaps, as one doctor put it, by "eating things that are not particularly well cleaned" or "drink[ing] water from a river."[21] I want to highlight the role played, again, by consumption. By incorporating certain objects (contaminated food, for instance) one might develop a biological advantage, an "immune strength" that "allows some people to feel especially potent." Martin calls this attitude "a kind of immune machismo," according to which "notions of the perfectability of this complex system" attach "to the notion that some kinds of people are superior to others."[22]

This line of reasoning has not faded in the intervening decades. In fact, it characterizes the remarkably diverse and widespread antivaccination movement of the twenty-first century, which the historian Traci Brynne Voyles notes "is less a unified political project . . . than it is a discursive contagion," another "storytelling strain" that informs such disparate individuals and groups as the far-right Georgia congresswoman Marjorie Taylor Greene and the liberal comedian Jim Carrey, the QAnon conspiracy phenomenon and *Mothering* magazine, fundamentalist Christians and urban professionals.[23] What links these "otherwise distant . . . contingents," Voyles notes in an interview, is the "notion that vaccines somehow represent chemical or technological pollution that is more dangerous than what are perceived as 'natural' germs."[24] The anti-vaxxer platform that one should "develop immunity to contagious diseases 'naturally,' without vaccination," the essayist Eula Biss adds, proceeds largely from a belief that "vaccines are inherently unnatural." In truth, vaccination did not emerge from modern medicine, but in fact pre-dates it. It originated in the folk practice of variolation, which developed independently worldwide before entering Western medicine through imperial channels. Variolation involves intentionally instigating a mild case of disease to mitigate future (and more deadly) illness. Farmers in early modern England found that exposure to livestock pus protected them from severe smallpox. (Counterparts in India, China, Africa, and elsewhere had been systematically taking advantage of this observation for centuries.) Most anti-vaxxers don't oppose inoculation itself. They merely find "natural," intentional exposure to disease more trustworthy than synthetic vaccines, given that "this form of inoculation," Biss writes, "resembles variolation, the real thing."[25]

Conceiving of variolation as the "real thing," however, more accurately creates a boundary between what is natural and what is artificial than it does represent one, based on other, preexisting sociocultural preoccupations. It is somewhat beside the point that vaccines do not really contain mercury or antifreeze (let alone the fact that countless studies have demonstrated that no link exists between them and autism). These substances, Biss writes, "speak to anxieties about our industrial world . . . evok[ing] the chemicals on which we now blame our bad health . . . and the pollutants that now threaten our environment."[26] We might view antivaccination as yet another iteration of recurring antimodernist malaise. But individuals and organizations within the movement have also appropriated rhetoric from the antitoxics and environmental justice movements to support their claims, linking exposure to industrial contaminants to what one woman refers to as "toxic shots."[27] Such appeals are ironic given that they constitute a denial not only of the ecological reality that humans always, unavoidably, exist in microbial interaction with their surroundings but also of the fact that the "lives and privileges" of the demographics most likely to shun vaccines are, Voyles points out, "*produced through* chemicals and technologies that pollute less privileged peoples' environments"— the main critique of the environmental justice movement to begin with.[28] It seems that what is at stake for such figures is not necessarily health itself but "an environmental imaginary that posits at its center a pure, 'natural' body unpolluted by the technology of vaccines"—one that is "better equipped to navigate the natural world of disease and infection . . . than one 'polluted.'"[29]

This fetish for self-optimization is inherited, in part, from earlier, New-Age (and eugenic) ideas about health, wellness, and nature of the sort described in the last chapter. Bodily "trainings" such as variolation not only enable one to avoid modern pollutants but also distinguish adapted humans from maladapted ones in the face of the ecological crises of a hypermodern world. In *The Future of the Body* (1992), Michael Murphy, cofounder of the Esalen Institute, argues that humans "can extrapolate from physiological changes" mastered by figures such as athletes, ascetics, and "shamans" to "imagin[e] somatic developments required for high-level change."[30] Such ideas are mainstays in contemporary online wellness networks, which overlap considerably with the anti-vax movement. Health in general and immunity in particular emerge in such circles as matters of choice, of personal (and, especially in wellness spaces, market-based) control over a bounded—and superior—body. Cultivation of "greater life . . . latent in the human race" through training, Murphy writes, is even "a sign of having evolved to a higher order of being," akin to that achieved through the consumption of psychedelic compounds for gurus like Stephen Harrod Buhner.[31]

This approach to adaptation, Martin notes, is "based on practice and potentially available to anyone. Unlike Darwinism, the outcome is not linked to the original biological material with which one was born." And yet such "training" nonetheless "takes money, time, information, and opportunity, things in short supply for many people."[32] And for many who subscribe to this notion, those who do not or cannot comply come to represent the pollution of which the pure have cleansed themselves. Take, for instance, the erroneous link between vaccines and autism. Children on the spectrum often function in such discourse almost as bodily manifestations of the contaminated, synthetic, artificial, and modern: everything inimical to the "natural." Voyles points out that such prescriptive distinctions are not only "profoundly ableist" but also "deeply racist." Investment in "protection of purity from any kind of contamination" not only has "been a mechanism by which toxins are diverted into nonwhite spaces," but also carries the eugenic torch of "racial projects that weaponize cultural notions of cleanliness, health, and good hygiene," which earlier chapters glossed.[33] In an allegedly "colorblind" era, persistent assumptions about class, health, and purity maintain inequities in terms of race and disability while ignoring access (or lack thereof) to medical, economic, and educational resources. As one man put it during the AIDS/HIV epidemic, "people without a good living standard need vaccines, whereas vaccines would only clog up the more refined immune systems of middle-class or upper-class people."[34]

This sort of prejudice has not diminished in the intervening thirty years. "I don't smoke and I don't drink," claims Catherine Gabitan, a popular (and representative) social media wellness influencer, in an interview. "I spend a lot of money investing in the highest-quality foods available to me. I believe in natural immunity and supporting my immune system. I've taken radical responsibility for that. . . . [T]here are other people out there who are still drinking alcohol and smoking cigarettes who want me to protect their health, but they won't even protect their own."[35] Gabitan's hyperindividualistic conception of health ignores questions of disability and age in the face of Covid-19, consigning persons constrained by these factors to an unfit, even immoral status, unworthy of survival. She also breathlessly passes by her own acknowledgment that the self-optimization on which she prides herself requires resources to which many do not have access. "Illness has long been blamed on the ill," the biophysicist Joseph Osmundson notes. Even cancer "carries a hint of . . . condemnation": people "*should know* to avoid carcinogens."[36] But what strikes me about rhetoric like Gabitan's is its suggestion not only that pure people are pure because they consume more natural foods or other substances than others (the subject of past chapters), but also that we might all contract the same pathogen but in different ways and, as such, to different effect. The babble surrounding vaccination centers on exactly this idea. One must consume a "real" version of a virus or bacterium rather than a synthetic vaccine to qualify as natural and, in the long term, for survival, regardless of social differences that render some more vulnerable than others.

Such an idea exacerbates those inequalities even as it reinforces a facile distinction between nature and artifice. It also does so in both explicitly white-supremacist and everyday expressions. "Some Americans," Osmundson notes, "take glee in the fact that not wearing their masks will kill Black and Brown and Indigenous people"— but, by the same token, the "first pivot" out of Covid-19 lockdowns "came as we were realizing who was most at risk" (i.e., the sort of people figures like Gabitan are "willing to let die for American normalcy").[37] Such a dismissal relies on narratives of health, strength, and disposability that do not require a far-right affiliation, a point to which the philosophically diverse field of anti-vaxxers attests. Some observers admit to being "baffled" that QAnon, for example, has "infiltrated" the wellness market, "historically a hippy, countercultural space." But the ideal of natural purity to which these parties subscribe defies partisan distinctions. Many activists otherwise at loggerheads pursue it for the same reason, too: out of a reasonable yet overdetermined distrust of "big pharmaceutical companies . . . primarily concerned with finances over health" and the entrenched political and economic arrangements that reward them.[38] (The wellness industry's own corporate operations seem lost on them, perhaps because of its canny facility with purity rhetoric.) In any event, past pandemics have made the effect of such narratives tragically clear: "When health becomes an identity," Biss writes, "sickness becomes not something that happens to you, but who you are," such that disease "happens to other people ... who are not good or clean."[39] The deep ecology movement's AIDS controversy and, more recently, the anti-vax movement's appropriation of environmental justice rhetoric furnish just two examples of such a conclusion's material effects on marginalized communities at times of intersecting ecological and viral crisis.

Microbial Consumption in *Parasites Like Us*

Writing in 1994, Martin observed "an apocalyptic tone to [popular] writing, a sense that the world as we have known it is going to come to an end in some disaster wrought by microbes. But ... there is more than a hint that *some* people with the right kind of immune systems will survive."[40] In *Parasites Like Us,* Adam Johnson dramatizes this theme, pushing it to its extremes in the context of rapid ecological change—specifically anthropogenic species extinction but also, as the novel's first sentence declares, the era in which "the climate [i]s warming" more generally.[41] Johnson is hardly the only twenty-first-century writer to consider contagion alongside the prospect of social collapse and themes of ecological abuse. Novels such as Emily St. John Mandel's *Station Eleven* (2014) and Ling Ma's *Severance* (2018) have more recently contributed to a booming subgenre of speculative fiction in this vein. What distinguishes *Parasites* for the purposes of this discussion is the extent to which Johnson's extensive reading of such texts as "survival narratives" and "hunting guides"—as well as, more abstractly, what the deep ecologist Paul Shepard called the "Pleistocene paradigm"—shaped his writing of it. It was survivalist sentiment, in the form of a doctor obsessed with the feasibility of performing surgery with hand-carved stone blades, that introduced Johnson to the Clovis people, possibly the first arrivals to the Americas over the Bering land bridge over 10,000 years ago and the object of the doctor's fascination—and *Parasites'* characters', too.[42]

The novel seizes on the uncertainty surrounding the Clovis to explore intersections among themes of human nature, environmental overdraft, and fitness for survival, among others. It starts with a specific archaeological detail: "[I]n 1929, at a site near Clovis, New Mexico, a mammoth bone was found with a large spear point embedded in it." In the intervening century, theories have abounded as to how the Clovis reached the continent and what became of them.

But the fossil record does confirm that within "three centuries . . . most of the large mammals of North America had been eradicated," Johnson writes, "leaving . . . future generations without the animals needed for domestication, transportation, and agriculture."[43] This observation underwrites the Hardinian thesis proposed by the novel's narrator, Hank Hannah, a washed-up anthropologist at a South Dakota university, in his book *The Depletionists*: that it was not climate change or disease that wiped out megafauna at the end of the last ice age, but inherent human vice. Hannah's colleagues generally agree that "if the Clovis had brought just one diseased animal with them . . . a virus could have decimated North American mammal populations" (115). But Hannah himself insists that the Clovis hunted to extinction thirty-five species of large mammal indigenous to North America. And "once they had consumed everything in sight," he remarks, "they disbanded . . . into small groups that would form the roughly six hundred Native American tribes that exist today" (1). This self-imposed collapse, Johnson explains, "is the metaphor at the heart of the book: a people came to a new frontier and built a grand culture based on natural resources, and once those resources were depleted, the culture fell apart, leaving their descendants impoverished."[44] As Hannah puts it, the Clovis "plundered the first sunny days of humanity, just as we . . . [a]re plundering the last" (125).

Parasites, that is, features a protagonist fond of declaring that "we're the virus." (Even the novel's title announces its interest in this perspective.) For Hannah, the species writ large shoulders blame for its oversized ecological footprint. Only fitfully does he come to recognize how histories of imperialism and structural inequity unevenly distribute that violence's sources and effects. But as a hemorrhagic plague ravages the earth late in the novel, he feels slightly vindicated. Humans rapidly eliminate whole species of hogs and birds, fearing their role in spreading a virus more accurately promulgated by industrial conditions and transportation technologies. Hannah and a small circle of acquaintances survive, however—the only humans to do so. Their resilience hinges on their inoculation against the plague, administered through appropriately "natural" methods. It is this combination—of a perspective that humans are a virus with another that certain people, by virtue of a bodily optimization characterized by closeness to the earth, are fit to live—that I want to emphasize. Hannah and company emerge absolved, intentionally or otherwise, of modernity's excesses. Worth noting, though, is the fact that Johnson understands his novel as a work of satire. Hannah—insistent upon his hypothesis that intrinsic human rapacity inevitably destroys human communities—must be read, at least in part, as an object of critique. Also worth noting is the fact that Johnson is deeply interested in the social effects of cultural narratives that reinforce the mystical unity of a chosen group of people. His 2012 *Orphan Master's Son*, a novel about North Korea, won the Pulitzer Prize for this sort of examination. At least one interviewer has noticed the extent to which this attention defines his entire oeuvre. "If *The Orphan Master's Son* is a critique of the problems of a communist society," he writes, the author's other stories often stage a similar appraisal "of American capitalism and suburban culture."[45] What I want to suggest, then, is that we can read *Parasites'* characters much as I read Margaret Atwood's Gardeners: not as fascists or even supremacists, but as everyday people who nonetheless advance narratives that promote their own survival at the expense of others' in times of crisis.

They are also people fixated on origins: of human cultures in the Americas, professionally, but also, in a more mystical sense, of humanity more generally, in terms of unalienated living with the earth and each other, unmarred by modern technologies and social structures. Hannah's student Eggers best captures this preoccupation in the novel. The man's celebrated dissertation project is "to exist using nothing but Paleolithic technology for an entire year." He wears "goatskin breeches and a giant poncho of dark, matted fur," hides he tanned himself using only other animal and plant materials. When he discovers a Clovis spearpoint in a nearby ravine, he demands that they test its famed potency on a prizewinning hog, the only remaining mammal in the Dakotas representative of Pleistocene megafauna. "This is the hunt," Eggers explains. "This is what connects us to the ancient ones" (26). When they find human remains in the same gully, he insists that they excavate using only paleolithic technology. Another graduate student, Trudy, excitedly proclaims "the birth of a whole new field . . . *paleo*-paleo-anthropology," in which the conspirators, rather than "dragging bones into the cold light of the modern age," go "back . . . *in situ* with the bones" (99). Hannah frets over how Eggers will "authenticate the find" and "win . . . esteem," but the man responds that his work "isn't about my reputation" (64). Trudy and Eggers both speak, throughout the novel, to what they are looking for instead. Hannah's book might be a bit "New Age-y," they acknowledge, but they admire its dedication to "shining the light of inquiry into the darkness of prehistory" and "unearthing the truth of who we are" (26, 65). For Eggers, this goal is a matter of accessing an unalienated, "organic" condition in relation to both the earth and other humans. "I've taken a vow of poverty," he proclaims. "I possess nothing but my friends, my loyalty, and twelve thousand years of history" (196).

The characterization of Hannah's theories as "New Age-y" strikes me as significant in the context of Eggers's objectives. It aligns this aspect of the novel with a perspective advanced by a loose contingent of New-Age thinkers and radical ecologists in the final decades of the twentieth century (leading up to *Parasites'* publication), who, despite their differences, "locate[d] the origin of human alienation as far back as the advent of agriculture during the Neolithic Revolution."[46] Spurred by the antimodernist anxieties that fueled the 1960s and 1970s political and environmental movements that earlier chapters explored, biocentric and anarcho-primitivist thinkers such as Paul Shepard, J. Baird Callicott, and—yes—Ernest Callenbach offered a series of often contradictory yet consistently ambitious narratives of humanity's fall from nature in the prehistoric past. Some have suggested that a return to Neolithic agrarianism or even hunter-gatherer life is tantamount to species and planetary survival. (Some, who came up briefly in the last chapter, have linked this reversion to the pulverization of symbolic faculties.) "A journey to our primal world may bring answers to our ecological dilemmas," Shepard writes in his posthumous *Coming Home to the Pleistocene* (1998). "We can go back to nature . . . because we never left it. . . . The genome is our Pleistocene treasure. . . . Possibilities lie within us."[47] The statement not only neglects the fact that countless cultures have successfully maintained sustainable, large-scale social organization even despite the recent history of Western imperialism, but also posits certain modes of living as matters of DNA, casting all deviations from the writer's own idea of nature as unnatural, for the biosphere and for its human inhabitants. Shepard did not hold this view alone. Kirkpatrick Sale, for example, insisted in 1980 that particular modes of "human scale community" are hardwired in "the human brain."[48]

The thread running through such perspectives is not necessarily the idea that human values are intrinsically irreconcilable with biotic ones (which Garrett Hardin argued, on dubious empirical grounds, around the same time). It is one that more closely resembles the argument made by *The Avengers*' Thanos, who contends that most people are either not willing or not strong enough to sacrifice human values for ecological ones. It is also, then, implicitly an argument about who *is* willing or strong enough, and therefore capable (or worthy) of survival in a changed world. Figures like Shepard, Michael Trask argues, "call less for a Thoreauvian retreat from sociality . . . than for a new (or very old) kind of polis": an ostensibly originary form of social organization in which the will of the people (and the earth) finds seamless expression in its activity. Trask connects this paleolithic nostalgia to aspects of post-1960s libertarianism, but what I want to emphasize is that it also invokes a mystical, unified conception of community (even nation) that resonates with organicist identity narratives of the sort promulgated by classical fascist movements. It also unfolds as a tale of rebirth facilitated by a modern recovery of old technologies. (Not incidentally, Trask links this perspective to Callenbach's *Ecotopia*, too.)[49] In truth, "human societies before the advent of farming were not confined to small, egalitarian bands," David Graeber and David Wengrow point out. Archaeological evidence overwhelmingly confirms that "the world of hunter-gatherers as it existed before the coming of agriculture was one of bold social experiments."[50] Grand narratives of human development tend to fuel alternating—and facile—assumptions about humans' inherent inequality or egalitarianism. While these beliefs seem at odds—representative of right-wing accelerationism and left-leaning anarcho-primitivism, respectively—they both arise from similar arguments about "natural" human vitality. Those who don't make the cut are excluded from both visions (if not explicitly targeted for violence) regardless.

These ideas have come to saturate mass culture through similar channels as wellness fixes and antivaccination sentiment, and for similar reasons: these trends all emerged from apparently antimodern angst and proffer a reinvigorated vision of nature (in prescriptive terms of both human and ecological health). "It might have taken three or four decades for these insights to make their way to TED stages," the journalist Gideon Lewis-Kraus writes, "but the paleo diet," for example, "became a fundamental require-ment of any self-respecting Silicon Valley founder."[51] Within such techno-utopian spaces (and beyond), the conservation practice of rewilding, or "restor[ing] land to an uncultivated state," has also come to refer to the restoration of what the nonprofit Rewild.com calls "ancestral ways of living" that very rarely reflect actual, ex-isting alternatives to neoliberal economics (and more often than not reproduce its logics).[52] Johnson caricatures this contradic-tion in *Parasites,* in which Eggers proposes to "reintroduce tigers, elephants, sloths, and so on" in a "Pleistocene World" attraction organized around his excavation site. "Tourists go crazy for this stuff . . . maybe, in ten thousand years, things will have taken their course, things will be back the way they were" (94–5). Rewilding becomes a matter of both entrepreneurship and playacting. One could argue that the latter also occurs in Shepard's writing when he entreats readers to "single out those many things, large and small, that characterized the social and cultural life of our ancestors—the terms under which our genome itself was shaped—and incorpo-rate them as best we can."[53]

Such statements beg the question of how one might know how to live like a Clovis, for example, without the scholarly technology required to investigate the matter—or, in Eggers's case, without the financial resources his university throws at him. The character indeed "cheats" over the course of his project, using dental floss rather than catgut to bind points to spears, bathing in the river with soap, and situating his hut on top of vents from the campus steam tunnels. He also hails from a filthy rich family, and when the period of his "research" ends, not just his dress but also "his whole demeanor" change, "as if he'd traded in cool and capable for cocky and posturing" (244). Pleistocene life, it seems, is not merely a matter of intensely hyperindividualistic lifestyle choices, but also, like nature, whatever the speaker says it is. In both respects, fan-tasies about it avoid addressing difficult systemic questions about ecological disruption. Eggers's sojourn in prehistory, then, reads in part as a matter of consumption similar to the Ecotopians'. His acquisition and incorporation of certain tools and clothing func-tions as a metonym for a plethora of activities and ideals related to emplaced identity and avowed virtue.

The novel features a different sort of paleolithic encounter—but one still legible in terms of self-incorporation—at the moment the plot turns from that of a campus novel to one more typical of apocalypse fiction. At their dig site, Hannah, Eggers, and Trudy discover two clay orbs, one of which law enforcement immediately confiscates. It later shows up at a cursory "ceremony" arranged to inaugurate a new casino on whose property the trio discovered the artifacts. An unspecified Native elder smashes it open, and a black soot floats out and over the audience (mostly attendees of a meat wholesalers conference). Eggers, watching on television, speculates that the powder is what's left of ancient meat, "blood and meal weathered down to an oily dust." Hannah privately wonders if maybe it was the unearthed corpse's own "organ meat . . . that had gritted their hair and gotten under their skin" (247). Whatever it is, it contains a petrified plague, now free to spread across the globe through channels of international trade. Humanity falls swiftly, taking the hogs and birds who help spread it with them.

"Exposure" is a more conventional word than "consumption" to use in reference to a deadly microbe. Every human individual on earth is indeed ultimately exposed to *Parasites'* plague—including Hannah, Eggers, Trudy, and a few others who survive. They do so, however, precisely because they incorporate the contagion rather than succumb to it. In fact they doubly consume it, in terms of both assimilation and ingestion. Hannah and Eggers discover corn kernels in the other orb, which presumably contain trace amounts of the same pathogen. Eggers prepares them as he argues the Clovis would: by popping them. Hannah initially attempts to dissuade him: "Remember the *National Geographic* team who discovered that galleon in the North Sea? They celebrated by drinking a jug of wine from its hold, and everything was one big party until they became the first people in five hundred years to contract the Thames strain of the black plague." Eggers, however, is unfazed. "Dr. Hannah, my worms have worms," he responds. "My amoebas have dysentery. Over the past year, I've devoured frogs, ducklings, and minnows, still wriggling. . . . I had squirrel fever for three weeks" (199). The novel pre-dates the most recent wave of "Green Our Vaccines" rhetoric among wellness gurus and more militant anti-vax activists, but this passage strikingly resonates with the preceding decade's mounting interest in exposure—to contaminated water, for example—as a method for "training" natural immunity. Eggers himself seems convinced by such reasoning, even if the novel complicates it. "Cooking the corn," Trudy muses, "must've somehow killed the disease" (301). Preparing ancient grains according to hyperspecialized knowledge of different cultural systems would seem to trouble the line between nature and modern technologies rather than reinforce it. Eggers's project is a matter of different forms of human technology, not a wholesale rejection of it. But what matters for the character is the notion that exposure, unmediated by modern medical innovations, strengthens his body by welcoming microbes. For real-world anti-vaxxers, the flip side is that synthetic derivatives weaken it in the face of the real thing.

The novel dramatizes this very argument. Medically unmediated exposure induces illness but preempts fatal infection. The handful of people who ingest the corn spend the night violently purging. "The fever that gripped us was savage," Hannah reports, but "[l]uckily, the illness left as quickly as it struck" (241). Later, as humanity perishes en masse, the man can still "hear it, down there in my lungs" (265). Its presence, though uncomfortable, protects him. Meanwhile, a flurry of hastily engineered vaccines and antibiotics prove woefully ineffective, even counterproductive. Not only does their distribution through modern industrial networks hasten the pandemic, but also synthetic solutions have softened individual bodies, weakening them to unforeseen threats. Eating paleolithic food, on the other hand, hardens the immune systems of Hannah's group.

Parasites raises and explores urgently relevant questions about these themes more than it attempts to provide answers (which would be difficult to do in a single novel in any case). Tensions involving the appropriate use of medical and other technologies, as well as the role of the state and corporations in such affairs, are not easily resolved, and indeed contribute to genuinely progressive critiques as well as to the propagation of deeply hierarchical anti-vaxxer rhetoric. What I want to emphasize about the novel is how it supplements scenes of inoculation with the fact that its characters appeal to nature to justify their own expectations for human ontology, social behavior, and group belonging before and after the local government brutally enforces its own at the height of the pandemic. Municipal officials quickly declare a state of emergency in the novel. "Law and order itself is under threat," the sheriff tells Hannah. "Measures are called for" (271). Those measures resemble the "lifeboat ethics" Hardin proposed to safeguard resources for a privileged few. Officers erect barricades "to keep the citizens out." Hannah also notices that "they were all men. Where were the women?" (272–3). The rigid gender hierarchy of the new, short-lived regime quickly becomes clear, as the police instate what they understand as a proper order not only pitting insiders against outsiders, but also stratifying men and women. But throughout the novel, Hannah frequently naturalizes social gender differences himself. Beyond his casual sexism, he imagines Trudy "as a prototypical Clovis woman . . . her body in motion as she hunted," admiring physical features that render her, for him, biologically superior to others (17). Trudy herself stresses the roles played by power and context in how a culture defines what is natural, arguing that a Clovis diorama on campus "is more about the Northern European male who created it than the culture he thought he was depicting" (56). Hannah himself does not quite take Shepard's position that it is "futile to pronounce, at the end of fifteen million years of hominid evolution, that men and women are alike."[54] But he does close the novel with an address to future generations that acknowledges his own caprice in defining the traits of the new "organic community" that he, by virtue of his survival, helps to found: "[F]orget not that you are all descended from me, that I myself am the source of your laws" (295).

The novel indeed ends with the characters' fetish for origins intact, despite the fact that it plays out as a discovery, on their part, of what a world without modern medicine might look like. The survivors resolve to turn away "from the depopulated plains of North America. . . . the journey ahead would shuttle us off this continent by the same road that had brought the Clovis" (341). And they come to understand their survival—first of the contagion, then of a world bereft of present conveniences—as contingent upon certain "primal" behaviors and interactions (as Shepard might put it), including exposure to disease. Hannah appeals to his students' abilities in this vein: "Look at the pathetic fire you built," he commands Eggers. "Observe its lack of heat. . . . That's what you learned from your dissertation?" Trudy knows how to "throw a spear, yet [she] settle[s] for cold beans from a can. What happened to the woman as . . . hunter?" (320). These scenes bespeak a revision in Hannah's perspective on humanity's inherent rapacity. He ultimately admits that "his theory that the Clovis vanished as a result of resource depletion has been dealt a serious blow by the contagion we have witnessed"—and indeed, throughout the novel, he develops a more nuanced understanding of the uneven distribution of blame for and the effects of ecological turmoil (322). When he studies the "bloated excess" of wealthy casino patrons, "the irony struck [him] that these were the real Clovis: people who used for themselves the resources of many, who exploited their environment to depletion, and, once everything they wanted was gone, would skip town" (89). Eggers "was no Clovis," Hannah decides. "The Clovis took and took and took, leaving six hundred generations of descendants to fend for themselves in an impoverished world." The man is, instead, "a romantic, his dissertation an exercise in nostalgia" (89). Somewhat paradoxically, this quality is what makes Eggers, for Hannah, *truly* paleolithic by the end. He is exempt from the alienation modernity has visited upon the species since the dawn of agriculture, and therefore innocent of the destruction the species enacts upon the world—and worthy of inheriting it. This evaluation itself encodes a call to or acceptance of violence implicit in the work of some real-world biocentrists: as Trask puts it, those "who would . . . return to the hunting life assume that they will be alone in their pursuit, the world having been nearly purged of human megafauna."[55] The novel ultimately calls into question the desirability of such a romance, but it arguably spares the process by which the characters arrive at the same critique, rehearsing cultural narratives about contagion and immunity that reserve survival for a "natural" elect.

Optimal Survivors in *Future Home of the Living God*

It bears mention that for all their fixation on the supposed lifestyles of North America's original peoples, *Parasites'* characters privilege the Pleistocene Clovis over still-living Indigenous peoples, who seem, for some of them, as alienated from a state of nature as Euro-Americans. And they meet the same fate: in the aftermath of the pandemic, Hannah and his fellow survivors "moved through the Sioux Reservation, windy and quiet. If only they'd harbored an atavistic gene of immunity . . . there would have been some delicious justice" (330). That Johnson refers to "justice" signals that the novel does pay some attention to the legacies of settler colonialism, such as the appropriation, commodification, and mockery of Native peoples in the form of school mascots and the cavalier treatment of stolen museum artifacts. It also situates European conquest within the discourse of contagion and immunity with which it engages, noting that, in the centuries following Christopher Columbus's arrival, upwards of 93 percent of the Native population in the Americas perished, most of them victims of an imported "all-star team" of smallpox, cholera, typhus, and other diseases (326). One can argue, as Emily Martin does, that ideas about superior immunity—and even genetic development related to it—have also broadly underwritten the settler-colonial entitlement to land that so often anchors national identity in the United States, in the form of a warrant that "it was the Europeans' more potent germs that made the conquests possible" and that their own "immune systems had evolved to a higher state as a result of being challenged by more evolved . . . nastier germs."[56] Louise Erdrich, in a 2017 interview, inverts that claim to make a point about Native resilience in the face of settler colonialism: "Every Native person knows that nine of every ten of their ancestors died of European diseases. We are descended of that one person in ten who . . . somehow survived the various government policies that first meant to eradicate and then assimilate all Native people." She intends this statement more as a condemnation of imperialism than as a glorification of her own hardiness compared to others': "[E]xistence for most Native people in this country," she adds, remains "an unrelenting struggle."[57]

Her novel *Future Home of the Living God,* however, toys with the notion that Native people possess an inherently more robust capacity for survival—but not necessarily because Erdrich takes this notion seriously. The novel explores this idea as a facet of contemporary settler fantasies about Indigenous peoples' closeness to the earth and the extent to which settler proximity might not only open access to this fitness, but also, through it, establish one's authentic belonging on American land and survival on a climate-changed planet. The novel dramatizes an unfolding ecological crisis linked vaguely to prehistoric pathogens released by thawing global temperatures, advanced enough that an "unusually cool day for August" in Minnesota is now ninety degrees (55). Genetically speaking, "our world is running backward. Or forward. Or maybe sideways" (3). Animal and plant genomes have, "on the molecular level," begun "skipping around . . . shuffling through random adaptations." Something that looks like a saber-toothed cat pulls a dog into a tree, an apparent archaeopteryx lands in a backyard, and humans and domesticated animals have stopped "breeding true," resulting in both miscarriages and "physically adept" yet not-quite-human infants who "grab things earlier" and "walk sooner" (44, 163). Experts and laypeople alike teleologically frame the problem as "regression," a matter of "humanoid figures growing hunched as they walked into the mists of time" (52). Regression is not something for which many of the novel's characters, unlike *Parasites'*, yearn. Returning to a prior episode of human history is a cause not for celebration but for individual and national concern—an interpretation with historical precedent. Margaret Atwood notes in dialogue with Erdrich that genetic regression "was a possibility that afflicted the Victorian mind right after the theory of evolution became generally accepted"—and a chief impetus behind eugenic race science.[58] *Future Home* explores this sort of reaction, too, as a Christian theocracy seizes power and begins to incarcerate pregnant women, hoping to identify viable infants with at least one white parent and salvage the racial and sociocultural composition of a reborn nation that fictively institutionalizes the real-world ambitions of the extreme, explicitly fascist right.

Despite Erdrich's self-conscious adoption of the label "dystopian" for the novel, however, she stresses the extent to which she means for it to capture everyday dilemmas faced especially by Native peoples in the climate change era. In an interview, she explains that she "wanted to write" about "a time very like the days we are experiencing now. We know that climate chaos is happening and that things are going to disintegrate in unknown ways. We know that some of this is too late to stop . . . and that this has already started. We try to guess how this will affect us personally, our families, and our children. We don't know."[59] She began writing in 2002, soon after the passage of the Patriot Act and President George W. Bush's instatement of the global gag rule targeting nongovernmental organizations that offer abortion counseling or services. "To sow fear" of diversity and secularity is, for Erdrich, the goal of such policies—part of a broader effort to strengthen national security and promote religious values threatened by the legal and cultural accomplishments of the late twentieth century's new social movements. After a long hiatus, she resumed writing around the 2016 presidential election, again prompted to consider the relationship among the reactionary, the authoritarian, and the everyday—an undertaking for which she believed dystopian fiction well suited. "As a genre with a particularly strong connection to culture and politics," Silvia Martínez-Falquina writes, "dystopia mediates between past, present, and future: grounded in the anxieties of the present, it speculates on the future consequences of current events and actions."[60] But like countless other Native scholars and artists, Erdrich adds that "Indigenous people in the Americas are descended of relatives who survived the dystopia of genocide. To us, dystopia is recent history. (For many, it is the present.)"[61] Speculative dystopia offers, for her, an opportunity to examine the more prosaic ways that ideas about the natural and unnatural reinforce logics of national or territorial belonging and individual survival in terms of race, gender, and the legacies of settler colonialism. The "world ends," her protagonist Cedar Songmaker remarks, with "everything crazy yet people doing normal things" (25).

Prevalent among those "normal things," early in the novel, is middle-class handwringing over the purity of vaccines. Cedar's adoptive mother Sera fears for her safety after having "refused to vaccinate" her as a child, suspicious "that additives in the shots or the vaccines themselves cause autism." Cedar had in fact acquired the standard shots herself when she turned eighteen, worried about "Native susceptibility to European viruses. . . . As a descendent of that tough-gened tenth person I had some natural inherent immunity, but still" (58). Vaccines (or technology in general) are not, for Cedar, inimical to nature, as they are for her mother and real-world anti-vax organizers. Nor does she swagger her own "inherent immunity." I belabor these points because, in the novel, they bear a relationship to class and Indigeneity. "Upper-class delusionals can afford to indulge their paranoias only because the masses bear the so-called dangers of vaccinations," Cedar tells Sera (59), telegraphing the critique of anti-vax rhetoric I sketched above, as well as referencing a pervasive lack of healthcare on Native reservations across North America.

Despite this fact, Cedar speaks to an association among her parents' (and others') attitudes about nature, health, and their daughter's identity, about which "they're overeager in some aspects. They want a piece of Native pie and I don't really have any pie at all" (57). Her "ethnicity" is "celebrated in the sheltered enclave of my adoptive . . . family. Native girl! Indian Princess! . . . I was rare, maybe part wild," and "star of my Waldorf grade school," too. "I always felt special. . . . My observations on birds, bugs, worms, clouds, cats and dogs, were quoted. I supposedly had a hotline to nature" (4–5). Her peers, guardians, and, later, boyfriend Phil often view her in terms of what Shepard Krech calls the "ecological Indian stereotype," but by adulthood her own romantic self-image has shattered.[62] She "heard stories. Addictions. Suicides." The material realities of contemporary Native life put the lie to the archetype by which others understand her, but to varying degrees, many non-Native figures continue to posit a special relationship between her and the earth by virtue of her Native ancestry—a fetish for the "natural" that coexists comfortably with Sera's antivaccine sentiment. Atwood, in her interview with Erdrich, notably describes Cedar's parents as "New Age-y" (gesturing toward an overlap between Johnson's and Erdrich's critique).[63] Cedar herself refers to Sera and her husband Glen as "green in their very souls," vegan and "phobic about food additives" (4). As lawyers, they specialize in midwifery and environmental protection, and are "shrewd as only market-based society suspicious trust-fund liberals can be" (57)—a tongue-in-cheek dig at a left-of-center mainstream that advances hyperindividualist solutions to systemic problems. From Cedar's vantage, one of those solutions seems to involve sponsoring (and romanticizing) a Native child, although she "never understood how [she] was adopted." The 1978 Indian Child Welfare Act (ICWA), which ended the forced, abiding removal of Native children from their families and cultures through expropriation to and assimilation in non-Native foster care, adoptive homes, and boarding schools, "had to . . . apply to me" (4). (As it turns out, Glen is her biological father.)

The novel foregrounds relationships among child custody, settler colonialism, and cultural identity especially in its treatment of reproductive politics, the stakes of which have grown higher following the U.S. Supreme Court's 2022 ruling overturning the constitutional right to abortion in *Dobbs v. Jackson's Women's Health.* In *Future Home,* the state compels women to give birth to maintain not only species viability but also the population and assumed cultural (and implicitly racial) character of the nation. Like *Parasites'* sheriff, the president declares a "state of emergency" and then martial law (8, 45). Deriving authority from the Patriot Act, the House and Senate vote to "seize entire library and medical databases in order to protect national security" and "determine who is pregnant throughout the country" (72). Cedar is among them, four months expecting with Phil's child when the state begins "round-ing us up" (72). Prisons across the country are emptied of inmates, most of them euthanized, to make space for the newly incarcerated women. Calls for "Womb Volunteers" give way to a "womb draft" for all women of childbearing age (159, 187). The headquarters of an "Unborn Protection Society" replaces Minneapolis City Hall, and the radio encourages listeners to call its "tip-line" with information about truants (124). "You can get picked up for running a stoplight," one woman remarks at the novel's end. "I'm here for shoplifting. . . . I needed food" (252), she adds, illuminating a relationship between reproductive unfreedom and class in the novel that reflects the fact that, as Martínez-Falquina notes, "it is poor and marginalized women who are most at risk of the recent regression in women's rights."[64] In all cases, state forces emphasize that this unfreedom benefits the nation. "I wonder if you have the courage to save the country we love," asks Mother, an anonymous agent responsible for encouraging women to volunteer (and pursuing those who don't). "We need you to be a Patriot" (90).

What I want to emphasize is the rhetorical homology Erdrich establishes between *Future Home*'s regime and what Carol Mason has referred to as the "apocalyptic narrative" of right-wing "pro-life" politics since the 1970s. "Pro-life retribution," she writes, is, on the far right, often "seen as a way to restore the order of God"—and, with it, a certain vision of a Christian (and, implicitly or explicitly, often white) nation—to a fallen United States, even in situations that don't necessarily involve abortion.[65] (Doug Wilson, the Christian Reconstructionist pastor, argues something similar about sexuality.) Mother captures this resonance in the novel, appealing to "the divinely infused eternal soul that you carry within you." The federal government collapses amid social and financial panic, and a "Church of the New Constitution" wins power in the ensuing struggle. Street names change to Bible verses. Women who die in childbirth *served the future* as "martyrs" (254). Mother spices this macabre religious spiel with a dose of inspiration evocative of social-media wellness rhetoric targeted at new mothers. "Women are powerful," she declares to a room of prisoners: "empowered to the max. Women are heroes" (255). This juxtaposition is striking given the history of pro-life discourse, whose apocalyptic narrative, Mason notes, migrated in the 1990s from extremist antiabortion terrorists to mainstream contexts, displacing otherwise liberal appeals to the rights of the fetus (which themselves often neglect the health, well-being, rights, and liberties of the women in question). In many circumstances, abortion became a matter not of individual rights but of God's creation—or "nature." Accordingly, pro-life politics broadly "narrate[s] some people as warriors" *for* and others as "enemies" *against* that nature. Even in everyday contexts, to be "pro-life" has largely come to signify being pure or natural. "More than mere demonizing, this narration of 'un-American' enemies seeks to interpellate them," Mason writes.[66]

For this very reason, this discourse also encodes assumptions about race, gender, and sexuality. Mason traces this warrior/enemy binary to the "revitalization" of Protestant millennialism, paramilitary movements, and white supremacy in the late twentieth century, a minefield of reaction that earlier chapters considered in light of the relationship between the socioeconomic upheavals of the past five decades and the history of racialization in the United States. In the novel, Erdrich links militia activity to everyday insecurities related to masculinity, involving economic dislocation and the erosion of gendered power structures—both enemies, as Mason puts it, of life, conflated with a specific vision of national culture. Male-dominated militias install the Church of the New Constitution after many years during which men had "in general . . . become militantly insecure . . . forming supersecret clubs" (79). At an emergency session of Congress, "men in dark suits" fret about not just abnormal fetal maturation but also, more specifically, "what it means that male sexual organs are not developing properly," if "at all" (69). Erdrich leaves open the possibility that when Cedar's doctor exclaims "We've got one" during a sonogram, he is referring to a fetus with testicles (50). The swift rollback in *only* women's rights, and their consignment to their proper status as incubators for patrilineal and national bloodlines, represents an institutional, biopolitical imposition of the sort of assumptions about "natural" gender roles explored throughout this book in less overtly authoritarian contexts. For Erdrich, "it's so obvious" that pro-life rhetoric is less "about religious faith" than "controlling women's bodies."[67] The Church takes the infants. The women disappear. Most do not survive childbirth, but imprisoned women speculate that those who do likely end up murdered and dumped, their impressionable infants of greater worth to the far-right regime than they are.

Erdrich also highlights the historically racialized dimensions of that control. It is only when the Ojibwe Cedar tells her doctor that Phil is white "as milk" that he cautions her to "get the hell out of here," attempting to protect her from the state's interest (51). Later, Cedar's roommate in a hospital-prison shares that the father of her child, too, is a "waspy . . . guy" (170). And at one point, an unspecified militant announces over the radio that she and her associates have "liberated" the "leftover" embryos "not labeled Caucasian" from an in-vitro clinic: "We're not killing any" (90). The Church, it seems, seeks out only developmentally normative children with at least one white parent, literally disposing of the rest. This detail, too, finds its basis not just in the history of eugenic race science (and the sterilization programs targeting Black, Native, and poor women that emerged from it) but also in a great deal of contemporary pro-life rhetoric. The Ku Klux Klan—an important interlocutor with (and component of) paramilitary movements since long before the 1970s—continues to "attribute abortion to white people's propensity for 'racial suicide,'" arguing that reproductive justice, feminism, and the legalization of homosexuality all contribute to "white genocide" in the form of declining white birthrates. Many members nonetheless proclaim their willingness "to pay higher taxes to pay for . . . abortions" if it would mean "a whiter and brighter future."[68] To expand Erdrich's point about pro-life hypocrisy, for many on the far right it is not abortion itself that is the issue, just abortion among white Euro-Americans. Such attitudes circulate among figures like the El Paso and Buffalo shooters today, too, but it would be a mistake to pretend that they're confined to the crypto-fascist margins. Illinois Representative Mary Miller declared the Supreme Court's *Dobbs* decision a "victory for white life" at a 2022 rally.[69] "The term *fetal protection* . . . encompasses a double meaning" in this respect, Mason writes: "protect those fetuses who would emerge as wholly pure in the genetic sense and holy pure in the spiritual sense," but also "protect us *from* the fetuses who would be born as members of degenerate races."[70]

Cedar's fetus is nonetheless desirable in the novel: Phil is white. But I would argue that it is through the character of Phil that Erdrich makes a subtler critique—one that involves the two threads of *Future Home* on which I've focused: the state's fixation on national survival and bodily optimization, paired with eugenic assumptions about race, and the fetishization of Cedar's Native ancestry. Phil captures both preoccupations quite explicitly. By the end of the novel, Cedar's birth and adoptive parents have evacuated her to the reservation, and Phil, in the time between her arrest and their reunion, has become something of an apologist for the regime. "After all, it's a global crisis, it's the future of humanity, so you can see why they need to keep an eye on women," he explains. Survival, for Phil as well as for the Church, is contingent upon the state of emergency according to which violence against some is necessary to safeguard the future of not only the nation but also its privileged inheritors.[71] Cedar might indeed be carrying "one of the originals . . . a regular baby," he tells her. "The thing is . . . you have a treasure, Cedar, if our baby is normal. We would be in charge of things. . . . [T]he sky's the limit." Cedar is alarmed. "We could seize power and found a dynasty," she scoffs (245–7). But Phil confirms this goal, subscribing to the notion that optimized bodies should survive and perhaps even rule.

I want to suggest that Erdrich establishes a homology between the Church and Phil similar to the one Atwood draws between Crake and the Gardeners, and to similar effect: it draws attention to everyday iterations of ecofascistic logic. In the Church, Erdrich literalizes twenty-first-century fears of a fascist resurgence. The regime not only resonates with recent rollbacks in reproductive freedom but also fictionalizes the rhetoric of the classical movements scrutinized by comparative studies of fascism. But Erdrich juxtaposes this new ethnostate with Phil for a reason. For purposes of survival, of nation or family, both privilege certain bodies over others, and both in terms of race and ethnicity as well as physical fitness and developmental normativity. Phil does not necessarily prioritize white bloodlines as the Church does, however. In fact, he participates in the same liberal fetishization of Cedar's Indigeneity as her classmates and, to a lesser extent, her parents. Phil "took a vow," Cedar remarks. "Do no harm, to anything or anyone. Save nature. He decided to dedicate himself to preserving bird habitat, and got an advanced degree in ecology. Since then, he has tried to protect the natural world whenever possible," including as a member of Earth First!–style groups "beyond the law." And Erdrich intimates that Phil understands his proximity to Cedar as a sort of benediction on this work, as well as the fulfillment of a sexual fantasy. He "was raised on dairy products bearing the image of the Land O'Lakes Butter Maiden." As a child, he "folded her knees up to make breasts." Later, he confesses to Cedar "that after he met me, the Butter Maiden started to haunt his dreams. . . . She looked like me" (83). The intersection Erdrich installs between Phil's sexual and epistemological interests in Cedar's Indigeneity places both on a sliding scale of settler-colonial entitlement. Phil's fantasy registers, for Cedar, as a recolonization, through intercourse, of a Native body. Read alongside it, his interest in her ostensible closeness to nature communicates something similar. This detail, taken together with Phil's comments about their fitness for survival in the face of extinction, signifies that unlike the Church, Phil values Cedar's fetus not because it has one white parent but because it also has a Native one. It is proximity to—or even consumption of—Native bodies that, for Phil, renders one fit to survive at the expense of others.

Consuming the Ecological Indian

I do not link these aspects of Phil's character haphazardly. This theme is one that Erdrich explores across her corpus, including in her most recent novel, *The Sentence* (2021), which also takes contagion, specifically Covid-19, for a subject. It also explicitly articulates questions that *Future Home* and *Parasites* only subtly explore: During times of crisis, including pandemics, who is most likely to survive, and why? According to what systemic constraints? Due to what histories? Two characters in *The Sentence* muse over "reports . . . that those who died had underlying health issues. That was probably supposed to reassure some people—the super-healthy, the vibrant, the young." One gets "an automatic point for being . . . ten years younger." Another "lose[s] a point for having asthma." In light of numbers coming out of nearby reservations and concurrent Black Lives Matter protests, being Native appears, for these two, to remain a liability in the United States. The plot nonetheless revolves, however, around what the narrator describes as "a stalker—of all things Indigenous," a "persistent wannabe" who effaces her European ancestry by inconsistently reporting, on one hand, that her grandmother, ashamed of her true Indigeneity, passed as white, and, on another, "that she had been an Indian in a former life." When the woman learns that her predecessor was not a Native woman but a white madam who ruthlessly abused and commercialized Native women, her "identity turned upside down.

Everything that she'd concocted about herself turned out to be its opposite."[72] The woman's desire to be Native, Erdrich suggests, represents yet another settler-colonial act—one that itself papers over and thereby reinforces settler-colonial histories.

I want to end this chapter with the suggestion that what Erdrich dramatizes, in *Future Home* and *The Sentence,* is the extent to which Native people themselves have functioned as threshold objects in cultural narratives across U.S. history. The performative (and commercial) consumption of Native stereotypes, iconography, and even bodies is certainly not a new phenomenon. Nor am I the first to draw attention to its centrality to U.S. mythmaking since at least the late nineteenth century. Kim TallBear (Sisseton Wahpeton Oyate) considers how, in the recent market for genetic testing, Native "blood" or ancestry has become a "desired object" whose "loss would be lamented, as the 'First American' is central to the country's nation-building project—to constructing moral legitimacy and a uniquely American identity."[73] Shari Huhndorf refers to this program as "going native," a "widespread conviction that adopting some vision of native life . . . is necessary to regenerate and to maintain European-American racial and national identities."[74] Ernest Thompson Seton founded the Boy Scouts of America in 1910 "partly on the idea that young men would acquire American virtue by learning the austere disciplines and woodcraft of 'little savages.'"[75] More broadly, writers like James Fenimore Cooper, seeking to establish an authentic U.S. literary tradition, posited in the nineteenth century the emergence of a "new race," as D. H. Lawrence put it in 1923, "from a rapprochement between Europeans and Native Americans."[76] This "American race," Roxanne Dunbar-Ortiz writes, would be "born of the merger of the best of both worlds" but "involv[e] the dissolving of the Indian" as the last of the "noble" Natives bequeathed nature and the territory said to epitomize it to their Euro-American usurpers.[77]

I've presented examples of what Philip Deloria calls "playing Indian" before: in *Ecotopia,* for instance, in which characters don knockoff Native styles as an expression of their unalienated relationship to the land, in part as a critique of Western capitalism. Such behavior has negotiated cultural ambivalence concerning modernity at least since the birth of the conservation movement. Even as social-Darwinist and patently eugenic screeds lionized the technological advancement and cultural dominance of the white race, the socioeconomic imbalances generated by industrial capitalism and attenuation of national identity heralded by both the closing of the frontier and the genocidal violence required to achieve it "created a nostalgia for origins." In texts like Cooper's, retreat from modernity is not really the "ultimate goal," Huhndorf argues. "By adopting Indian ways, the socially alienated character uncovers his own 'true' identity" on the land—and "redeems Euro-American society" in the process.[78] That ambition has not faded with time. Before his 1964 presidential bid, Barry Goldwater regularly engaged in Native "redfacing" in his involvement with the "Smoki People," an "alchemy of white men's social club, post-conquest cultural expropriation, anti-Indian sacrilege, and colonialist frontier theater," as Dylan Rodríguez describes it.[79] And a decade later, Forrest Carter, formerly the Ku Klux Klan leader Asa Carter, published *The Education of Little Tree* (1976), seemingly a pivot from his rabid white supremacy to an embrace of simplified Native custom. In both cases, however, apparent appreciation of Native peoples "serve[d] to reassert white dominance even as it conceal[ed] a profoundly racist project." Neither Goldwater nor Carter renounced their regard of their own racial purity. They simply sought to emplace it through a different rhetorical "alchemy" by which proximity to Native stereotype (though rarely actual Native people) would symbolically confirm their organic belonging upon U.S. soil. What I want to point out, however, is that this tendency has never been limited to overt white supremacists. As I noted in chapter 2, communalists of the same era enacted similar performances (often effacing the lived experience of actual Native peoples). Political affiliation matters less than the fact that all these parties subscribed to a "conviction that the world has gone awry in spiritual, racial, economic, and ecological terms"—and told a similar story about how to revitalize it.[80]

Such lopsided engagements with Indigeneity function, in this respect, in part as appeals to palingenetic rebirth—one of fascism's principal generic characteristics. But as previous examples have demonstrated, likeminded ideas surface in more recent, everyday contexts as well, in some cases promoting the notion that one can expect to survive conditions of ecological crisis as other, insufficiently *un*alienated people die. Too many anti-vaxxer moms imply something similar when they promote variolation over vaccination. Erdrich situates Phil among *Future Home*'s conflicts and themes in such a way that he makes the same case. Like Johnson, Erdrich writes a character fixated on optimization for survival in the face of rapid ecological change as well as widespread disease. For Phil, however, what proves his fitness for survival—even for rule—is not exposure to pathogens, but rather his intimacy with a romanticized Native ancestry. It is not just the possibility that Cedar is carrying "a regular baby" that excites him, but also the fact that the fetus represents a closeness to the earth for which he also fetishizes its mother. He "want[s] a piece of Native pie," as Cedar puts it. For Phil, that means ecological innocence, belonging on the land, fitness for survival, even license to dominate whoever remains. Bodies themselves become threshold objects. The Christian state consumes women like Cedar to preserve what it takes to be beneficial—i.e., their life-giving capacity—in the form of their (white) offspring. The nation consumes bodies, that is, for the purposes of its own perpetuation and control, effacing Indigenous and women of color themselves. (To name just one other example, one could argue that Cherie Dimaline explores a kindred conflict in her 2017 young adult novel *The Marrow Thieves*.) Phil does something quite similar. He privileges Native ancestry for the sake of *his* continuity and control.

Though fictional, the implications of this logic have taken on new urgency in contemporary relations between the United States and sovereign Indigenous nations. On the one hand, *Future Home* seems to reverse the country's eugenic tradition of forced sterilization among Native, Black, Latinx, and poor women, dramatizing instead the fact that the nation has always depended on—and horrifically exploited—their labor (especially that of Black women confined to the system of chattel slavery). But on the other, the novel resonates with a variety of recent and ongoing threats to Native identity and sovereignty as well as reproductive freedom. In addition to announcing its decision in *Dobbs*, the U.S. Supreme Court also heard oral arguments for *Haaland v. Brackeen* in 2022. The suit (which was ultimately decided in favor of the defendant) sought to overturn the Indian Child Welfare Act of 1978—the one Cedar mentions in *Future Home* that compels state officials to ensure that Native children remain with family members or guardians of the same nation or ancestry. The act passed with bipartisan support and remained uncontroversial for years, but numerous challenges have risen against it in the twenty-first century. The plaintiffs argued that the law violates the Fourteenth Amendment's equal-protection clause, citing racial discrimination against white adoptive parents.[81] Beyond the fact that child welfare experts overwhelmingly view the ICWA as an exemplar, the problem is that sovereign Native nations do not comprise a racial category but a political one, a status like that of other nation-states. (*Future Home* highlights this double standard. Officials raid Native reservations for pregnant women but not other countries, maintaining U.S. claims to unceded land.) Critics view the case as one (failed) move in an ongoing chess match organized by a variety of interests, including not only private adoption firms but also rightwing policy thinktanks, corporate energy and land speculators, and unabashed hate groups, whose endgame is to "gut the legal rights of Indigenous nations" wholesale. "The potential domino effect of the lawsuit" lay in the extent to which it sought "to reframe tribal membership as a racial rather than a political category," Rebecca Nagle (Cherokee) writes. Reservation status, land use, water rights—in effect, tribal sovereignty writ large—would have become "questionable" had the suit succeeded.[82]

Land and fossil fuel resources indeed attracted the plaintiffs' supporters and sponsors at a macro scale, but coverage made clear that, at the micro, the white evangelical Brackeen family really did just want a Native child. Erdrich raises the question of whether such desires constitute yet another form of "going native." Prior to the ICWA's passage, the federal government removed roughly a third of Native children from their families under the authority of the boarding school system, midcentury Termination and Relocation policies, and other programs. Ever since, Native children have proven far more likely than others to remain in their communities.[83] "There is a deep irony," the journalist Elie Mystal writes, to claims of prejudice by the white plaintiffs, who were "in essence the beneficiaries of centuries of theft, discrimination, and outright genocide of Native peoples."[84] A character like Phil (and his potential real-world resonances) continues that tradition, making it a matter of environmentalist virtue—even identity. He is, in this regard, not so different from the Native "wannabe" of *The Sentence*, whose ghost "trie[s] to enter" the protagonist in a seeming possession. She "wanted to *be* . . . to exist inside of a Native body. But a certain kind of Indigenous body, big and tough."[85] Both Phil and the ghost identify Native people with fitness and resilience, intrinsic and essential not only to weathering ecological crises but also to organically belonging on American soil and the earth itself in their aftermath. They imagine that, "by some clever manipulation," as Vine Deloria Jr. (Standing Rock Sioux) puts it, they "achieve an authenticity that cannot ever be" theirs.[86]

For Erdrich, however, "authenticity" does not seem to be a realistic quality for anyone to claim—a fact that doesn't rule it out for other Native writers. The question of blood, for example—and its relation to land—is a matter of debate among Indigenous scholars as well as Euro-American consumers. Blood and land, Chadwick Allen writes, "name primary and interrelated sites in the struggle over defining indigenous minority identities." They also function as important tropes "to counter and, potentially, to subvert dominant settler discourses"—sometimes controversially, given that talk of blood can "raise disturbing issues of essentialism, racism, and genocide," as well as marginalize "large numbers of 'mixed-blood' individuals and communities." What is worth emphasizing is that different Native writers recombine and deploy these "emblematic figures" in ways that are contextually specific in terms of both communal histories and contemporary material realities. Many Native writers and activists—such as Glen Coulthard, Leanne Simpson, Winona LaDuke (Mississippi Band Anishinaabeg), and Robin Wall Kimmerer (Potawatomi)—themselves mobilize variations on the ecological Indian figure. Very rarely do they do so, however, as a matter of "conformity . . . to a given set of standards," let alone presumptions of purity or innocence."[87] The narrator of *The Sentence* holds traditional lands in reverence but idealizes neither environment nor her Native ancestors. People and peoples are complicated, prone to conflict as much as to cooperation—with the land and each other. Land relations have differed wildly over history, from people to people, and culturally specific practices of reciprocity with environment have developed over time rather than springing, fully formed, from the ground. For Erdrich, idealization is a liability, not a point of pride—a perspective she attributes to her experience as a woman. In *Future Home,* the antagonistic Mother's declaration that women are "heroes" reflects the fact that social media platitudes are not merely frivolous slogans. They can also reinforce strict, materially consequential gender ideals, "male creations . . . constructed," Erdrich writes, "to thrash the rest of us."[88] The same goes for Native peoples, she adds elsewhere: "The thing is, most of us . . . have to consciously pull together our identities," especially after "centuries of being erased . . . in a replacement culture."[89] As Cedar remarks in *Future Home*, her biological grandmother "seems to have lived out many versions of her own history" through the narration of stories she "probably tells and retells all the time." This "narrative is all that matters" when it comes to her understanding of self, people, and relations with environment (35).

Phil, by contrast, seeks to acquisitively access something intrinsic—some blood that will link him to the soil. In doing so, he ignores actual Native institutions and traditions, even as they play out around him at the end of the novel. Despite the consolidation of existing patterns of power by Christian fundamentalists, an alternative social structure emerges on the Ojibwe reservation: one based on both reproductive and nonreproductive kinship structures and systems of reciprocity and responsibility organized around mutual aid. *"Quite a number of us see the governmental collapse as a way to make our move and take back the land,"* writes Eddy, Cedar's stepfather (95). Later, he explains how the Dawes Act of 1887 "removed land from communal ownership," even after years of loss through treaties. "We're just taking back the land within the original boundaries of our original treaty," housing Ojibwe without shelter or living in substandard conditions and welcoming "urban relatives" who bring their own expertise in education, medicine, law, and other fields to the reservation (214). "We're gonna be self-sufficient," he says, "like the old days" (227). He remains optimistic despite concerns that crops and livestock, bred to fragile specificity, will themselves genetically shuffle: "Indians have been adapting since before 1492 so I guess we'll keep adapting." Cedar is skeptical: "But the world is going to pieces," she says. "It is always going to pieces," he responds. "We'll adapt" (28).

The sentiment reflects the fact that, though apocalypse might be a new experience for many in the United States, Indigenous peoples have lived through the continual destruction of their ways of life at least since 1492. "As Native people, we have endured some of the darkest chapters in history and emerged knowing who we are, where we come from, and what we stand for," writes Julian Brave NoiseCat (Secwepemc and St'at'imc).[90] This sentiment is not necessarily a form of idealism itself. For Cedar, "humanity is going forward," not back (225)—a rejection of romantic essentialism on the one hand, and, in light of her grandmother and stepfather's

reflexive perspectives on identity, history, and survival, of teleological narratives of nation, race, and environment on the other.

We would do well to apply that sort of perspective to narratives about contagion, immunity, survival, and crisis in general,
too. The idea that "nature was healing" from a "human virus" at
the height of the Covid-19 pandemic is only "one viral story," Joseph Osmundson writes: one of "consumption, illness, death." But
"[I]sn't this a true story?" he asks. "[W]e're ruining the planet—
our host—to replicate ourselves or our culture or to maximize our
wealth." He quickly gestures to the issue with this telling—and to
a more sophisticated explanation: "There's a pretty obvious way
to fix the problem of too many humans and it's called genocide,"
he writes. "But what's being produced isn't too many humans, it's
too many humans with extreme, obscene wealth; maybe *they* are
the virus, or capitalism itself." But this narrative, too, seems insufficient. "In the story of capitalism or racism as a virus, we are
naming a virus as a thing of excessive self-interest, a thing that
will overwhelm the whole, a thing that will kill, a thing *against* life
itself"—this, despite the fact that we require microbes to live just
as they require us.[91] The viral metaphor, that is, denies our complex interconnection with other species—as well as with other
humans—at every level, animating a misleading story of a pure us
versus an impure them, no matter the context.

Conclusion

The concept of ecofascism remains hotly contested in both scholarly and popular debate. It is, for many, "a 'fringe phenomenon' that has little impact on the existing political landscape." Still, for Sam Moore and Alex Roberts, we might nonetheless study and write about it "in anticipation of politics to come" while "reflecting on the politics of today."[1] And in any event, declaring the idea a "fringe phenomenon" not only misclassifies a broad cultural process as a clearly articulated right-wing ideology but also seems somewhat belated. Joseph Henderson, the social scientist mentioned in the Introduction, sees increasingly explicit gestures toward environmentally motivated political violence not just among vocal white supremacists but also among many of his students. They "fully understood the science of climate change," he writes. But it "doesn't follow that if you teach people about climate change, they're all of a sudden going to create a world that is more just. They're going to integrate it into their existing politics." It would be naive to limit this response to "alienated young white m[en]" who "sit online and get drunk and watch really horrific videos on 4chan and 8chan." Most of his students "took it places that were illiberal" and "antidemocratic" because doing so, he adds, accords with an "existing politics" that transcends distinctions between left and right.[2] The storytelling patterns through which many Americans come to understand and express relationships among self, belonging, and environment lay groundwork for a variety of possibilities—some of them just, some of them not. Many of them are indeed deeply rooted in longstanding assumptions about entitlement to land, social and environmental purity, and—yes—the potential for rebirth through violence. One cannot neatly divorce the "politics of today" from "politics to come," but nor can one straightforwardly disentangle spectacular violence from the cultural narratives that inform them. And engaging those narratives is often a quotidian affair.

Everyday Ecofascism has made a case that, as for fascism more broadly, ecofascism is not reducible to the far right. What makes it unique is that it emerges in large part from certain social conditions and the stories told in reaction to them, not from a central ideological source or camp. The spectacular, manifestly white-supremacist activity we customarily (and increasingly) refer to as "ecofascism"—racialized political violence in the name of both "palingenetic ultranationalism" and environment, together—is in part an effect of slow, complex, discursive processes that often remain obscure. Even if it is only the relatively small number of actors who explicitly call for and perpetrate such violence who qualify (or self-identify) as ecofas*cists*, ecofas*cism*, as a phenomenon or process, is inclusive of both these effects and the cultural narratives that inform them. I began this book with a provocation that casual speech flirts with this territory when it links certain people with certain environments in an apparently antimodernist mode, implicitly advocates palingenetic violence in the process, and reinforces existing systems of power and inequality as it does. After a period of ecological disruption, a privileged population asserts its innocence and positions itself for survival and rebirth at the expense of other, often marginalized peoples who stand to lose the most. In the United States, such narratives often crystallize around figures I've referred to as threshold objects, whose consumption ostensibly enables one to establish their belonging to this organic community. Throughout this book, I've explored how numerous objects fulfill this function for a variety of speakers: land, tools, foods, drugs, microbes, and even romanticized human bodies and bloodlines.

In other words, consumption, broadly conceived, operates as a metaphor for accessing an exclusive state of purity and safety in times of ecological crisis. I want to end *Everyday Ecofascism* by considering what other metaphors might be available for responding to ecological disruption—and what other visions of identity, belonging, and resilience these alternatives might offer. I want to expand, that is, on a theme that emerges in this book's two Interludes: a focus, still, on scenes of consumption (especially of food), but one that foregrounds neither ingestion nor other forms of incorporation, but rather invention. Threshold object narratives revise yet consecrate and reinforce existing patterns of power, affiliation, ownership, and hierarchy along lines of race, class, ability, and normative codes of gender and sexuality. By contrast, writers like Gloria Anzaldúa, Jeff Mann (at his best), and others advance the collaborative design of nonnormative (and often queer) kinship structures inclusive of nonhuman creatures and environments, frequently in the form of a recipe.

I'll close this book with a final example: the Kumeyaay poet Tommy Pico's Teebs tetralogy (*IRL, Nature Poem, Junk,* and *Feed,* published from 2016 to 2019). The four volumes expand on the narrative patterns I've observed throughout this book by both centering images of consumption and specifically by doing so in ways that foreground the same sort of romanticization that Louise Erdrich explores in *Future Home of the Living God*: that of Native ancestry or even living Native people as a means to establishing an organic connection to the earth. Pico's work "offer[s] acute observations of the everyday," Min Hyoung Song writes, especially of "the many ways in which Indigeneity has been made to stand for nature itself."[3] One can describe it, as Kaleem Hawa does, as a "poetry of consumed indigeneity." Pico's pervasive use of food and eating motifs draws a parallel between systemic appropriations and erasures of Native lands, knowledges, and peoples on the one hand, and his own experiences as a gay man on the other. At the same time, however, it also figures scenes of consumption as "site[s] of community-building" and "pleasure."[4] As always, mode of representation matters—and in this case, makes a difference in terms of how belonging is articulated or achieved.

Nature Poem, especially, unfolds as a critique of consumption not only of land but also of romantic representations of it. "I swore to myself I would never write a nature poem," declares the speaker—a Pico alter-ego named Teebs.[5] To do so, for him, would be to contribute to a cultural economy that trades in imagery of untouched wilderness and of noble savages intrinsically attuned to it, and therefore to render himself complicit in erasures of actual, lived experiences of Native life in the Americas (*NP* 2, 50). But Pico extends the consumption metaphor further when he frames U.S. history writ large (and the identities it has engendered) as a recipe that takes Native land as one of its ingredients. "If the dish is, 'subjugate an indigenous population,'" he writes, the principal "ingredient" is to "alienate us from our traditional ways" of gathering, growing, harvesting, and cooking food, as well as from water and other resources—an intervention that has had catastrophic effects on Native self-determination and health across the reservation system (*F* 11). Both literal food traditions and eating metaphors stand in for broader matters of identity, sovereignty, imperialism, and environment.

Pico is concerned with this sort of consumption of nature and its imagery not only because it erases the asymmetrical environmental challenges faced by his reservation due to settler-colonial land management, but also because such representations tend to nonetheless identify Native people like himself *with* environmental purity. Throughout his four volumes, Pico, like Cedar in *Future Home of the Living God,* confronts the ecological Indian stereotype. He describes a moment when a student refers to him as "*such a good Indian*" after he picks up a piece of trash, and another when a white man asks if he feels a greater affinity with the natural world because he's Native (*NP* 24, 15). What I want to emphasize about this second example is how the passage ends: with Teebs sleeping with the man regardless, "bit[ing] him on the cheek" and "reify[ing] savage lust." Two details about this line merit attention. First, the word "bite" ropes sex into the eating idiom that also arranges food, landscapes, and settler-colonial history in Pico's writing, juxtaposing acts of cruising online for sex with eating metaphors so that bodies themselves become a matter of incorporation. Eating comes to function in the volumes, as it does in Mann's essays and poems, "as a metalanguage for genital pleasure and sexual desire."[6]

For Pico, however, Indigeneity adds a dimension to the sexual consumption of bodies. He frames the marketplace of intimacy among queer men as a matter of ingestion: "*he def has an edible butt*" is the colloquial expression he works with—one that suggests that "some butts are edible," or overarchingly desirable, and some are not (*J* 11). The story Pico tells across his poetry is in large part one about negotiating what makes Teebs "edible," or about how he has needed to present himself to seem desirable for sex. Over time, he divulges that he finds it useful "*to lead with something pastoral*" when chatting with white men over dating apps or drinks (*J* 38). By the time *Junk* ends, Pico has enumerated a variety of roles Teebs's partners have expected him to play, including that of environmentalist, shaman, even noble savage itself (48). These details illustrate my second point about that "savage lust" line above. Teebs acknowledges that in the bedroom, many of his white partners expect him to actively play a "savage" role.

Sex is also a kind of consumption, Pico suggests, and for many of the men he meets, Pico himself is doubly fulfilling, providing both sexual gratification and a sort of environmentalist exoneration. He adopts the name "Teebs" not just as a nod to his real-life nickname but also as a self-conscious reference to the elaboration of authorial and other personae, at times as a matter of social expectation (*F* 43–4). Part of his creation of those personae involves both a recognition of and compliance with the ecological Indian stereotype as a fetish, a way of being attractive to certain progressive gay men. Teebs interprets his suitors' fixation on his ostensibly innate environmentalism as a pathway to sex but struggles with the implications: in some cases, from the perspective of the lover, sex with Teebs offers a share in his ostensibly pure ecological existence. These scenes might seem innocuous or even playful, but they raise important questions that I've asked throughout this book: What do people consume and why? What effect do they intend that consumption to have? And in cases where the answer is innocence, belonging, or both, who becomes virtuous and at whose expense? What argument is being made in relation to environment and ecological disruption?

Perhaps most importantly, what more pernicious myths might that consumption uphold or give rise to? In not only romanticizing Indigeneity as a site of environmental purity but also sleeping with it, Teebs's hookups perpetuate longstanding frontier myths of the land as a body (typically a woman, though in this case a feminized gay man) to be conquered, possessed, and exploited. (Something similar happens in the 2018 novel *Jonny Appleseed* by the Two-Spirit, Oji-nêhiyaw writer Joshua Whitehead.) For Teebs, ecological Indian stereotypes deflect attention from real, material challenges facing Indigenous peoples, maintaining exclusive settler-colonial sovereignty and, ultimately, possessive relations with land. What disturbs him is not promiscuity but the fact that more men sleep with him when they can fetishize him, feel that they're good environmentalists for screwing an Indian, then block him on their dating apps—in other words, consume him, exploit him, then erase him. This activity strikes me as a form of "going native" that maps over what Zita Nunes describes as eating's metaphorical function as an expression of mastery, the "assimilation of what is ingested and the reassertion of the identity of the ingester."[7] If cruising is about finding an "edible butt" to consume, the nutrients many of Teebs's lovers seem intent on absorbing, before tossing him aside, are his environmentalist credentials.

Throughout the four volumes, however, Pico ultimately comes to pull Teebs out of these liaisons through an altogether different engagement with food motifs: the restitution of Kumeyaay recipe traditions that settler colonialism erased through new ones reflexively designed and shared with friends—a focus on invention rather than ingestion. Of course, such scenes always involve a measure of both creation (in the form of storytelling, at the very least) and consumption itself—even the previous, colonialist instances considered earlier in this book. And championing invention might seem to overestimate human creativity at the expense of elements of passivity and need that not only anchor human life but also ecologically intertwine it with nonhuman others. As usual, however, I am concerned with mode of representation. For Pico, as for Anzaldúa and Mann (at his best), the emphasis is on collaboration in times of need rather than individualistic assimilation in situations of existing pretense to mastery. "I says to them around the table . . . I don't have food stories. With / you, I say, I'm cooking new ones," Pico writes in *Feed,* inviting the reader to join (11). A recipe can be generative, a metaphor for self-determination as well as for literary transmission. "If it is to be believed that feeding on something necessarily means the end of that thing, then a death impulse is baked into consumption," Hawa writes. "But we also 'consume to continue,' and reading poetry must also nourish and translate."[8] Pico, as both writer and reader, himself becomes something of a recipe in this respect. His stance is much like Erdrich's: he insists that identity (in terms of self, group, and/or place) is not and has never been static, let alone a matter of blood and soil. It is changeful, subject to revision and negotiation over time, if also to material histories and constraints.

I don't mean this point to absolve settler colonialism of its brutal offenses but to foreground a different perspective on identity, belonging, and environment than that which the mechanisms and legacies of settler colonialism have tended to impose or instill. Identity and its relation to place can never be pure. It is not just the case that historical study puts the lie to notions of a mythic ethnonational past. The ecological and geological sciences do the same for ideas about nature. Identity and place are themselves processes—recipes all. Belonging, as such, can't be predicated on

purity either. Purity, Pico writes, "is so fascist" (*J* 43). It also inheres only in the stories told about it—including narratives that
center the consumption of threshold objects. Across Pico's poetry,
"it becomes evident that it's not 'nature' I really have a problem
with," he notes in an interview. "It's racism, colonialism, homophobia, misogyny, etc."—and all the ideas about purity bound up with
them.[9] Pico quite directly responds to and contests the premises of
threshold object narratives, offering in their place everyday stories
of "collective continuance"—what Kyle Whyte defines as "a society's capacity to self-determine how to adapt to change in ways
that avoid reasonably preventable harms." Such narratives function not to purify but to represent "interdependence" as Whyte
understands it: that is, as a network of "caretaking responsibilities
to . . . relatives, human and nonhuman," rather than as a fixed regime of "organic" blood-and-soil ties, with all the social stratifications and forms of violence that have historically accompanied it
and continue to do so.[10]

What Pico, Anzaldúa, and Mann offer are catalogs rather than
consumptions. Catalogs give voice to a plethora of identity positions that might come together to testify to shared experiences of
social and ecological destabilization. Fascist politics, Jason Stanley
writes, "invariably claims to discover its genesis" in "a pure mythic
past tragically destroyed."[11] But as Adeline Johns-Putra points out,
one of the most important things that multiple identity narratives
reveal, when gathered together as they might be in the form of
a catalog, is the "irrecoverability of the past" to which they often
speak. Environments change, have always changed, and will continue to change, and with them, so do place-based identities. To
approach them through divergent yet overlapping experiences is
to "acknowledge that what we call nature is just as radically contingent as human identity . . . while still locating non-human and human beings within the same ethical universe."[12] Such a perspective
respects difference in identity and has the potential to clarify systems of interdependence while considering shared environmental
futures—a direction more indicative of environmental justice than
ecofascism. I do not mean to suggest that, as a form, the catalog
in general (or recipe in particular) constitutes the only or even the
best response to ecofascist narrative logics. My point is that there
do exist representational and material alternatives to consumption, which so often functions both literally and figuratively: on

the one hand, in the form of concrete acts of dispossession and other acts of political violence, and, on the other, in stories of self-purification often told in implicit reference to them. Consumption, that is, underwrites not only ecofascist reactions to ecological disruptions, but also the very exigencies of those challenges: the intertwined histories of settler colonialism and extractive racial capitalism.

Fascism "was not the dominant mode in which far-right ecologism worked" in a postwar era characterized by a distinct "absence of political mobilized masses," Moore and Roberts write. In the meantime, though, "[l]arge numbers of people committed to mainstream right politics, most substantially in the US, have been lied to by those who denied climate change." Moore and Roberts speculate that when they "confront this—and . . . discover that in many cases this suppression of the truth imperils everything that their politics works to hold together—they are likely to radicalize . . . [to] revolt against those who have got us into this mess *and simultaneously* . . . attempt to hold on to what some people already have, either as individuals or, more worryingly, as racial groups."[13] The activities of fringe figures such as the El Paso and Buffalo shooters indicate that at least some individuals and groups have begun to more boldly prod their own version of environmentalism in this direction. Their methods seem less like outliers in our present political moment than they do specific yet representative snapshots of it. "Organic nationalism and the adoption of paramilitary forms, committed to ethnic and political cleansing, at present moves many thousands of people across the world to commit supposedly 'idealistic' . . . acts against neighbors . . . whom they call 'enemies,'" Michael Mann wrote in 2004.[14] In the years since, paramilitary activity has escalated in the United States, too—at times quite explicitly in the name of environment.

So have vast economic inequalities and ecological disruptions, just as they did in the decades leading up to the rise of the classical interwar fascist movements and regimes. The conditions that generated those phenomena "are still present" in Europe, the United States, and other so-called developed nations, Mann writes. Pervasive wealth disparity and its attendant social crises continue to kindle a "sense of betrayal of citizen rights" among otherwise privileged classes, who turn their anger, in some cases fairly but in others misguidedly, to "elites, big business, and immigrant newcomers." It is "rather fortunate," Mann writes, "that 'statism' . . . is greatly out of fashion." And yet, in the early twenty-first century, he mused that, "[g]iven time for a supposedly stateless neoliberalism to do similar damage to parts of the world" as rapid industrialization and wealth accumulation did in the early twentieth, "this rejection of the powerful state will probably fade"—especially, Walter Laqueur adds, in light of "the failure of democratic systems to resolve the problems facing them."[15] Not only the right but also U.S. liberalism in general have persevered for over a century on a shaky alliance between what Corey Robin calls conservatism's "political" and "economic" wings, which champion a hierarchical "elitism of the masses" and "the accumulation of wealth and exchange of commodities . . . associated with unfettered capitalism," respectively. The mainstream acceptance of that partnership in the United States has come under duress in recent years. President Donald Trump's "critique of plutocracy," in word if not in deed, and his "articulated sense of the market's wounds were among the most noteworthy innovations of his campaign," Robin suggests. "If nothing else," they "signal that the sun of Reaganomics—which saw in the unfettered market the answer to the political, economic, and cultural stagflation of the 1970s—no longer warms the lower orders of the right."[16] For Laqueur, writing in the 1990s, anticapitalism was "sure to come to the fore among the extreme Right," despite its lack of coherent economic alternatives to capitalism or socialism. "It might be enough," he cautioned, for "neofascists to appear as the party of order, of national regeneration, and of the defense of their country . . . against rapacious or parasitic aliens," not least in an era of rapid climate and other ecological changes.[17]

Literary interventions do much to lay bare the narrative conventions of ecofascism as a cultural process, dramatize the effects to which they might (or do) give shape, and offer alternative ways of representing identity and its relationship to place and environment. But cultural narratives run deep. They are difficult if not impossible to excise. But we can strive to rework them, just as farright actors do. This work might ultimately amount to little, however, if we do not at the same time collectively address the social conditions that incubate fascist genres to begin with. It would be impossible to simplify the complex, interlocking economic, political, cultural, and ecological factors that have, over the years, decades, and even centuries, culminated in this historical moment,

characterized by ethnonationalist revanchism, paramilitary mobilization, targeted and mass gun violence, and open and racialized insurrection. And it would also be irresponsible to generalize
the diverse exigencies, motives, and reasoning behind these and
other forms of reaction, whether they materialize among vocal
white supremacists or disgruntled ranchers or lonely young men
watching extremist videos online. But there is one thing that these
and other constituencies, across lines of race, ethnicity, nationality, and other social forms, have in common: a shared experience,
however stratified, of mounting inequality and disenfranchisement in a global economic system that favors corporate power and
the ongoing exploitation of resources and people over collective
human and nonhuman well-being—and of an increasingly unpredictable global ecosystem that is also its result. It is not enough
to focus only on violence as an effect. How do people come to it?
Why? According to what stories about themselves and the world?
To think through such questions is to think through fascism as a
process that implicates a variety of people—right, left, and center.
As Laqueur puts it, fascism, classic or contemporary, eco- or otherwise, "is not primarily an ideology or a political party." It is more
like "an alternative way of life"—a complicated dyad of political
genre and its variegated effects.[18] All fascism is everyday fascism.
All ecofascism is everyday ecofascism.

Acknowledgments

Writing and publishing a second book is arguably a smoother process than doing it the first time around. In my experience, it's also one in which the writer is far more aware, from the beginning, of all the other people who make it possible. My thinking on the matters covered in this book has changed considerably since I began to explore them. No one deserves more credit for helping me to work through them—in conversations and collaborations as pleasurable and entertaining as they have been serious—than April Anson, Cassie Galentine, Shane Hall, Jane Henderson, and Bruno Seraphin. Our work together is proof that academic labor is often most generative when pursued together, with the goals of public education in mind.

My colleagues in the Department of English at the University of Connecticut were perhaps the first with whom I shared the project in its earliest coherent form, and their enthusiasm propelled it forward. For their continued support—of both this manuscript and my career more broadly—I am especially grateful to Ellen Carillo, Dwight Codr, Tom Deans, Serkan Görkemli, Bob Hasenfratz, Oliver Hiob-Bansal, Clare Costley King'oo, Kathy Knapp, Ellen Litman, Grégory Pierrot, Greg Semenza, Victoria Ford Smith, Kathleen Tonry, Chris Vials, and Sarah Winter. Beyond UConn, Michael Trask proved, as always, to be an incisive reader at a decisive moment in the project's development, and Virginia Blum an encouraging interlocutor even at a distance. Sarah Dimick was kind enough to read and provide formative feedback on a draft as I turned my attention from writing to publishing. Conversations at meetings of the Modern Language Association, American Studies Association, Association for the Study of Literature and Environment, and Society for the Study of the Multi-Ethnic Literature of the United States with her and others—including Kyle Boggs, Kai Bosworth, Rebecca Evans, Travis Franks, Sage Gerson, Matthew

Henry, Tom Hertweck, Jamie Jones, and Cassidy Thomas—enriched the book immeasurably. I've been fortunate to share portions of this work in other venues as well, including the Cornell University American Studies Spring Colloquium; the Nature, Science, and Society Seminar at UConn; the Fordham University American Studies Department; and the Queer Scholars Series at the University of Massachusetts Dartmouth.

Leah Pennywark and Anne Carter at the University of Minnesota Press deserve special recognition for their patience and keen advice when guiding this manuscript through revision and publication, as do two anonymous readers whose incredibly generous, thorough engagement with my argument not only strengthened it in ways I was struggling to do but also demonstrated, to my mind, genuine excitement about the project. I'd also like to thank every copyeditor, draftsperson, artist, designer, and other member of the production team who worked on this book. Appreciation is due to other presses as well. I am grateful to *Mosaic* and to Duke University Press for granting permission to republish material here I would also like to thank the University of Connecticut Humanities Institute for contributing financial support toward this book's publication.

There are plenty of folks beyond the profession who also deserve thanks. Rachel Mihuta Grimm, Erin Newell, and Beth Lehr continue to provide rich conversation in which to test ideas about social, cultural, and political promises and fears. Countless others provide support in innumerable other ways, including by simply putting up with my nonsense. On that note, thank you last of all—and most importantly—to Vince, who makes work like this worth doing.

Notes

INTRODUCTION

1. Daniel Woodley, *Fascism and Political Theory*, 182, 162.
2. Sarah Jaquette Ray, "Climate Anxiety."
3. See Kathryn Joyce, "What Is 'Ecofascism'?"
4. "An Interview with Out of the Woods."
5. Peter Staudenmaier, *Ecology Contested*, 11–3. See also Bernhard Forchtner and Balša Lubarda, "Eco-Fascism 'Proper.'"
6. Glen Sean Coulthard, *Red Skin, White Masks*, 15.
7. Walter Laqueur, *Fascism*, 121–2.
8. Kai Bosworth, *Pipeline Populism*, 42.
9. Lauren Berlant, *The Female Complaint*, 4.
10. Bosworth, 38, 42.
11. Min Hyoung Song, *Climate Lyricism*, 51, 163. See also Ketan Joshi, "Watch Out for This Symptom."
12. Nira Yuval-Davis, "Belonging and the Politics of Belonging," 204–5, 202.
13. Staudenmaier, 22.
14. Bosworth, 42, 38.
15. Yuval-Davis, 202.
16. See Benedict Anderson, *Imagined Communities*.
17. On the subject of responsibility, see Rob Nixon, *Slow Violence*.
18. Bosworth, 34–5.
19. I do not address storytelling concerning the consumption of fossil fuels given that the figures I examine, on the left and right, tend to oppose it, even if, in practice, their politics ultimately support the economic status quo (i.e., a carbon economy). Stephanie LeMenager's *Living Oil: Petroleum Culture in the American Century* (2016) addresses such storytelling and its own social effects, which might indeed take fascist, if not *eco*fascist, forms—a contention Andreas Malm and the Zetkin Collective make in *White Skin, Black Fuel*.
20. Alexander Reid Ross, *Against the Fascist Creep*, 2.
21. Sarah Manavis, "Eco-Fascism."
22. See Malm and the Zetkin Collective.
23. See Jonathan Olsen, *Nature and Nationalism*.

24. Sam Moore and Alex Roberts, *The Rise of Ecofascism*, 13–6, 35.

25. Bernhard Forchtner, "Far-Right Articulations of the Natural Environment," 2.

26. See, for example, Beth Gardiner, "White Supremacy Goes Green."

27. Moore and Roberts, 78.

28. See Blair Taylor, "Alt-Right Ecology," 283–4.

29. See, for example, Manavis.

30. Janet Biehl and Peter Staudenmaier, *Ecofascism Revisited*, 125.

31. Biehl and Staudenmaier, 17. For the Pagan Liberation League statement, see 97. For the quote about the "true essence of National Socialist Thought," from Ernst Lehmann, a professor of botany, see 13.

32. George Mosse, *The Crisis of German Ideology*, 101.

33. Sarah Jaquette Ray, *The Ecological Other*, 1, 3, 6.

34. Biehl and Staudenmaier, 31.

35. Olsen, 29.

36. Biehl and Staudenmaier, 46, 26, 19.

37. Staudenmaier, 24.

38. Ruth Wodak, "The Trajectory of Far-Right Populism," 30.

39. Blair Taylor, 276–7.

40. Anthony Giddens, *The Consequences of Modernity*, 21.

41. Staudenmaier, 26.

42. Blair Taylor, 278.

43. See Taylor Eggan, *Unsettling Nature*, 50.

44. Lawrence Buell, *Writing for an Endangered World*, 6–7.

45. Moore and Roberts, 122.

46. Matthew Lyons, *Insurgent Supremacists*, ix.

47. Lyons, viii.

48. See Michael Mann, *Fascists*.

49. Laqueur, *Fascism*, 7.

50. Michael Mann, 14, 23, 7.

51. Figures such as Carl Schmitt, for example, loom large in radical right-wing thought. For Schmitt, state sovereignty is fundamentally rooted in an identitarian distinction between *us* and *them*. The ability to identify internal and external enemies—and declare a "state of exception" permitting extreme violence against them—defines sovereignty and justifies its consolidation in the form of an authoritarian leader. See especially Giorgio Agamben, *State of Exception* (2005). For Agamben, this situation is not incidental to political organization, but foundational to the nation-state form.

52. Woodley, 2.

53. Bosworth, 31.

54. See Jeffrey Herf, *Reactionary Modernism*.

55. George Mosse, "Toward a General Theory of Fascism," 77.

56. Roger Griffin, *The Nature of Fascism*, 13.

57. See Jason Stanley, *How Fascism Works,* xvi–xvii, 4–5.
58. Griffin, 26, 33, 37.
59. Robert O. Paxton, *The Anatomy of Fascism,* 23.
60. Michael Mann, 6.
61. Michael Mann, 13.
62. Constantin Iordachi, "Comparative Fascist Studies," 24.
63. Paxton, 13, 209.
64. George Mosse, "The Genesis of Fascism," 19, and "Toward a General Theory of Fascism," 83–4.
65. Woodley, 2.
66. Woodley, 180.
67. Bosworth, 29–30.
68. Woodley, 180.
69. In "Defining Ecofascism," Kristy Campion "canvasses" distinctions and resonances among fascism, ecologism, and ecofascism, highlighting ecofascism's amalgamation of fascism and ecologism as a "regional symbiosis of people and place" (19). She does not, however, consider everyday instances of this interaction.
70. Quoted in Manavis.
71. Blair Taylor, 279.
72. Keith Makoto Woodhouse, *The Ecocentrists,* 7.
73. James F. Jarboe, "The Threat of Eco-Terrorism." The scope of what constitutes ecoterrorism is also a matter of debate. Can one include, for example, colonized peoples fighting on behalf of their land who do *not* identify as "environmentalists" (which is largely a modern, Western affiliation)?
74. Biehl and Staudenmaier, 87, 95.
75. Moore and Roberts, 12.
76. Forchtner, 5.
77. Coulthard, 171, 13.
78. Christophe Bonneuil and Jean-Baptiste Fressoz, *The Shock of the Anthropocene,* 279–80.
79. See Nixon, *Slow Violence.*
80. "An Interview with Out of the Woods." See also Cedric Robinson, *Black Marxism.* "The bourgeoisie that led the development of capitalism," Robinson writes, "were drawn from particular ethnic and cultural groups; the European proletariat and the mercenaries of the leading states from others; its peasants from still other cultures; and its slaves from entirely different worlds. The tendency of European civilization through capitalism was thus not to homogenize but to . . . exaggerate regional, subcultural, and dialectical differences into 'racial' ones" (26).
81. Moore and Roberts, 311.
82. Malm and the Zetkin Collective, 174, 172.

83. Chadwick Allen, *Blood Narrative*, 15ff., 1, 9.
84. See Coulthard, 91–2.
85. Coulthard, 156; Taiaiake Alfred, *Peace, Power, Righteousness*, xviii.
86. Alfred, xviii.
87. Raquel Kennon, "Uninhabitable Moments," 30.
88. Eduardo Bonilla-Silva, *Racism without Racists*, 3.
89. Michael Omi and Howard Winant, *Racial Formation in the United States*, 64.
90. Erin James and Eric Morel, "Introduction," 1.
91. John Levi Barnard, "The Bison and the Cow," 378; Kyle Powys Whyte, "Settler Colonialism," 141.
92. Barnard, 384.
93. Betsy Hartmann, *The America Syndrome*, 21.
94. Whyte, "Against Crisis Epistemology," 52
95. Allison Carruth, *Global Appetites*, 5.
96. See Bonilla-Silva.

1. LAND

1. John Hultgren, *Border Walls Gone Green*, 3.
2. Hultgren, 1.
3. Hultgren, 104.
4. Neel Ahuja, *Planetary Specters*, 21.
5. Matthew Lyons, *Insurgent Supremacists*, v.
6. Daniel Woodley, *Fascism and Political Theory*, 170.
7. Lyons, 159.
8. Hultgren, 28, 94, 5, 27.
9. Lorenzo Veracini, *Settler Colonialism*, 3–4.
10. Zak Cope, *Divided World, Divided Class*, 294.
11. Rowland Keshena Robinson, "Fascism & Anti-Fascism."
12. Patrick Wolfe, *Settler Colonialism and the Transformation of Anthropology*, 163.
13. Veracini, 3.
14. Hultgren, 9, 5.
15. Taylor Eggan, *Unsettling Nature*, 5.
16. Dina Gilio-Whitaker, *As Long as Grass Grows*, 7.
17. See James Pogue, *Chosen Country*, 117–8.
18. Kyle Boggs, "The Rhetorical Landscapes of the 'Alt Right,'" 302.
19. Quoted in Maxine Bernstein, "Ammon Bundy's Lawyer Argues for His Client's Right to Wear Cowboy Boots."
20. See Philip J. Deloria, *Playing Indian*.
21. See, for example, "Hundreds March in Arizona."
22. Pogue, 57, 243.
23. April Anson, "Master Metaphor," 69.

24. See Kyle Keeler, "Colonial Theft."
25. Anson, "Master Metaphor," 60, 65.
26. Gilio-Whitaker, 43.
27. Dorceta Taylor, *The Rise of the American Conservation Movement*, 21–2. For the Roosevelt quote, see 353.
28. Ray, *The Ecological Other*, 13.
29. See Dorceta Taylor, 346–7. The Save the Redwoods League has changed considerably since its founding. Once a hotbed of eugenics, the organization purchased 523 acres of redwood forest in Mendocino County, California, in 2022, which they granted to ten sovereign Indigenous nations (see Rachel Treisman, "A California Redwood Forest").
30. Nancy Ordover, *American Eugenics*, xxiv.
31. Madison Grant, *The Passing of the Great Race*, 97.
32. Sam Moore and Alex Roberts, *The Rise of Ecofascism*, 26.
33. Kimberly Smith, *African American Environmental Thought*, 105, 109–10.
34. Laqueur, *Fascism*, 24.
35. Ordover, xxvii, xiii.
36. Shane Burley, *Fascism Today*, 50.
37. Anson, "Master Metaphor," 69.
38. Blair Taylor, "Alt-Right Ecology," 284–5.
39. Burley, 115.
40. See Ray, *The Ecological Other*, 24.
41. John Muir, *My First Summer in the Sierra*, 303–6. For more on the equation between whiteness and cleanliness, see Carl A. Zimring, *Clean and White*.
42. Dorceta Taylor, 360–1.
43. Dorceta Taylor, 10–2.
44. Jeffrey Myers, *Converging Stories*, 32.
45. Dorceta Taylor, 12.
46. Myers, 36, 42–3, 33–4.
47. Dorceta Taylor, 11.
48. Myers, 36.
49. Roxanne Dunbar-Ortiz, *An Indigenous Peoples' History of the United States*, 34–5.
50. Gilio-Whitaker, 25.
51. Dunbar-Ortiz, 108–9.
52. Jack Forbes, "Fascism," 16.
53. Daniel Martinez HoSang and Joseph E. Lowndes, *Producers, Parasites, Patriots*, 138.
54. Lyons, vii, xiii.
55. HoSang and Lowndes, 12, 17, 104.
56. HoSang and Lowndes, 134, 139, 141–2.

57. Woodley, 7–8.
58. Jason Stanley, *How Fascism Works*, xvii, 177. In Nazi Germany, this injunction included disabled as well as racialized others.
59. Pogue, 103–4, 131, 286.
60. Boggs, 195, 294–5.
61. Lyons, 154, 144.
62. Quoted in Lyons, 139.
63. Burley 100, 59, 99, 57–8. Burley notes that "the artificial construct of whiteness overwhelms other forms of ethnic identity as [many on the far right] look for some type of 'Pan-European' unity" (57–9).
64. Quoted in Lyons, 137.
65. Ursula K. Heise, "The Virtual Crowds," 2.
66. Reece Jones, *White Borders*, 99, 112.
67. Aric Mcbay, Lierre Keith, and Derrick Jensen, *Deep Green Resistance*, 206. See also Ahuja.
68. Garrett Hardin, "Human Ecology," 471–2. On Hardin's (and Malthus's) shaky reasoning, see especially the work of the political economist Elinor Ostrom, recipient of the 2009 Nobel Prize in Economics. Critique of Malthus is hardly new. The political economist Henry George, for instance, declared in his 1879 tract *Progress and Poverty* that "the injustice of society, not the niggardliness of nature, is the cause of the want and misery which the current theory attributes to overpopulation" (104).
69. Rob Nixon, "Neoliberalism," 593.
70. Betsy Hartmann, *The America Syndrome*, 223. See also David Graeber and David Wengrow, *The Dawn of Everything*, 250.
71. These debates began in the 1960s and 1970s, around the time of Ehrlich's writing. One of the most recent iterations corresponded with an ultimately unsuccessful "hostile takeover" of the organization by Tanton and his allies between 1998 and 2005, during which they packed the Club with members of twenty white supremacist organizations (see Reece Jones, 129ff.).
72. Hardin, "The Tragedy of the Commons," 1244.
73. Hardin, "Human Ecology," 473.
74. Hardin, "Tragedy," 1247.
75. Nixon, "Neoliberalism," 594.
76. Ray, *The Ecological Other*, 10.
77. Hultgren, 4, 14.
78. Hardin, "Lifeboat Ethics."
79. This point clarifies why self-identified ecofascists, though deeply concerned with climate change, are contemptuous of climate policy as such. As Amitav Ghosh points out in *The Great Derangement*, international discussion trends toward negotiation related to "an equitable regime of emissions" established through, for example,

"a fair apportioning of the world's remaining 'climate budget.'" But self-identified ecofascists, unconcerned with their own consumption habits, reject the "resulting equity" envisioned by such measures. Ghosh worries that governments will themselves operate in accordance with a "lifeboat ethics": "from the point of view of a security establishment . . . [t]he tasks of the nation-state . . . will be those of keeping 'blood-dimmed tides' of climate refugees at bay" (143).

80. Boggs, 301, 298.
81. Boggs, 305.
82. Quoted in Boggs, 297.
83. Samantha Senda-Cook and Danielle Endres, "A Place of One's Own," 143, 147.
84. Ray, *The Ecological Other*, 30.
85. See Anson, "The President Stole Your Land."
86. Pogue, 288, 82.
87. See, for example, Ewan Palmer, "Jake Angeli Will Be Fed Organic Shaman Diet."
88. Hartmut Berghoff, "Shades of Green," 14.
89. Ray, *The Ecological Other*, 4.
90. Chris Vials, "Margaret Atwood's Dystopic Fiction," 237.
91. Jim Igoe, *The Nature of Spectacle*, 12.

INTERLUDE I

1. Roxanne Dunbar-Ortiz, *An Indigenous Peoples' History of the United States*, 5.
2. Blair Taylor, "Alt-Right Ecology," 281–2. Other sorts of partnerships have formed and thrived among Indigenous and settler populations. For example, Mi'kmaq coalitions with New Brunswick locals of French and English descent successfully fought back extractive industries that threatened the health of their human and nonhuman communities in the early 2010s (even after brutal race riots against the Mi'kmaq just a decade earlier).
3. Cary Wolfe, *Ecological Poetics*, xiii, x.
4. Gloria Anzaldúa, *Borderlands/La Frontera*, 25. Cited in text for the remainder of Interlude I.
5. Vanessa Fonseca-Chávez, *Colonial Legacies in Chicana/o Literature and Culture*, 133.
6. See Dorceta Taylor, *The Rise of the American Conservation Movement*, 15–6. For a specific account of the connection among labor, race, and deportation, see especially Francisco E. Balderrama and Raymond Rodríguez, *Decade of Betrayal: Mexican Repatriation in the 1930s*.
7. Priscilla Solis Ybarra, *Writing the Goodlife*, 116.
8. See Ybarra, 137, 141, 21–3.

9. See also Andrea Lunsford, "Toward a Mestiza Rhetoric," 9.
10. Hultgren, *Border Walls Gone Green*, 29.
11. Anzaldúa, "Speaking across the Divide," 286.
12. Ybarra, 10.
13. Ybarra, 173.
14. Bosworth, *Pipeline Populism*, 53.
15. Whyte, "Against Crisis Epistemology," 53.

2. TOOLS

1. Timothy Miller, *The 60s Communes*, 20, 52.
2. Susan Sontag, "Fascinating Fascism."
3. Miller, *The 60s Communes*, 1, 7.
4. See Philip Deloria, *Playing Indian*, 100ff.
5. Miller, *The 60s Communes*, 157, 153. See also Coulthard, *Red Skin, White Masks*.
6. See Susannah Crockford, "Q Shaman's New Age–Radical Right Blend."
7. Robert O. Paxton, *The Anatomy of Fascism*, 13.
8. Michael Mann, *Fascists*, 13.
9. See Rebecca E. Klatch, *A Generation Divided*.
10. Andrew G. Kirk, *Counterculture Green*, 187, 9.
11. Timothy Miller, *Communes in America*, 139.
12. See Blair Taylor, "Alt-Right Ecology."
13. Karen Svensson, "What Is an Ecovillage?", 10.
14. See Miller, *The 60s Communes*, 69–70.
15. Blair Taylor, 280. Numerous far-right organizations, such as True Cascadia and the Northwest Front, have taken up this strategy, known as the "Northwest Territorial Imperative."
16. See, for example, Graeber and Wengrow, *The Dawn of Everything*, 22–3.
17. Miller, *Communes in America*, 49–50.
18. Ernest Callenbach, *Ecotopia*, 180, 85, 3. Cited in text for the remainder of chapter 2.
19. Dorceta Taylor, *The Rise of the American Conservation Movement*, 30.
20. Malcolm Margolin, "Foreword," iv.
21. Harvey Wasserman, "A Green-Powered Trip through Ecotopia."
22. Wasserman.
23. Roger Ivar Lohmann, "Fiction in Fact," 179.
24. Lohmann, 179.
25. See Heinz Tschachler, "Despotic Reason in Arcadia?"
26. In the novel, italicized passages indicate material from Weston's private journal, as opposed to his public columns.
27. Tschachler, 305.

28. See Miller, *The 60s Communes*, 151.
29. Miller, *Communes in America*, xviii, and *The 60s Communes*, 149–50.
30. Miller, *The 60s Communes*, 152.
31. Theodore Roszak, *From Satori to Silicon Valley*, 2–3 (emphasis added).
32. Biehl and Staudenmaier, *Ecofascism Revisited*, 21.
33. Walter Laqueur, *Young Germany*, 41.
34 Amitav Ghosh, *The Great Derangement*, 132.
35. See Klatch, 3.
36. Klatch, 33, 45, 30.
37. See Klatch, 118–9.
38. Kirk, 204–5.
39. Miller, *Communes in America*, 1.
40. Roszak, 25, 32.
41. Stewart Brand, "Introduction"; Edward Abbey, *Desert Solitaire*, 185.
42. Kirk, 2, 191, 11–2.
43. Thomas Frank, *The Conquest of Cool*, 7, 6, 26, 28.
44. Frank, 55.
45. Kirk, 204.
46. Fred Turner, *From Counterculture to Cyberculture*, 5, 7.
47. Kirk, 183, 188.
48. Blair Taylor, 286.
49. See James Lovelock, *The Revenge of Gaia*.
50. Moore and Roberts, *The Rise of Ecofascism*, 65.
51. Roszak, 65.
52. Roszak, 9, 50–1.
53. Miller, *The 60s Communes*, 25.
54. Corey Robin, *The Reactionary Mind*, 36.
55. See Ray, *The Ecological Other*.
56. Margolin, vi.
57. Nicole Seymour, *Strange Natures*, 7.
58. Adeline Johns-Putra, *Climate Change and the Contemporary Novel*, 21–3.
59. Philip Deloria, 7.
60. Margolin, vi.
61. Hannah Holleman, *Dust Bowls of Empire*, 98–9.

3. FOOD

1. Theodore Roszak, *From Satori to Silicon Valley*, 4.
2. Gloria Anzaldúa, *Borderlands*, 83.
3. David Graeber and David Wengrow, *The Dawn of Everything*, 123–4.
4. Jeff Mann, *Loving Mountains, Loving Men*, 83, 132. Cited in text for the remainder of chapter 3 and the following Interlude.
5. Kilian Melloy, "A Surly Bear Speaks Out."

6. Scott Herring, *Another Country*. See also Jack Halberstam, *In a Queer Time and Place*.

7. Brock Thompson, *The Un-Natural State*, 9.

8. See Rachel Garringer, "We're Fabulous and We're Appalachians," 81.

9. Allison E. Carey, "Food in *Finding H.F.*," 171.

10. David Bell and Gill Valentine, *Consuming Geographies*, 3.

11. Kyla Wazana Tompkins, *Racial Indigestion*, 3–4, 11

12. In the essays of *Loving Mountains, Loving Men,* Mann uses the word "queer" to refer collectively to cisgender gay men and lesbian women as a coherent population.

13. See Michelle Niemann, "Organic Farming's Political History."

14. Corinna Treitel, "Organic Origin Story." See also Gregory A. Barton, *The Global History of Organic Farming,* and Philip Conford, *The Origins of the Organic Movement*.

15. Niemann. See also Sam Moore and Alex Roberts, *The Rise of Eco-fascism*, 36.

16. Shane Burley, *Fascism Today*, 98–9.

17. Blu Buchanan, "Gay Neo-Nazis," 491, 499, 502–3, 505–6.

18. Moore and Roberts, 83.

19. Jeff Mann, *Endangered Species*, 306.

20. Moore and Roberts, 81–2.

21. Gary Paul Nabhan, *Coming Home to Eat*, 23.

22. I use the word "kinship" to refer specifically to Judith Butler's understanding of the concept in *Antigone's Claim* as an "action of kinship" rather than an identity derived "from kinship" (58), emphasizing the performative and, more specifically, narrative acts by which one or more subjects claim new, nonnormative relationships rather than reify normative ones that might exclude them.

23. Jonathan Cohn, "Yet Again."

24. Matthew S. Henry, "Extractive Fictions and Postextraction Futurisms," 403.

25. Mann, *Endangered Species*, 70.

26. Henry, 404.

27. Chad Montrie, *To Save the Land and People*, 4, 156.

28. Montrie, 16. See also 2–3, 12–5.

29. Wendell Berry, *A Continuous Harmony*, 172.

30. See Allison Carruth, *Global Appetites*.

31. Wendell Berry, *The Gift of Good Land*, x.

32. Berry, *A Continuous Harmony*, 90.

33. Carruth, 7.

34. Carruth, 1.

35. Wendell Berry, *Home Economics*, 125, 131.

36. See, for example, Heather Niday, "Save the Forest."

37. Carruth, 158–60.

38. Berry, *Home Economics,* 185.
39. Barbara Kingsolver, *Animal, Vegetable, Miracle,* 209.
40. Stephen Pearson, "'The Last Bastion of Colonialism,'" 165–6.
41. Montrie, 3–5, 13.
42. Pearson, 165–6.
43. Roxanne Dunbar-Ortiz, *An Indigenous Peoples' History of the United States,* 52.
44. Pearson, 177.
45. Tompkins, 5.
46. Mann, *Endangered Species,* 69.
47. Susan J. Leonardi, "Recipes for Reading," 340.
48. Rafia Zafar, "The Signifying Dish," 450.
49. Stephen Vider, "Oh Hell," 879. Carruth notes an important gendered aspect to representations or even literary forms involving food: "Scholars of the American pastoral and agrarian traditions have emphasized male writers . . . particularly when their interest is in how rural literature treats the sweeping forces of industrialization," while "critics have defined [culinary literature] primarily around the spaces of the kitchen and the table . . . bracketing it from the wider food system" (8).
50. Lucille Clifton, "cutting greens," line 15.
51. Elspeth Probyn, *Carnal Appetites,* 4.
52. Tompkins, 3–4.
53. Mann, *Endangered Species,* 267. See also 260 for the racial diversity of his understanding of Appalachia.
54. Katharina Vester, *A Taste of Power,* 200.
55. Annalee Newitz and Matt Wray, "Introduction," 1.
56. Carl A. Zimring, *Clean and White,* 46, 80–1.
57. Daniel Martinez HoSang and Joseph E. Lowndes, *Producers, Parasites, Patriots,* 16–7.
58. Ray, *The Ecological Other,* 3, 9.
59. Annalee Newitz, "White Savagery," 134.
60. Jeff Mann, "Appalachian Subculture," 19.
61. Montrie, 14.
62. Anthony Harkins, *Hillbilly,* 7.
63. Carol Mason, "The Hillbilly Defense," 42.
64. Mann, "Appalachian Subculture," 19.
65. Nancy Isenberg, *White Trash,* 270.
66. Jason Ezell, "Returning Forest Darlings," 73.
67. Scott Herring, "Out of the Closets," 342, 346.
68. Loyal Jones, *Appalachian Values,* 13, 24, 99.
69. Sarah Jaquette Ray, *The Ecological Other,* 14.
70. Camille Bégin, *Taste of the Nation,* 81.
71. Mark F. Sohn, *Appalachian Home Cooking,* 90, 92.

72. Bégin, 75.
73. Mann, *Endangered Species*, 234.
74. Ezell, 87.
75. Scott Lauria Morgensen, "Settler Homonationalism," 106.
76. Dianne Chisholm, "Biophilia," 159.
77. Mann, *Endangered Species*, 28, 14.
78. Melloy.
79. Mann, *Endangered Species*, 194–5.
80. Mann, *Endangered Species*, 333, 3, 14, 231. See also Maureen O'Connor, "The Philosophical Fascists of the Gay Alt-Right."
81. Mann, *Endangered Species*, 123, 4, 237, 211ff., 235.
82. Forbes argues that the Confederate States of America was in fact "the first independent fascist society in North America. It was a state founded in militarism . . . where non-whites were to be forever excluded from basic human rights by means of sheer terror" (16).
83. Mann, *Endangered Species*, 235, 242.
84. Berry, *A Continuous Harmony*, 61–3.
85. Mann, *Endangered Species*, 214
86. Joe Bageant, *Deer Hunting with Jesus*, 187, quoted in Mann, *Endangered Species*, 234.
87. Mann, *Endangered Species*, 237, 224, 206, 218, 204, 209.

INTERLUDE II

1. Kyla Wazana Tompkins, *Racial Indigestion*, 10.
2. Donna Haraway, *When Species Meet*, 15.
3. Sarah Ensor, "Terminal Regions," 41.
4. Ensor, 43, 46–7, 51–3.
5. Guido Pezzarossi, Ryan Kennedy, and Heather Law, "'Hoe Cake and Pickerel,'" 201, 204.

4. DRUGS

1. Margaret Atwood, *The Year of the Flood*, 141. Atwood frequently insists that she anchors her fiction in events, ideas, and technologies that either already exist or realistically could. The Gardeners are no exception. She chose Christianity as the basis for their theology rather than pagan derivatives not only to situate their radicalism in broadly recognizable terms but also because green Christianity, she notes, is "a trend," pointing to the 2008 Green Bible as an example (Jill Owens, "The Powells.com Interview"). The Evangelical Climate Initiative, Interfaith Power and Light organization, and Pope Francis's 2015 *Laudato si'* are others.
2. Shelley Boyd, "Ustopian Breakfasts," 162.

3. See, for example, Michelle Zacaria, "The Ecological Fascism of Thanos."

4. Isabel Slone, "Who Survives, Who Doesn't?"

5. Countless descriptors have emerged over the years to label psychoactive compounds, including the familiar *hallucinogenic* ("vision inducing") and more obscure *psychotomimetic* ("madness mimicking") and *psycholytic* ("psyche loosening"). I stick with *psychedelic,* not just because the term is recognizable, but because its meaning, "mind manifesting," arguably best balances accuracy with breadth.

6. Shayla Love, "If Everyone Tripped on Psychedelics."

7. Jesse Jarnow, *Heads,* x, 325.

8. Ariel Levy, "The Secret Life of Plants," 31

9. See Ralph Metzner, *Ayahuasca,* 106, 112

10. Alex Halperin, "More Real Than Real."

11. Ira Israel, "The Problem with Ayahuasca."

12. Chris Elcock, "From Acid Revolution to Entheogenic Evolution," 297.

13. See William A. Richards, *Sacred Knowledge,* 3–4, 140.

14. Atwood, *MaddAddam,* 221; Dennis J. McKenna and Terence K. McKenna. *The Invisible Landscape,* 102. Atwood's *Oryx and Crake, The Year of the Flood,* and *MaddAddam* cited in text for the remainder of chapter 4 as *OC, YF,* and *MA,* respectively.

15. Axel Goodbody and Adeline Johns-Putra, "The Rise of the Climate Change Novel," 234.

16. Molly Wallace, *Risk Criticism,* 5, 20, 13.

17. Michael Trask, *Ideal Minds,* 2–3.

18. Levy, 31.

19. Margaret Atwood, *Payback,* 41.

20. Hope Jennings, "The Comic Apocalypse of *The Year of the Flood,*" 11.

21. Carol Osborne, "Compassion, Imagination, and Reverence for All Living Things," 32.

22. Jennings, 11.

23. Stacy Alaimo, *Bodily Natures,* 2, 20.

24. Elcock, 307.

25. Richards, 10.

26. Timothy Leary, Ralph Metzner, and Richard Alpert, *The Psychedelic Experience,* 3.

27. Michael Pollan, *How to Change Your Mind,* 85.

28. Ralph Metzner, *Allies for Awakening,* 9, 11.

29. Theodore Roszak, *From Satori to Silicon Valley,* 47.

30. Michael Pollan, *This Is Your Brain on Plants,* 244.

31. See Pollan, *How to Change Your Mind,* 25.

32. Pollan, *How to Change Your Mind,* 25.

33. Albert Hofmann, *LSD, My Problem Child,* 126.

34. Terence McKenna, *Food of the Gods,* 248.

35. Leary, Metzner, and Alpert, 3.
36. Richard Louis Miller, *Psychedelic Medicine*, 3.
37. Richards, 11, 61.
38. Pollan, *How to Change Your Mind*, 303, 305–7.
39. See Metzner, *Ayahuasca*, 65–6.
40. Pollan, *How to Change Your Mind*, 289–90.
41. Françoise Bourzat, *Consciousness Medicine*, 247, 32.
42. Stephen Harrod Buhner, *Plant Intelligence and the Imaginal Realm*, 166, 238. Buhner is the author of numerous texts on "plant medicine," as well as Native American traditions from which he draws his own conclusions. He and one of his collaborators, Brooke Medicine Eagle, have drawn criticism over representations of Native spirituality and identity (as well as Eagle's claims to Indigenous ancestry) from several organizations, most notably the American Indian Movement.
43. Bourzat, 22.
44. Bourzat, 26.
45. Murray Bookchin, "Between the 30s and the 60s," 250; Bourzat, 27.
46. See Pollan, *This Is Your Brain on Plants*, 270.
47. Bourzat, 251.
48. Buhner, 417.
49. Elanor Cummins, "The Worst Answer to Climate Anxiety."
50. See Pollan, *How to Change Your Mind*, 124.
51. Buhner, 224.
52. Bourzat, 248.
53. Richard Miller, 3.
54. Jane Ciabattari, "Disease and Dystopia in Atwood's *Flood*."
55. Chris Vials, "Margaret Atwood's Dystopic Fiction," 237–8.
56. Betsy Hartmann, *The America Syndrome*, 216, 220.
57. Heather I. Sullivan, "The Dark Pastoral," 56.
58. Blair Taylor, "Alt-Right Ecology," 285.
59. Blair Taylor, 285.
60. Sullivan, 47–8.
61. Hartmann, 23, 41–2, 214.
62. Levy, 34.
63. Ralph Metzner, "Hallucinogenic Drugs," 334.
64. McKenna and McKenna, 12.
65. Terence McKenna, *True Hallucinations and The Archaic Revival*, 11, 65–6.
66. Pollan, *How to Change Your Mind*, 175.
67. McKenna, *True Hallucinations and the Archaic Revival*, 49.
68. Daniel Pinchbeck, "Introduction," xiii.
69. Leary, Metzner, and Alpert, 24.

70. Buhner, 166, 220.
71. Pollan, *How to Change Your Mind*, 314.
72. Richard Evans Schultes and Albert Hofmann, *Plants of the Gods*, 59.
73. William Burroughs and Allen Ginsberg, *The Yage Letters*, 57.
74. Terence McKenna, *Food of the Gods*, 39, xvi, xx.
75. Buhner, 361.
76. Bourzat, 246.
77. Charles Grob, "The Psychology of Ayahuasca," 214. Researchers indeed observe neurological parallels between psychedelic experience and psychosis.
78. Elcock, 303.
79. There is no standard Native American interaction with psychedelic plants, either. Cultural practices differ not only by nation and geography but also over time. Spanish colonizers viciously suppressed centuries-old traditions in the Americas. Contemporary peyote rituals are, by contrast, relatively recent inventions— perhaps a recovery, but one that required lobbying for religious freedom within the constraints of the U.S. legal system and cultural norms.
80. Buhner, 359–60.
81. Pollan, *How to Change Your Mind*, 193–4.
82. Israel.
83. Terence McKenna, *True Hallucinations and the Archaic Revival*, 68, 72, 39.
84. Terence McKenna, *Food of the Gods*, 98.
85. Richard Miller, 186.
86. Pollan, *This Is Your Brain on Plants*, 284.
87. Matthew Rothschild, "Margaret Atwood Interview."
88. See Metzner, *Ayahuasca*, 73.
89. Burroughs and Ginsberg, 60.
90. Raoul Adamson, "Initiation into Ancient Lineage," 49.
91. Diana Coole and Samantha Frost, "Introducing the New Materialisms," 9.
92. Hannes Bergthaller, "Limits of Agency," 39–40.
93. Rosi Braidotti, *The Posthuman*, 136, 134, 137.
94. Buhner, 402–5. The Gaia hypothesis itself in fact has roots in this sort of reasoning. As Leah Aronowsky explains in "Gas Guzzling Gaia," Lovelock articulated his theory with the blessing of fossil fuel executives, who welcomed the idea that, no matter how much damage one does, the earth will always bounce back.
95. Atwood, *Surfacing*, 195.
96. Ursula K. Heise, *Imagining Extinction*, 203.
97. Rothschild.

5. CONTAGION

1. Sam Moore and Alex Roberts, *The Rise of Ecofascism*, 93.
2. Blair Taylor, "Alt-Right Ecology," 288–9. The Christchurch shooter titled the conclusion of his manifesto "Destabilization and Accelerationism."
3. Quoted in Alex Amend, "Blood and Vanishing Topsoil." Survivalist communities have long had close ties to the radical right. Kurt Saxon, founder of *The Survivor* magazine, once claimed membership in the American Nazi Party.
4. Cedric Johnson, "Preface," xii.
5. Quoted in Amend.
6. Anson, "No One Is a Virus."
7. Amend.
8. See Amend.
9. Quoted in Stephan Harding, *Animate Earth*, 12.
10. Quoted in Moore and Roberts, 10.
11. Roderick Frazier Nash, *The Rights of Nature*, 159.
12. Robert Pois, *National Socialism and the Religion of Nature*, 40.
13. See Amend.
14. See Moore and Roberts, 10, and Amend.
15. Adam Trexler, *Anthropocene Fictions*, 10.
16. Louise Erdrich, *Future Home of the Living God*, 8. Cited in text for the remainder of chapter 5.
17. Anson, "No One Is a Virus."
18. Quoted in Leah Sottile, "As a Plague Sweeps the Land."
19. Emery Jenson, "Why Are Anti-Vaxxers Obsessed with the 'Natural'?"
20. Emily Martin, *Flexible Bodies*, 229, 50, 54, 51, 69–70.
21. Quoted in Martin, 235, 237.
22. Martin, 236, 81.
23. Traci Brynne Voyles, "Green Lovin' Mamas Don't Vax!," 2.
24. Jenson.
25. Eula Biss, *On Immunity*, 41, 52–3, 117.
26. Biss, 14.
27. Quoted in Jenson.
28. Jenson.
29. Voyles, 3.
30. Michael Murphy, *The Future of the Body*, 157.
31. Murphy, 30, 157.
32. Martin, 239–40.
33. Jenson.
34. See Martin, 235.
35. Sirin Kale, "Chakras, Crystals and Conspiracy Theories."
36. Joseph Osmundson, *Virology*, 148–9.

37. Osmundson, 206, 182.
38. See Kale.
39. Biss, 135, 138.
40. Martin, 231.
41. Adam Johnson, *Parasites Like Us*, 1. Cited in text for the remainder of chapter 5.
42. See Adam Johnson, "*Parasites Like Us* Reader's Guide."
43. Adam Johnson, "Reader's Guide."
44. Adam Johnson, "Reader's Guide."
45. Jamie Acevedo, "Adam Johnson."
46. Taylor Eggan, *Unsettling Nature*, 17.
47. Paul Shepard, *Coming Home to the Pleistocene*, 153–4.
48. Kirkpatrick Sale, *Human Scale*, 182–4.
49. Michael Trask, *Ideal Minds*, 75, 77.
50. David Graeber and David Wengrow, *The Dawn of Everything*, 4.
51. Gideon Lewis-Kraus, "Early Civilizations Had It All Figured Out."
52. Eggan, 20.
53. Shepard, *Coming Home to the Pleistocene*, 154.
54. Paul Shepard, *The Tender Carnivore and the Sacred Game*, 120.
55. Trask, 2.
56. Martin, 232.
57. Christian A. Coleman, "Interview."
58. Margaret Atwood and Louise Erdrich, "Inside the Dystopian Visions." *Future Home* has invited comparisons to Atwood's work, especially *The Handmaid's Tale,* which also dramatizes the rise of a theocratic autocracy that places women's bodies under special surveillance, rendering them little more than vessels for breeding. *Future Home,* however, arguably treats with the history of reproductive politics more accurately than Atwood does, given its focus on the disproportionate violence experienced by women of color in North America, from chattel slavery to the forced sterilization and adoption measures faced by Black, Latina, and Native women across the twentieth century.
59. Coleman.
60. Silvia Martínez-Falquina, "Feminist Dystopia and Reality," 270.
61. Coleman.
62. See Shepard Krech, *The Ecological Indian.*
63. Atwood and Erdrich.
64. Martínez-Falquina, 272.
65. Carol Mason, *Killing for Life*, 4–5.
66. Mason, *Killing for Life*, 4, 7.
67. Bethanne Patrick, "Louise Erdrich Discusses Her New Novel."
68. See Mason, *Killing for Life*, 33–4, 42.
69. See Jill Colvin, "Rep. Mary Miller."

70. Mason, *Killing for Life*, 6 (emphasis added).
71. Erdrich's characters' responses to ecological and social crisis fall across lines of gender "in ways that have almost become generic patterns," Ana-Karina Schneider writes. In apocalyptic fiction by men, she notes, male characters typically try to survive and rebuild. Women writers, on the other hand, more often scrutinize the extent to which heteropatriarchy, colonialism, and capitalism precipitate those very disasters ("Clinging to Flesh," 13–4).
72. Erdrich, *The Sentence*, 183–4, 36.
73. Kim TallBear, *Native American DNA*, 46.
74. Shari Huhndorf, *Going Native*, 8.
75. See Jedediah Purdy, *This Land Is Our Land*, xix.
76. See Eggan, 126.
77. Roxanne Dunbar-Ortiz, *An Indigenous Peoples' History of the United States*, 104.
78. Huhndorf, 2, 14.
79. Dylan Rodríguez, *White Reconstruction*, 127–9.
80. Huhndorf, 17.
81. Notably, the Court neglected to address this argument, instead ruling in favor of the defendants in part on the basis of states' rights.
82. Rebecca Nagle, "The Story of Baby O."
83. See Nagle.
84. Elie Mystal, "This Supreme Court Case."
85. Erdrich, *The Sentence*, 308–9.
86. Vine Deloria Jr., "Foreword."
87. Chadwick Allen, *Blood Narrative*, 15, 12.
88. Atwood and Erdrich. This is not to say that Erdrich demonizes motherhood as such—just certain narratives that surround it. Cedar actively wants her child despite the state's intervention and the biological "regression" that might threaten it precisely because she does *not* see species, nation, or gender as fixed, inflexible ontologies.
89. Erdrich, *The Sentence*, 347.
90. Julian Brave NoiseCat, "How to Survive an Apocalypse."
91. Osmundson, 34.

CONCLUSION

1. Sam Moore and Alex Roberts, *The Rise of Ecofascism*, 39.
2. See Kathryn Joyce, "'What Is 'Ecofascism'?"
3. Min Hyoung Song, *Climate Lyricism*, 161, 171.
4. Kaleem Hawa, "Open Wide!"
5. Tommy Pico, *Nature Poem*, 1. *Nature Poem, Junk*, and *Feed* cited in text for the remainder of the Conclusion as *NP, J*, and *F*, respectively.
6. Kyla Wazana Tompkins, *Racial Indigestion*, 5.

7. Zita Nunes, *Cannibal Democracy*, 17–8.
8. Hawa.
9. Tobias Carroll, "'I Said What I Had to Say.'"
10. Kyle Powys Whyte, "Settler Colonialism," 131, 128.
11. Jason Stanley, *How Fascism Works*, 4.
12. Adeline Johns-Putra, *Climate Change and the Contemporary Novel*, 27, 29.
13. Moore and Roberts, 45, 5–6.
14. Michael Mann, *Fascists*, 4.
15. Michael Mann, 4, 369; Walter Laqueur, *Fascism*, 5.
16. Corey Robin, *The Reactionary Mind*, 241–4.
17. Laqueur, *Fascism*, 94–5.
18. Laqueur, *Fascism*, 121–2.

Bibliography

Abbey, Edward. *Desert Solitaire: A Season in the Wilderness.* 1968. New York: Ballantine, 1971.

Acevedo, Jamie. "Adam Johnson." *Superstition Review,* no. 10 (2012). https://superstitionreview.asu.edu/issue10/interviews/adamjohnson.

Adamson, Raoul. "Initiation into Ancient Lineage of Visionary Healers." In *Ayahuasca: Hallucinations, Consciousness, and the Spirit of Nature,* edited by Ralph Metzner, 46–57. Philadelphia: Running Press, 1999.

Agamben, Giorgio. *State of Exception.* 2003. Chicago: University of Chicago Press, 2005.

Ahuja, Neel. *Planetary Specters: Race, Migration, and Climate Change in the Twenty-First Century.* Chapel Hill: University of North Carolina Press, 2021.

Alaimo, Stacy. *Bodily Natures: Science, Environment, and the Material Self.* Bloomington: Indiana University Press, 2010.

Alfred, Taiaiake. *Peace, Power, Righteousness: An Indigenous Manifesto.* New York: Oxford University Press, 2009.

Allen, Chadwick. *Blood Narrative: Indigenous Identity in American Indian and Maori Literary and Activist Texts.* Durham, N.C.: Duke University Press, 2002.

Amend, Alex. "Blood and Vanishing Topsoil: American Ecofascism Past, Present, and in the Coming Climate Crisis." *Political Research Associates,* July 9, 2020, https://politicalresearch.org/2020/07/09/blood-and-vanishing-topsoil.

Anderson, Benedict. *Imagined Communities.* 1983. New York: Verso, 2006.

Anson, April. "'Master Metaphor': Environmental Apocalypse and the Settler States of Emergency." *Resilience: A Journal of the Environmental Humanities* 8, no. 1 (2020): 60–81.

Anson, April. "No One Is a Virus." *Environmental History Now,* October 21, 2020, https://envhistnow.com/2020/10/21/no-one-is-the-virus-on-american-ecofascism/.

Anson, April. "The President Stole Your Land: Public Lands and the Settler Commons." *Western American Literature* 54, no. 1 (2019): 49–62.

Anzaldúa, Gloria. *Borderlands/La Frontera: The New Mestiza.* 1987. San Francisco: Aunt Lute Books, 2007.

Anzaldúa, Gloria. "Speaking across the Divide." In *The Gloria Anzaldúa Reader,* edited by AnaLouise Keating, 282–94. Durham, N.C.: Duke University Press, 2009.

Aronowsky, Leah. "Gas Guzzling Gaia, or: A Prehistory of Climate Change Denial." *Critical Inquiry* 47 (2021): 306–27.

Atwood, Margaret. *MaddAddam.* 2013. New York: Anchor, 2014.

Atwood, Margaret. *Oryx and Crake.* 2003. New York: Anchor, 2004.

Atwood, Margaret. *Payback: Debt and the Shadow Side of Wealth.* Toronto: House of Anansi Press, 2008.

Atwood, Margaret. *Surfacing.* 1972. New York: Anchor, 1998.

Atwood, Margaret. *The Year of the Flood.* 2009. New York: Anchor, 2010.

Atwood, Margaret, and Louise Erdrich. "Inside the Dystopian Visions of Margaret Atwood and Louise Erdrich." *Elle,* November 14, 2017, https://www.elle.com/culture/books/a13530871/future-home-of-the-living-god-louise-erdrich-interview/.

Bageant, Joe. *Deer Hunting with Jesus: Dispatches from America's Class War.* New York: Three Rivers, 2007.

Balderrama, Francisco E., and Raymond Rodríguez, *Decade of Betrayal: Mexican Repatriation in the 1930s.* Albuquerque: University of New Mexico Press, 2006.

Barnard, John Levi. "The Bison and the Cow: Food, Empire, Extinction." *American Quarterly* 72, no. 2 (2020): 377–401.

Barton, Gregory A. *The Global History of Organic Farming.* Oxford: Oxford University Press, 2018.

Bégin, Camille. *Taste of the Nation: The New Deal Search for America's Food.* Champaign: University of Illinois Press, 2016.

Bell, David, and Gill Valentine. *Consuming Geographies: We Are What We Eat.* New York: Routledge, 1997.

Berghoff, Hartmut. "Shades of Green: A Business-History Perspective on Eco-Capitalism." *Green Capitalism? Business and the Environment in the Twentieth Century,* edited by Hartmut Berghoff and Adam Rome, 13–32. Philadelphia: University of Pennsylvania Press, 2017.

Bergthaller, Hannes. "Limits of Agency: Notes on the Material Turn from a Systems-Theoretical Perspective." In *Material Ecocriticism,* edited by Serenella Iovino and Serpil Oppermann, 37–50. Bloomington: Indiana University Press, 2014.

Berlant, Lauren. *The Female Complaint: The Unfinished Business of Sentimentality in American Culture.* Durham, N.C.: Duke University Press, 2008.

Bernstein, Maxine. "Ammon Bundy's Lawyer Argues for His Client's Right to Wear Cowboy Boots at Trial." *Oregon Live,* September 7, 2016, https://www.oregonlive.com/oregon-standoff/2016/09/ammon_bundys_lawyer_argues_for.html.

Berry, Wendell. *A Continuous Harmony: Essays Cultural and Agricultural.* 1970. Berkeley, Calif.: Counterpoint, 2012.

Berry, Wendell. *Home Economics.* Berkeley, Calif.: North Point, 1987.

Berry, Wendell. *The Gift of Good Land: Further Essays Cultural and Agricultural.* Berkeley, Calif.: Counterpoint, 1981.

Biehl, Janet, and Peter Staudenmaier. *Ecofascism Revisited: Lessons from the German Experience.* 1995. Porsgrunn, Norway: New Compass, 2011.

Biss, Eula. *On Immunity: An Inoculation.* Minneapolis: Graywolf, 2014.

Boggs, Kyle. "The Rhetorical Landscapes of the 'Alt Right' and the Patriot Movements: Settler Entitlement to Native Land." In *The Far Right and the Environment: Politics, Discourse and Communication,* edited by Bernhard Forchtner, 293–309. New York: Routledge, 2020.

Bonilla-Silva, Eduardo. *Racism without Racists: Color-Blind Racism and the Persistence of Racial Inequality in America.* 2003. Lanham, Md.: Rowman & Littlefield, 2018.

Bonneuil, Christophe, and Jean-Baptiste Fressoz. *The Shock of the Anthropocene.* 2013. New York: Verso, 2017.

Bookchin, Murray. "Between the 30s and the 60s." *Social Text,* nos. 9/10 (1984): 247–51.

Bosworth, Kai. *Pipeline Populism: Grassroots Environmentalism in the Twenty-First Century.* Minneapolis: University of Minnesota Press, 2022.

Bourzat, Françoise. *Consciousness Medicine: Indigenous Wisdom, Entheogens, and Expanded States of Consciousness for Healing and Growth.* Berkeley, Calif.: North Atlantic Books, 2019.

Boyd, Shelley. "Ustopian Breakfasts: Margaret Atwood's *MaddAddam.*" *Utopian Studies* 26, no. 1 (2015): 160–81.

Braidotti, Rosi. *The Posthuman.* Cambridge: Polity, 2013.

Brand, Stewart. "Introduction." *The Essential Whole Earth Catalog.* New York: Doubleday, 1986.

Buchanan, Blu. "Gay Neo-Nazis in the United States: Victimhood, Masculinity, and the Public/Private Spheres." *GLQ: A Journal of Lesbian and Gay Studies* 28, no. 4 (2022): 489–513.

Buell, Lawrence. *Writing for an Endangered World: Literature, Culture, and Environment in the U.S. and Beyond.* Cambridge, Mass.: Belknap, 2001.

Buhner, Stephen Harrod. *Plant Intelligence and the Imaginal Realm: Beyond the Doors of Perception into the Dreaming of Earth.* Rochester, Vt.: Bear & Company, 2014.

Burley, Shane. *Fascism Today: What It Is and How to End It.* Chico, Calif.: AK Press, 2017.

Burroughs, William, and Allen Ginsberg. *The Yage Letters.* 1963. San Francisco: City Lights Books, 2006.

Butler, Judith. *Antigone's Claim: Kinship between Life and Death.* New York: Columbia University Press, 2000.

Callenbach, Ernest. *Ecotopia.* 1975. Berkeley, Calif.: Heyday, 2014.

Campion, Kristy. "Defining Ecofascism: Historical Foundations and Contemporary Interpretations in the Extreme Right." *Terrorism and Political Violence* 35, no. 4 (2021): 926–44.

Carey, Allison E. "Food in *Finding H.F.* and *Secret City* by Julia Watts: The Food of Home and the Food of the Big City." *Journal of Appalachian Studies* 20, no. 2 (2014): 170–80.

Carroll, Tobias. "'I Said What I Had to Say': An Interview with Tommy Pico." *Vol. 1 Brooklyn,* June 14, 2017, https://vol1brooklyn.com/2017/06/14/i-said-what-i-had-to-say-an-interview-with-tommy-pico/.

Carruth, Allison. *Global Appetites: American Power and the Literature of Food.* Cambridge: Cambridge University Press, 2013.

Chisholm, Dianne. "Biophilia, Creative Involution, and the Ecological Future of Queer Desire." In *Queer Ecologies: Sex, Nature, Politics, Desire,* edited by Catriona Mortimer-Sandilands and Bruce Erickson, 359–81. Bloomington: Indiana University Press, 2010.

Ciabattari, Jane. "Disease and Dystopia in Atwood's *Flood,*" *National Public Radio,* September 10, 2009, https://www.npr.org/2009/09/10/112706370/disease-and-dystopia-in-atwoods-flood.

Clifton, Lucille. "cutting greens." *Poetry Foundation,* 1987. https://www.poetryfoundation.org/poems/54590/cutting-greens.

Cohn, Jonathan. "Yet Again, Florida Proves That It Prefers White Supremacy to Being above Sea Level." Twitter.com, November 6, 2018, 8:37 a.m.

Coleman, Christian A. "Interview: Louise Erdrich." *Lightspeed Magazine,* no. 91 (2017), https://www.lightspeedmagazine.com/nonfiction/interview-louise-erdrich/.

Colvin, Jill. "Rep. Mary Miller Calls Roe Decision 'Victory for White Life.'" *Associated Press,* June 25, 2022, https://apnews.com/article/2022-midterm-elections-abortion-illinois-congress-rodney-davis-b5ea16788dd89de6fe3ef5366fbefb4d.

Conford, Philip. *The Origins of the Organic Movement.* Edinburgh: Floris Books, 2001.

Coole, Diana, and Samantha Frost. "Introducing the New Materialisms." In *New Materialisms: Ontology, Agency, and Politics,* edited by Diana Coole and Samantha Frost, 1–43. Durham, N.C.: Duke University Press, 2010.

Cope, Zak. *Divided World, Divided Class: Global Political Economy and the Stratification of Labour Under Capitalism.* Montreal: Kersplebedeb, 2015.

Coulthard, Glen Sean. *Red Skin, White Masks: Rejecting the Colonial Politics of Recognition.* Minneapolis: University of Minnesota Press, 2014.

Crockford, Susannah. "Q Shaman's New Age–Radical Right Blend Hints at the Blurring of Seemingly Disparate Categories." *Religion Dispatches,* January 11, 2021, https://religiondispatches.org /q-shamans-new-age-radical-right-blend-hints-at-the-blurring -of-seemingly-disparate-categories/.

Cummins, Elanor. "The Worst Answer to Climate Anxiety: Wellness." *The New Republic,* July 29, 2020, https://newrepublic.com /article/158621/worst-answer-climate-anxiety-wellness.

Deloria, Philip J. *Playing Indian.* New Haven, Conn.: Yale University Press, 1998.

Deloria, Vine, Jr. "Foreword: American Fantasy." In *The Pretend Indians: Images of Native Americans in the Movies,* edited by Gretchen M. Bataille and Charles L. P. Silet. Ames: Iowa State University Press, 1980.

Dunbar-Ortiz, Roxanne. *An Indigenous Peoples' History of the United States.* Boston: Beacon, 2014.

Eggan, Taylor. *Unsettling Nature: Ecology, Phenomenology, and the Settler Colonial Imagination.* Charlottesville: University of Virginia Press, 2022.

Elcock, Chris. "From Acid Revolution to Entheogenic Evolution: Psychedelic Philosophy in the Sixties and Beyond." *Journal of American Culture* 36, no. 4 (2013): 296–311.

Ensor, Sarah. "Terminal Regions: Queer Ecocriticism at the End." In *Against Life,* edited by Alastair Hunt and Stephanie Youngblood, 41–61. Evanston, Ill.: Northwestern University Press, 2016.

Erdrich, Louise. *Future Home of the Living God.* New York: Harper Perennial, 2017.

Erdrich, Louise. *The Sentence.* New York: HarperCollins, 2021.

Ezell, Jason. "'Returning Forest Darlings': Gay Liberationist Sanctuary in the Southeastern Network, 1973–80." *Radical History Review,* no. 135 (2019): 71–94.

Fonseca-Chávez, Vanessa. *Colonial Legacies in Chicana/o Literature and Culture: Looking through the Kaleidoscope.* Tucson: University of Arizona Press, 2020.

Forbes, Jack D. "Fascism: A Review of Its History and Its Present Cultural Reality in the Americas." *Explorations in Ethnic Studies* 5, no. 1 (1982): 3–25.

Forchtner, Bernhard. "Far-Right Articulations of the Natural Environment: An Introduction." In *The Far Right and the Environment: Politics, Discourse and Communication,* edited by Bernhard Forchtner, 1–17. New York: Routledge, 2020.

Forchtner, Bernhard and Balša Lubarda. "Eco-Fascism 'Proper': The Curious Case of Greenline Front." *Centre for Analysis of the Far Right,* June 25, 2020, https://www.radicalrightanalysis.com/2020/06/25 /eco-fascism-proper-the-curious-case-of-greenline-front/.

Frank, Thomas. *The Conquest of Cool: Business Culture, Counterculture, and the Rise of Hip Consumerism.* Chicago: University of Chicago Press, 1997.

Gardiner, Beth. "White Supremacy Goes Green." *New York Times,* February 28, 2020, https://www.nytimes.com/2020/02/28/opinion/sunday/far-right-climate-change.html.

Garringer, Rachel. "'Well, We're Fabulous and We're Appalachians, So We're Fabulachians': Country Queers in Central Appalachia." *Southern Cultures* 23, no. 1 (2017): 79–91.

George, Henry. *Progress and Poverty: An Inquiry into the Cause of Industrial Depressions and of Increase of Want with Increase of Wealth: The Remedy.* Boston: D. Appleton and Company, 1879.

Ghosh, Amitav. *The Great Derangement: Climate Change and the Unthinkable.* Chicago: University of Chicago Press, 2017.

Giddens, Anthony. *The Consequences of Modernity.* Stanford, Calif.: Stanford University Press, 1990.

Gilio-Whitaker, Dina. *As Long as Grass Grows: The Indigenous Fight for Environmental Justice, from Colonization to Standing Rock.* Boston: Beacon, 2019.

Goodbody, Axel, and Adeline Johns-Putra. "The Rise of the Climate Change Novel." In *Climate and Literature,* edited by Adeline Johns-Putra, 229–45. Cambridge: Cambridge University Press, 2019.

Graeber, David, and David Wengrow. *The Dawn of Everything: A New History of Humanity.* 2021. London: Picador, 2023.

Grant, Madison. *The Passing of the Great Race.* New York: Charles Scribner's Sons, 1916.

Griffin, Roger. *The Nature of Fascism.* New York: Routledge, 1991.

Grob, Charles S. "The Psychology of Ayahuasca." In *Ayahuasca: Hallucinations, Consciousness, and the Spirit of Nature,* edited by Ralph Metzner, 214–49. Philadelphia: Running Press, 1999.

Halberstam, Jack. *In a Queer Time and Place: Transgender Bodies, Subcultural Lives.* New York: New York University Press, 2005.

Halperin, Alex. "'More Real Than Real': A Psychiatrist Discusses DMT." *WeedWeek,* November 17, 2020, https://www.weedweek.com/stories/a-psychiatrist-discusses-dmt/.

Haraway, Donna. *When Species Meet.* Minneapolis: University of Minnesota Press, 2007.

Hardin, Garrett. "Human Ecology: The Subversive, Conservative Science." *American Zoologist* 25, no. 2 (1985): 469–76.

Hardin, Garrett. "Lifeboat Ethics: The Case against Helping the Poor." *Psychology Today,* 1974.

Hardin, Garrett. "The Tragedy of the Commons." *Science* 162 (1968): 1243–8.

Harding, Stephan. *Animate Earth: Science, Intuition and Gaia.* London: Green Books, 2006.

Harkins, Anthony. *Hillbilly: A Cultural History of an American Icon.* New York: Oxford University Press, 2003.

Hartmann, Betsy. *The America Syndrome: Apocalypse, War, and Our Call to Greatness.* 2017. New York: Seven Stories, 2019.

Hawa, Kaleem. "Open Wide!: On Tommy Pico's *Feed* and the Poetry of Consumed Indigeneity." *The Adroit Journal,* November 5, 2019, https://theadroitjournal.org/2019/11/05/open-wide-on-tommy -picos-feed-and-the-poetry-of-consumed-indigeneity/.

Heise, Ursula K. *Imagining Extinction: The Cultural Meanings of Endangered Species.* Chicago: University of Chicago Press, 2016.

Heise, Ursula K. "The Virtual Crowds: Overpopulation, Space and Speciesism." *Interdisciplinary Studies in Literature and Environment* 8, no. 1 (2001): 1–29.

Henry, Matthew S. "Extractive Fictions and Postextraction Futurisms: Energy and Environmental Injustice in Appalachia." *Environmental Humanities* 11, no. 2 (2019): 402–26.

Herf, Jeffrey. *Reactionary Modernism: Technology, Culture and Politics in Weimar and the Third Reich.* Cambridge: Cambridge University Press, 1984.

Herring, Scott. *Another Country: Queer Anti-Urbanism.* New York: New York University Press, 2010.

Herring, Scott. "Out of the Closets, Into the Woods: *RFD, Country Women,* and the Post-Stonewall Emergence of Queer Anti-urbanism." *American Quarterly* 59, no. 2 (2007): 341–72.

Hofmann, Albert. *LSD, My Problem Child.* 1980. San Jose, Calif.: Multidisciplinary Association for Psychedelic Studies, 2009.

Holleman, Hannah. *Dust Bowls of Empire: Imperialism, Environmental Politics, and the Injustice of "Green" Capitalism.* New Haven, Conn.: Yale University Press, 2018.

HoSang, Daniel Martinez, and Joseph E. Lowndes. *Producers, Parasites, Patriots: Race and the New Right-Wing Politics of Precarity.* Minneapolis: University of Minnesota Press, 2019.

Huhndorf, Shari M. *Going Native: Indians in the American Cultural Imagination.* Ithaca, N.Y.: Cornell University Press, 2001.

Hultgren, John. *Border Walls Gone Green: Nature and Anti-Immigrant Politics in America.* Minneapolis: University of Minnesota Press, 2015.

"Hundreds March in Arizona in Solidarity with Climate Strikes around the World," *AZ Central,* September 20, 2019, https://www.azcentral. com/picture-gallery/news/local/arizona-environment/2019/09/20 /hundreds-march-arizona-solidarity-climate-strikes-around-world /2391592001/.

Igoe, Jim. *The Nature of Spectacle: On Images, Money, and Conserving Capitalism.* Tucson: University of Arizona Press, 2017.

"An Interview with Out of the Woods." *Journal of Aesthetics & Protest,* no. 11 (2020), https://www.joaap.org/issue11/OutoftheWoods.htm.

Iordachi, Constantin. "Comparative Fascist Studies: An Introduction." *Comparative Fascist Studies: New Perspectives,* edited by Constantin Iordachi, 1–50. New York: Routledge, 2010.

Isenberg, Nancy. *White Trash: The 400-Year Untold History of Class in America.* New York: Viking, 2016.

Israel, Ira. "The Problem with Ayahuasca." *Medium,* May 4, 2019, https://iraisrael.medium.com/the-problem-with-ayahuasca-91046b4ae3dd.

James, Erin, and Eric Morel. "Introduction: Notes Toward New Econarratologies." In *Environment and Narrative: New Directions in Econarratology,* edited by Erin James and Eric Morel, 1–24. Columbus: Ohio State University Press, 2020.

Jarboe, James F. "The Threat of Eco-Terrorism." Federal Bureau of Investigation, 2002, https://archives.fbi.gov/archives/news/testimony/the-threat-of-eco-terrorism.

Jarnow, Jesse. *Heads: A Biography of Psychedelic America.* Cambridge, Mass.: Da Capo, 2016.

Jennings, Hope. "The Comic Apocalypse of *The Year of the Flood.*" *Margaret Atwood Studies* 3, no. 2 (2010): 11–8.

Jenson, Emery. "Why Are Anti-Vaxxers Obsessed with the 'Natural'?" *Edge Effects,* February 17, 2022, https://edgeeffects.net/traci-brynne-voyles-anti-vaccination/.

Johnson, Adam. *Parasites Like Us.* New York: Penguin, 2003.

Johnson, Adam. "*Parasites Like Us* Reader's Guide." Penguin Random House, n.d., https://www.penguinrandomhouse.com/books/291208/parasites-like-us-by-adam-johnson/9780142004777/readers-guide/.

Johnson, Cedric. "Preface: Obama's Katrina." In *The Neoliberal Deluge: Hurricane Katrina, Late Capitalism, and the Remaking of New Orleans,* edited by Cedric Johnson, vii–xv. Minneapolis: University of Minnesota Press, 2011.

Johns-Putra, Adeline. *Climate Change and the Contemporary Novel.* Cambridge: Cambridge University Press, 2019.

Jones, Loyal. *Appalachian Values.* 1973. Ashland, Ky.: Jesse Stuart Foundation, 1994.

Jones, Reece. *White Borders: The History of Race and Immigration in the United States from Chinese Exclusion to the Border Wall.* Boston: Beacon, 2021.

Joshi, Ketan. "Watch Out for This Symptom of Corona Virus: Lazy Ecofascism." *Ketan Joshi: Posts about Climate and Energy,* March 20, 2020, https://ketanjoshi.co/2020/03/20/watch-out-for-this-symptom-of-corona-virus-lazy-ecofascism/.

Joyce, Kathryn. "What Is 'Ecofascism'—and What Does It Have to Do with the Buffalo Shooting?" *Salon,* May 18, 2022, https://www.salon.com/2022/05/18/what-is-ecofascism--and-what-does-it-have-to-do-with-the-buffalo-shooting/.

Kale, Sirin. "Chakras, Crystals and Conspiracy Theories: How the Wellness Industry Turned Its Back on Covid Science." *The Guardian,* November 11, 2021, https://www.theguardian.com/world/2021/nov/11/injecting-poison-will-never-make-you-healthy-how-the-wellness-industry-turned-its-back-on-covid-science.

Keeler, Kyle. "Colonial Theft and Indigenous Resistance in the Kleptocene." *Edge Effects,* September 8, 2020, https://edgeeffects.net/kleptocene/.

Kennon, Raquel. "Uninhabitable Moments: The Symbol of Serena Williams, Rage and Rackets in Claudia Rankine's *Citizen: An American Lyric.*" In *Challenging Misrepresentations of Black Womanhood: Media, Literature and Theory,* edited by Marquita M. Gammage and Antwanisha Alameen-Shavers, 28–52. New York: Anthem Press, 2019.

Kingsolver, Barbara. *Animal, Vegetable, Miracle: A Year of Food Life.* New York: HarperCollins, 2007.

Kirk, Andrew G. *Counterculture Green: The* Whole Earth Catalog *and American Environmentalism.* Lawrence: University Press of Kansas, 2007.

Klatch, Rebecca E. *A Generation Divided: The New Left, the New Right, and the 1960s.* Berkeley: University of California Press, 1999.

Krech, Shepard. *The Ecological Indian: Myth and History.* New York: W. W. Norton, 1999.

Laqueur, Walter. *Fascism: Past, Present, Future.* New York: Oxford University Press, 1996.

Laqueur, Walter. *Young Germany: A History of the German Youth Movement.* New York: Routledge, 1962.

Leary, Timothy, Ralph Metzner, and Richard Alpert. *The Psychedelic Experience.* 1964. New York: Citadel, 2007.

LeMenager, Stephanie. *Living Oil: Petroleum Culture in the American Century.* Oxford: Oxford University Press, 2016.

Leonardi, Susan J. "Recipes for Reading: Summer Pasta, Lobster à la Riseholme, and Key Lime Pie." *PMLA* 104, no. 3 (1989): 340–7.

Levy, Ariel. "The Secret Life of Plants." *New Yorker,* September 12, 2016, 30–6, https://www.newyorker.com/magazine/2016/09/12/the-ayahuasca-boom-in-the-u-s.

Lewis-Kraus, Gideon. "Early Civilizations Had It All Figured Out." *New Yorker,* November 8, 2021, https://www.newyorker.com/magazine/2021/11/08/early-civilizations-had-it-all-figured-out-the-dawn-of-everything.

Lohmann, Roger Ivar. "Fiction in Fact: Ernest Callenbach's *Ecotopia* and

the Creation of a Green Culture with Anthropological Ingredients."
Anthropology and Humanism 43, no. 2 (2018): 178–95.

Love, Shayla. "If Everyone Tripped on Psychedelics, We'd Do More about Climate Change." *Vice,* June 27, 2019, https://www.vice.com/en /article/j5w49p/if-everyone-tripped-on-psychedelics-wed-do-more -about-climate-change.

Lovelock, James. *The Revenge of Gaia: Why the Earth Is Still Fighting Back and How We Can Still Save Humanity.* New York: Penguin, 2006.

Lunsford, Andrea A. "Toward a Mestiza Rhetoric: Gloria Anzaldúa on Composition and Postcoloniality." *JAC* 18, no. 1 (1998): 1–27.

Lyons, Matthew. *Insurgent Supremacists: The U.S. Far Right's Challenge to State and Empire.* Oakland, Calif.: PM Press, 2018.

Malm, Andreas, and the Zetkin Collective. *White Skin, Black Fuel: On the Danger of Fossil Fascism.* New York: Verso, 2021.

Manavis, Sarah. "Eco-Fascism: The Ideology Marrying Environmentalism and White Supremacy Thriving Online." *New Statesman,* September 21, 2018, https://www.newstatesman.com/science-tech /2018/09/eco-fascism-ideology-marrying-environmentalism-and -white-supremacy.

Mann, Jeff. "Appalachian Subculture." *Gay & Lesbian Review,* September–October 2003, 19–21.

Mann, Jeff. *Endangered Species: A Surly Bear in the Bible Belt.* Amherst, Mass.: Lethe, 2019.

Mann, Jeff. *Loving Mountains, Loving Men.* Athens: Ohio University Press, 2005.

Mann, Michael. *Fascists.* Cambridge: Cambridge University Press, 2004.

Margolin, Malcolm. Foreword to *Ecotopia,* by Ernest Callenbach, iii–ix. Berkeley, Calif.: Heyday, 2014.

Martin, Emily. *Flexible Bodies: Tracking Immunity in American Culture— from the Days of Polio to the Age of AIDS.* Boston: Beacon, 1994.

Martínez-Falquina, Silvia. "Feminist Dystopia and Reality in Louise Erdrich's *Future Home of the Living God* and Leni Zumas's *Red Clocks.*" *European Legacy* 26, no. 3–4 (2021): 270–86.

Mason, Carol. "The Hillbilly Defense: Culturally Mediating U.S. Terror at Home and Abroad." *NWSA Journal* 17, no. 3 (2005): 39–63.

Mason, Carol. *Killing for Life: The Apocalyptic Narrative of Pro-Life Politics.* Ithaca, N.Y.: Cornell University Press, 2002.

Mcbay, Aric, Lierre Keith, and Derrick Jensen. *Deep Green Resistance: Strategy to Save the Planet.* New York: Seven Stories, 2011.

McKenna, Dennis J., and Terence K. McKenna. *The Invisible Landscape: Mind, Hallucinogens, and the I Ching.* New York: Seabury, 1975.

McKenna, Terence. *Food of the Gods: The Search for the Original Tree of Knowledge: A Radical History of Plants, Drugs, and Human Evolution.* New York: Bantam, 1992.

McKenna, Terence. *True Hallucinations and the Archaic Revival.* New York: MJF Books, 1998.

Melloy, Kilian. "A Surly Bear Speaks Out: BDSM Mountain Poet and Essayist Jeff Mann on Being an 'Endangered Species.'" *Edge Media Network,* 2019.

Metzner, Ralph. *Allies for Awakening: Guidelines for Productive and Safe Experiences with Entheogens.* Berkeley, Calif.: Regent, 2015.

Metzner, Ralph, ed. *Ayahuasca: Hallucinations, Consciousness, and the Spirit of Nature.* Philadelphia: Running Press, 1999.

Metzner, Ralph. "Hallucinogenic Drugs and Plants in Psychotherapy and Shamanism." *Journal of Psychoactive Drugs* 30, no. 4 (1998): 333–41.

Miller, Richard Louis. *Psychedelic Medicine: The Healing Powers of LSD, MDMA, Psilocybin, and Ayahuasca.* Rochester, Vt.: Park Street, 2017.

Miller, Timothy. *The 60s Communes: Hippies and Beyond.* Syracuse, N.Y.: Syracuse University Press, 1999.

Miller, Timothy. *Communes in America, 1975–2000.* Syracuse, N.Y.: Syracuse University Press, 2019.

Montrie, Chad. *To Save the Land and People: A History of Opposition to Surface Coal Mining in Appalachia.* Chapel Hill: University Press of North Carolina, 2003.

Moore, Sam, and Alex Roberts. *The Rise of Ecofascism: Climate Change and the Far Right.* Cambridge: Polity, 2022.

Morgensen, Scott Lauria. "Settler Homonationalism: Theorizing Settler Colonialism within Queer Modernities." *GLQ: A Journal of Lesbian and Gay Studies* 16, nos. 1–2 (2010): 105–31.

Mosse, George. *The Crisis of German Ideology: Intellectual Origins of the Third Reich.* New York: Penguin, 1964.

Mosse, George. "The Genesis of Fascism." *Journal of Contemporary History* 1, no. 1 (1966): 19–20.

Mosse, George. "Toward a General Theory of Fascism." In *Comparative Fascist Studies: New Perspectives,* edited by Constantin Iordachi, 60–94. New York: Routledge, 2010.

Muir, John. *My First Summer in the Sierra.* 1911. Boston: Houghton Mifflin, 1972.

Murphy, Michael. *The Future of the Body: Explorations into the Further Evolution of Human Nature.* New York: Tarcher, 1992.

Myers, Jeffrey, *Converging Stories: Race, Ecology, and Environmental Justice in American Literature.* Athens: University of Georgia Press, 2005.

Mystal, Elie. "This Supreme Court Case Is a Case Study in Conservative Hypocrisy." *The Nation,* December 12/19, 2022, https://www.thenation.com/article/society/tribal-rights-attacked/.

Nabhan, Gary Paul. *Coming Home to Eat: The Pleasures and Politics of Local Foods.* New York: W. W. Norton, 2002.

Nagle, Rebecca. "The Story of Baby O—and the Case that Could Gut

Native Sovereignty." *The Nation,* November 28/December 5, 2022, https://www.thenation.com/article/society/icwa-supreme-court -libretti-custody-case/.

Nash, Roderick Frazier. *The Rights of Nature.* Madison: University of Wisconsin Press, 1989.

Newitz, Annalee. "White Savagery and Humiliation, or A New Racial Consciousness in the Media." In *White Trash: Race and Class in America,* edited by Matt Wray and Annalee Newitz, 131–54. New York: Routledge, 1997.

Newitz, Annalee, and Matt Wray. "Introduction." In *White Trash: Race and Class in America,* edited by Matt Wray and Annalee Newitz, 1–12. New York: Routledge, 1997.

Niday, Heather. "Save the Forest, Get Paid." *100 Days in Appalachia,* August 18, 2020, https://www.100daysinappalachia.com/2020/08 /save-the-forest-get-paid-this-appalachian-farming-initiative -shows-people-how/.

Niemann, Michelle. "Organic Farming's Political History." *Edge Effects,* January 23, 2020, https://edgeeffects.net/organic-farmings -political-history/.

Nixon, Rob. "Neoliberalism, Genre, and 'The Tragedy of the Commons.'" *PMLA* 127, no. 3 (2012): 593–9.

Nixon, Rob. *Slow Violence and the Environmentalism of the Poor.* Cambridge, Mass.: Harvard University Press, 2013.

NoiseCat, Julian Brave. "How to Survive an Apocalypse and Keep Dreaming." *The Nation,* June 2, 2020, https://www.thenation.com /article/society/native-american-postapocalypse/.

Nunes, Zita. *Cannibal Democracy: Race and Representation in the Literature of the Americas.* Minneapolis: University of Minnesota Press, 2008.

O'Connor, Maureen. "The Philosophical Fascists of the Gay Alt-Right." *The Cut,* April 30, 2017, https://www.thecut.com/2017/04/jack -donovan-philosophical-fascists-of-the-gay-alt-right.html.

Olsen, Jonathan. *Nature and Nationalism: Right-Wing Ecology and the Politics of Identity in Contemporary Germany.* London: Palgrave, 1999.

Omi, Michael, and Howard Winant. *Racial Formation in the United States: From the 1960s to the 1980s.* 1986. New York: Routledge, 1994.

Ordover, Nancy. *American Eugenics: Race, Queer Anatomy, and the Science of Nationalism.* Minneapolis: University of Minnesota Press, 2003.

Osborne, Carol. "Compassion, Imagination, and Reverence for All Living Things: Margaret Atwood's Spiritual Vision in *The Year of the Flood.*" *Margaret Atwood Studies* 3, no. 2 (2010): 30–42.

Osmundson, Joseph. *Virology: Essays for the Living, the Dead, and the Small Things in Between.* New York: W. W. Norton, 2022.

Owens, Jill. "The Powells.com Interview with Margaret Atwood." *Powell's*

Books Blog, October 6, 2009, https://www.powells.com/post
/interviews/the-powellscom-interview-with-margaret-atwood.

Palmer, Ewan. "Jake Angeli Will Be Fed Organic Shaman Diet Following
Judge's Order." *Newsweek,* January 12, 2021, https://www.newsweek
.com/qanon-shaman-organic-diet-jake-angeli-1560754.

Patrick, Bethanne. "Louise Erdrich Discusses Her New Novel, *Future
Home of the Living God.*" *Los Angeles Times,* November 10, 2017,
https://www.latimes.com/books/jacketcopy/la-ca-jc-louise-erdrich
-20171110-story.html.

Paxton, Robert O. *The Anatomy of Fascism.* New York: Alfred A. Knopf,
2004.

Pearson, Stephen. "'The Last Bastion of Colonialism': Appalachian
Settler Colonialism and Self-Indigenization." *American Indian Culture
and Research Journal* 37, no. 2 (2013): 165–84.

Pezzarossi, Guido, Ryan Kennedy, and Heather Law. "'Hoe Cake
and Pickerel': Cooking Traditions, Community, and Agency at a
Nineteenth-Century Nipmuc Farmstead." In *The Menial Art of Cook-
ing: Archaeological Studies of Cooking and Food Preparation,* edited by
Sarah R. Graff and Enrique Rodríguez-Alegría, 201–29. Denver:
University Press of Colorado, 2012.

Pico, Tommy. *Feed.* New York: Tin House, 2019.

Pico, Tommy. *Junk.* New York: Tin House, 2018.

Pico, Tommy. *Nature Poem.* New York: Tin House, 2017.

Pinchbeck, Daniel. Introduction to *The Psychedelic Experience,* by
Timothy Leary, Ralph Metzner, and Richard Alpert, ix–xix. New
York: Citadel, 2007.

Pogue, James. *Chosen Country: A Rebellion in the West.* New York: Henry
Holt, 2018.

Pois, Robert. *National Socialism and the Religion of Nature.* London:
Palgrave Macmillan, 1985.

Pollan, Michael. *How to Change Your Mind.* New York: Penguin, 2018.

Pollan, Michael. *This Is Your Brain on Plants.* New York: Random House,
2021.

Probyn, Elspeth. *Carnal Appetites: FoodSexIdentities.* New York: Routledge, 2000.

Purdy, Jedediah. *This Land Is Our Land: The Struggle for a New Common-
wealth.* Princeton, N.J.: Princeton University Press, 2019.

Ray, Sarah Jaquette. "Climate Anxiety Is an Overwhelmingly White
Phenomenon." *Scientific American,* March 21, 2021, https://www
.scientificamerican.com/article/the-unbearable-whiteness-of
-climate-anxiety/.

Ray, Sarah Jaquette. *The Ecological Other: Environmental Exclusion in
American Culture.* Tucson: University of Arizona Press, 2013.

Richards, William A. *Sacred Knowledge: Psychedelics and Religious Experiences.* New York: Columbia University Press, 2016.

Robin, Corey. *The Reactionary Mind: Conservatism from Edmund Burke to Donald Trump.* 2011. New York: Oxford University Press, 2017.

Robinson, Cedric. *Black Marxism: The Making of the Black Radical Tradition.* 1983. Chapel Hill: University of North Carolina Press, 2020.

Robinson, Rowland Keshena. "Fascism & Anti-Fascism: A Decolonial Perspective." *Maehkōn Ahpēhtesewen,* February 11, 2017, https:// onkwehonwerising.wordpress.com/2017/02/11/fascism-anti -fascism-a-decolonial-perspective/.

Rodríguez, Dylan. *White Reconstruction: Domestic Warfare and the Logics of Genocide.* New York: Fordham University Press, 2020.

Ross, Alexander Reid. *Against the Fascist Creep.* Chico, Calif.: AK Press, 2017.

Roszak, Theodore. *From Satori to Silicon Valley.* San Francisco: Don't Call It Frisco Press, 1986.

Rothschild, Matthew. "Margaret Atwood Interview." *The Progressive,* December 2, 2010, https://progressive.org/magazine/margaret -atwood-interview/.

Sale, Kirkpatrick. *Human Scale.* New York: Coward, McCann & Geoghegan, 1980.

Schneider, Ana-Karina. "Clinging to Flesh: Embodied Experience in Contemporary Women's Dystopias." *Contemporary Women's Writing* 16, no. 3 (2022): 343–60.

Schultes, Richard Evans, and Albert Hofmann. *Plants of the Gods: Origins of Hallucinogenic Use.* New York: McGraw-Hill, 1979.

Senda-Cook, Samantha, and Danielle Endres. "A Place of One's Own." *Environmental Rhetoric and Ecologies of Place,* edited by Peter N. Goggin, 143–54. New York: Routledge, 2013.

Seymour, Nicole. *Strange Natures: Futurity, Empathy, and the Queer Ecological Imagination.* Champaign: University of Illinois Press, 2013.

Shepard, Paul. *Coming Home to the Pleistocene.* Washington, D.C.: Island, 2004.

Shepard, Paul. *The Tender Carnivore and the Sacred Game.* New York: Scribner, 1973.

Slone, Isabel. "'Who Survives, Who Doesn't?' An Interview with Margaret Atwood." *Hazlitt,* August 30, 2013, https://hazlitt.net /feature/who-survives-who-doesnt-interview-margaret-atwood.

Smith, Kimberly. *African American Environmental Thought: Foundations.* Lawrence: University Press of Kansas, 2007.

Sohn, Mark F. *Appalachian Home Cooking: History, Culture, and Recipes.* Lexington: University Press of Kentucky, 2005.

Song, Min Hyoung. *Climate Lyricism.* Durham, N.C.: Duke University Press, 2022.

Sontag, Susan. "Fascinating Fascism." *New York Review of Books,*

February 6, 1975, https://www.nybooks.com/articles/1975/02/06 /fascinating-fascism/.

Soper, Kate. *What Is Nature?* 1995. Oxford: Blackwell, 2004.

Sottile, Leah. "As a Plague Sweeps the Land, Zealots See a Gift from Heaven." *High Country News,* August 1, 2020, https://www.hcn.org /issues/52-8/extremism-as-a-plague-sweeps-the-land-zealots-see-a -gift-from-heaven/.

Stanley, Jason. *How Fascism Works: The Politics of Us and Them.* New York: Random House, 2018.

Staudenmaier, Peter. *Ecology Contested: Environmental Politics between Left and Right.* Porsgrunn, Norway: New Compass, 2021.

Sullivan, Heather I. "The Dark Pastoral: Goethe and Atwood." *Green Letters* 20, no. 1 (2016): 47–59.

Svensson, Karen. "What Is an Ecovillage?" In *Ecovillage Living: Restoring the Earth and Her People,* edited by Hildur Jackson and Karen Svensson, 10–12. London: Green Books, 2002.

TallBear, Kim. *Native American DNA: Tribal Belonging and the False Promise of Genetic Science.* Minneapolis: University of Minnesota Press, 2013.

Taylor, Blair. "Alt-Right Ecology: Ecofascism and Far-Right Environmentalism in the United States." *The Far Right and the Environment: Politics, Discourse, and Communication,* edited by Bernhard Forchtner, 275–92. New York: Routledge, 2019.

Taylor, Dorceta. *The Rise of the American Conservation Movement: Power, Privilege, and Environmental Protection.* Durham, N.C.: Duke University Press, 2016.

Thompson, Brock. *The Un-Natural State: Arkansas and the Queer South.* Fayetteville: University of Arkansas Press, 2010.

Tompkins, Kyla Wazana. *Racial Indigestion: Eating Bodies in the 19th Century.* New York: New York University Press, 2012.

Trask, Michael. *Ideal Minds: Raising Consciousness in the Antisocial Seventies.* Ithaca, N.Y.: Cornell University Press, 2020.

Treisman, Rachel. "A California Redwood Forest Has Officially Been Returned to a Group of Native Tribes." *NPR,* January 26, 2022, https://www.npr.org/2022/01/26/1075778055/california-redwood -forest-native-american-tribes.

Treitel, Corinna. "Organic Origin Story: Tracing the History of 'Natural' Eating." Center for the Humanities, Washington University in St. Louis, April 23, 2015, https://humanities.wustl.edu/features /Corinna-Treitel-Eating-Nature.

Trexler, Adam. *Anthropocene Fictions: The Novel in a Time of Climate Change.* Charlottesville: University of Virginia Press, 2015.

Tschachler, Heinz. "Despotic Reason in Arcadia? Ernest Callenbach's Ecological Utopias." *Science Fiction Studies* 11, no. 3, 1984, 304–17.

Turner, Fred. *From Counterculture to Cyberculture: Stewart Brand, the Whole Earth Network, and the Rise of Digital Utopianism*. Chicago: University of Chicago Press, 2006.

Veracini, Lorenzo. *Settler Colonialism: A Theoretical Overview*. London: Palgrave Macmillan, 2010.

Vester, Katharina. *A Taste of Power: Food and American Identities*. Berkeley: University of California Press, 2015.

Vials, Chris. "Margaret Atwood's Dystopic Fiction and the Contradictions of Neoliberal Freedom." *Textual Practice* 29, no. 2 (2015): 235–54.

Vider, Stephen. "'Oh Hell, May, Why Don't You People Have a Cookbook?': Camp Humor and Gay Domesticity." *American Quarterly* 65, no. 4 (2013): 877–904.

Voyles, Traci Brynne. "Green Lovin' Mamas Don't Vax! The Pseudo-Environmentalism of Anti-Vaccination Discourse." *Studies in the Humanities* 46, no. 1–2 (2020): 1–21.

Wallace, Molly. *Risk Criticism: Precautionary Reading in an Age of Environmental Uncertainty*. Ann Arbor: University of Michigan Press, 2016.

Wasserman, Harvey. "A Green-Powered Trip through Ecotopia." *CounterPunch*, June 5, 2009, https://www.counterpunch.org /2009/06/05/a-green-powered-trip-through-ecotopia/.

Whyte, Kyle Powys. "Against Crisis Epistemology." In *Routledge Handbook of Critical Indigenous Studies*, edited by Brendan Hokowhitu, Aileen Moreton-Robinson, Linda Tuhiwai-Smith, Chris Andersen, and Steve Larkin, 52–64. New York: Routledge, 2021.

Whyte, Kyle Powys. "Settler Colonialism, Ecology, and Environmental Injustice." *Environment and Society: Advances in Research* 9 (2018): 125–44.

Wodak, Ruth. "The Trajectory of Far-Right Populism—A Discourse-Analytic Perspective." In *The Far Right and the Environment: Politics, Discourse and Communication*, edited by Bernhard Forchtner, 21–37. New York: Routledge, 2020.

Wolfe, Cary. *Ecological Poetics; or, Wallace Stevens's Birds*. Chicago: University of Chicago Press, 2020.

Wolfe, Patrick. *Settler Colonialism and the Transformation of Anthropology: The Politics and Poetics of an Ethnographic Event*. London: Cassell, 1999.

Woodhouse, Keith Makoto. *The Ecocentrists: A History of Radical Environmentalism*. New York: Columbia University Press, 2018.

Woodley, Daniel. *Fascism and Political Theory: Critical Perspectives on Fascist Ideology*. New York: Routledge, 2009.

Ybarra, Priscilla Solis. *Writing the Goodlife: Mexican American Literature and the Environment*. Tucson: University of Arizona Press, 2016.

Yuval-Davis, Nira. "Belonging and the Politics of Belonging." *Patterns of Prejudice* 40, no. 3 (2006): 197–214.

Zacaria, Michelle. "The Ecological Fascism of Thanos in Marvel's *Infinity War*." *People's World*, May 3, 2018, https://www.peoplesworld.org /article/the-ecological-fascism-of-thanos-in-marvels-infinity-war/.

Zafar, Rafia. "The Signifying Dish: Autobiography and History in Two Black Women's Cookbooks." *Feminist Studies* 25, no. 2 (1999): 449–69.

Zimring, Carl A. *Clean and White: A History of Environmental Racism in the United States*. New York: New York University Press, 2015.

Index

Alexander Menrisky is assistant professor of English and affiliate faculty in American Studies at the University of Connecticut. He is author of *Wild Abandon: American Literature and the Identity Politics of Ecology.*